Adapting Regulation to Shortages, Curtailment, and Inflation

Adapting Regulation to Shortages, Curtailment, and Inflation

Edited by
John L. O'Donnell

1977
MSU Public Utilities Papers

Division of Research
Graduate School of
Business Administration
Michigan State University

The Institute of Public Utilities, Graduate School of Business Administration, Michigan State University, publishes books, monographs, and occasional papers as part of its program of promoting academic interest in the study of public utilities and regulation. The views and opinions expressed in these works are solely those of the authors, and acceptance for publication does not constitute endorsement by the Institute, its member companies, or Michigan State University.

ISBN: 0-87744-149-9

Library of Congress Catalog Card Number: 77-620033

Printed in the United States of America

Contents

FOREIGN EXPERIENCE WITH INFLATION AND PRICE STRUCTURE REFORM

EXPERIMENTS IN RATE STRUCTURE

Preface

In many ways 1965 marks a watershed for both regulated industries and their regulators. From that date the combined forces of inflation, fuel shortages, and consumer militancy all combined to transform the economic and political climate. As a result, regulatory lag no longer worked to the advantage of companies. Instead, operating and investment costs rose more rapidly than revenues so that reported earnings declined, accompanied by severe cash flow problems. By 1974 most utility common stocks (especially the electrics) were selling substantially below book values, and debt quality was seriously eroded.

There is now evidence that starting around 1974 the financial status of utilities began to improve in response to substantial rate increases. In addition, the period saw many departures from traditional regulation, such as a wider adoption of normalized accounting for depreciation, automatic adjustment clauses, the future test period, and special treatment of allowance for funds used during construction. Innovation and experimentation also has extended to rate design, with two major policy objectives in mind. First, there are pricing arrangements intended to give preferential treatment to low income and small volume consumers. In contrast, other experiments are concerned with peak-load pricing and load management in an effort to reduce energy consumption and the amount of new physical investment needed to support growth.

In short, the last twelve years have seen a succession of serious challenges to all parties involved in the regulated sector of our economy. It is therefore most appropriate that the Eighth Annual Conference of the Institute of Public Utilities should be entitled *Adapting Regulation to Shortages, Curtailments, and Inflation.* As might be expected, a great deal has already been written on the theoretical aspects of these problems, and even more remains to be explored. With this in mind, the main thrust of our conference was deliberately focused on the operational difficulties of implementing solutions, along with an evaluation of some of the experiments already under way in various parts of the country.

The collection of essays and commentaries contained in this volume forms the skeleton of a vigorous and creative debate that characterized the entire conference. The papers appear in the order presented at the conference, beginning with "The Impact of Inflation on Financial Reporting for Regulated Industries," presented by myself, and "Rate of Return Regulation in the Current Economic Environment," by Myron Gordon.

My paper traces the origins of current accounting techniques as applied to regulated industries. These techniques work reasonably well under normal circumstances but fail in eight major policy areas when rapid inflation takes over. The two most widely suggested accounting solutions are reviewed in the context of modern financial theory. It transpires that inflation magnifies differences between the size and timing of cash flows as compared with reported book earnings. It is therefore suggested that conventional accrual accounting statements be supplemented with well-designed quarterly cash flow statements. Taken together, the former provide data about corporate performance, while the latter meet the needs of financial decision makers.

Gordon's paper is a masterly summary of several separate but closely related topics. He begins with the problem of measuring the cost of equity capital and concludes that the best approach is to use dividend yield plus growth. He also believes that most experts will arrive at closely similar estimates of the growth factor by studying historic retention rates capitalized by corresponding rates of return earned on book. Gordon feels that the capital asset pricing model offers interesting possibilities for measuring relative risks, but he regards it as less accurate than the discounted cash flow approach for measuring the cost of capital. He then turns to the even more difficult and contentious problem of measuring the cost of equity for closely held corporations or corporate divisions. In these situations he advocates the use of income betas on the ground that they are highly correlated with security betas. The entire analysis seems very tenuous and admittedly subject to wide margins of error.

As far as historic versus general price level adjusted cost accounting is concerned, Gordon concludes that both lead to the same results if correctly implemented. He dismisses the notion that changes in the market value of monetary assets should be included in operating income. Finally, Gordon claims that the biggest deficiency of rate of return regulation is that it produces excess investment in the regulatory sector that should be countered by direct regulatory intervention in the allowed volume of new investment. Suffice it to say that all aspects of Gordon's excellent paper are subject to widely different interpretations.

The two discussants, William H. Fletcher and Richard Walker, are men of considerable experience. Fletcher stresses the belief that utilities are subject to competition and that financial leverage creates risks which should be reflected in higher rewards for equity holders. He sees no logic in Gordon's claim that utilities tend to overinvest. He also questions the validity of the efficient market hypothesis, although on this point he may be failing to recognize that the most widely accepted version of the theory allows that fraud and insider information can mislead investors. He also has problems with the publication of cash flow statements, which he sees as thoroughly misleading for reasons other than as vehicles for improving financial disclosure. These and other comments about nationalization undoubtedly reflect misunderstandings arising out of extemporaneous comments, as they have no foundations in the presented papers.

Walker's comments on the technical aspects of price level and replacement cost accounting are penetrating and to the point. He analyzes these problems against the background of a career which began when historic cost accounting was introduced as a measure (albeit an imperfect one) to counter financial scandals which once racked the utility industry. He advocates some form of adjusted historic cost data, but sees cash flow disclosure as largely redundant. Walker also notes circularity in the Gordon recommendation for determining the equity cost of capital for widely traded companies.

The second group of three papers is devoted to aspects of automatic adjustment clauses as a regulatory tool. Stanley Bazant of the New Mexico Commission staff contributes "The New Mexico Response to Inflation." This now celebrated experiment is perhaps the most comprehensive form of indexed regulation in the nation. Bazant points out that the New Mexico plan began by securing the strong support of leading consumer groups. He then itemizes the expected advantages of indexing the equity rate of return. In essence, the plan first establishes 13.5 to 14.5 percent as a fair rate of return range for common equity on the basis of a full-blown rate case. The realized rate is then reviewed ex post facto, and any needed adjustments in consumer charges are made automatically to ensure that the rate of return is brought up to 13.5 percent or reduced to 14.5 percent as the facts demand. In theory, this arrangement should keep the rate of return within the 13.5 to 14.5 percent range, stimulate company efficiency, and relieve the New Mexico Public Service Commission from the tyranny of revolving door rate cases. Bazant notes that at the time of writing, three cost of service index adjustments had been applied to the customer rates charged by the Public Service Company of New Mexico. There was evidence that the company's cost of debt and equity capital had appreciably declined.

"The Case against Automatic Adjustment Clauses as a Means for Improving Regulation," by Sylvia M. Siegel, is a completely uncompromising assault on both the philosophy and current implementation of all types of automatic adjustment clauses. She presents the history, alleged intent, and pros and cons for automatic adjustments with great lucidity. She has no difficulty in concluding that these clauses are thoroughly pernicious on all counts, especially since they inflate customer rates.

As the title suggests, William W. Lindsay's paper, "The Case for Automatic Adjustment Clauses as a Means for Improving Regulation," advocates such arrangements. As does Siegel, he explores all the basic arguments but concludes that automatic adjustments are a useful and needed method for contending with the impact of inflation on regulated industries.

J. M. Quigley comments on the three papers in this section from the viewpoint of an executive. He summarizes the cash flow problems that plague many utilities, and he cannot dismiss the need for specific adjustment clauses as an ancillary regulatory tool. At the same time he is skeptical about the New Mexico plan and related kinds of comprehensive indexing because they tend to set the regulatory goal in terms of a market-to-book target relationship.

Douglas N. Jones confines his remarks to the Lindsay and Bazant papers and is generally unsympathetic to automatic adjustment clauses. He sees them as an abdication of regulatory responsibility, if not representative of the decline of effective regulation itself. He feels that Lindsay has overstated the financial plight of utilities, and he would have liked more information on the philosophy employed by the Federal Power Commission governing its acceptance of automatic adjustment clauses. Jones is equally reserved about the New Mexico plan, which he notes had only been operative for about 18 months. He is particularly concerned about the 13.5 to 14.5 percent range as being somewhat high, especially since it was set without regard to any reductions in the cost of capital which the plan might cause. Finally, he sees the escalation of fuel costs as a national problem that must be shared by all segments of the community.

In the next section, the papers presented by B. H. F. Johnson, "The Impact of Inflation on the Electricity Industry in Great Britain," and by Mario P. Bhering and José D. Langier, "Inflation and Public Utilities in Brazil," provide insights into the problems of inflation and regulation in these two countries. Johnson's paper is a brilliant summation of the institutional structure, economic theory, and managerial policy of a large nationalized industry carrying out its mandate in the face of severe inflation. This mandate is interpreted to mean running the industry in a fashion that seems to conform to the best principles of free enterprise. One is also left with the impression that Great Britain's nationalized industry has been much more alert in anticipating the inevitable political pressures generated by inflation than have the investor-owned companies in this country.

The Bhering and Langier paper begins by tracing the historical development of the industry in a developing economy. Two factors now pervade all managerial decisions: the general indexing of all prices and a tax system designed to make customers the major source of financing. Although the authors deplore general indexing as a contributory factor to inflation, they conclude that, under prevailing conditions, it is a good simplified alternative to replacement cost accounting.

In commenting on the above two papers James R. Nelson stresses the differences between financing problems in a developing versus developed economy. He also feels that the hydroelectric potential in Brazil offers continued possibilities for growth with declining unit costs. Somewhat paradoxically, he sees it easier for utilities to contend with rampant rather than limited rates of inflation.

Joel R. Dirlam, on the other hand, is much more disturbed by the spectacle of state-owned industries functioning like private firms. He strongly questions the use of present value concepts as employed by Johnson to value assets and deplores the unlimited use of long-run marginal costing as a policy tool. He is critical of the financing techniques used by ELETROBRAS but sees no viable alternatives. Dirlam is encouraged by the fact that Brazilian policy seems directed at growth rather than income redistribution.

The last four papers in the volume are devoted to experiments in rate structure. As the title suggests, "Lifeline, an Unfair Share," by Frank S. Walters, concentrates largely on the technical problems inherent in achieving social ends through tariff design. Walters points out in detail that some beneficiaries of lifeline rates can easily be customers for whom the subsidies were not intended. In addition, these rates offend the cost-of-service principle. Walters demonstrates his points with interesting arithmetical examples and concludes that supplying services below cost involves a subsidy that should be solely a governmental responsibility.

"Lessons from the Los Angeles Rate Experiment in Electricity," by Jan P. Acton, Willard G. Manning, and Bridger M. Mitchell, is a highly technical paper describing current experiments in measuring demand response to peak-load tariffs. These experiments were initiated by the Los Angeles Department of Water and Power with solid support from several other prestigious bodies. The experiment covers about 1,800 households and involves 40 different experimental rates for a 30-month period. The authors give a clear account of their research methods and objectives in almost blueprint detail, including why they rejected analysis of variance techniques in favor of demand curves. Of particular significance is the authors' conviction that the results of the study will be applicable to other communities and thus of policy value to many utilities.

"Time of Day Pricing: An Empirical Study," by Larry L. Kehler, reports upon a pilot study which, if successful, may be extended to the entire Arkansas Power and Light Company service area. Stratified sampling was employed to select representative groups which were obliged to use tariffs testing the impact of summer-winter differentials, increased tail block energy tariffs, and time-of-day tariffs. Kehler explains in some detail how rates were developed in order to provide the maximum amount of data on consumer reactions. He reports considerable consumer suspicion with the new rates, indeterminate preliminary results, and a high percentage of mechanical failures with some of the special meters purchased for the experiment.

"Ratemaking Objectives and Rate Design Options," by Robert G. Uhler, attributes four major reactions to the escalation of oil prices.

One of these is the nationwide Electric Power Research Institute rate design study examining peak-load pricing and other aspects of load management. He outlines the background to this extensive research project, which is intended to produce a wide range of empirical data for future analysis. As a preliminary to describing the study he also reviews the essentials surrounding most academic debates about rate making, along with the policy conflicts and objectives that are an integral part of most rate structures.

The discussant, David McNicol, confines his attention to the question of lifeline rates. He presents a tightly reasoned case for direct rather than indirect income transfers and sees the basic issue of lifeline rates in the broader context of a social philosophy dedicated to a more equal distribution of income. His comments are a provocative and stimulating conclusion to this collection of essays.

On behalf of the Institute of Public Utilities, Graduate School of Business Administration, Michigan State University, I wish to thank all those persons who participated in the conference from which this collection was derived. In addition, I should like to express my thanks to Elizabeth Johnston for her timeless assistance in matters of style and format, plus many other details pertinent to the preparation of the book for publication. Similarly, I owe a debt of gratitude to the other Institute staff members who gave unstintingly of their time to make a success of this entire enterprise.

Financial Reporting and Rate of Return Regulation during Inflation

The Impact of Inflation on Financial Reporting for Regulated Industries

John L. O'Donnell

It is widely recognized that sustained changes in the value of money seriously affect real income. As a result, an ever increasing number of buyers and sellers are responding to inflation by attempting to incorporate cost of purchasing or cost of living clauses into the bargains they make with each other. Even the Justices of the Supreme Court have joined the parade. They are requesting that their salaries automatically be adjusted in line with changes in the cost of living. Apparently, this is necessary in order to meet a constitutional provision prohibiting any unilateral reduction in the salary paid a Supreme Court Justice.

The problems of allowing for changes in the value of money become especially complex when we turn to measuring business income. An Oxford economist, Sir John Hicks, has given us one of the most widely used definitions of *income*. He defines it as the amount which can be consumed during a period so that the economic unit is just as well off at the end of the period as at the beginning. For accountants this translates into the concept that income is the difference between balance sheet net worth as recorded at the beginning and end of an accounting period after appropriate adjustments for any distributions and capital contributions. Operationally, the problem becomes one of valuing assets that have not yet been expensed through the income statement. In short, the Hicksian definition is of little help except to the extent it describes a process and focuses attention on the fact that asset values and income are interrelated. If you have one, you have the other, and both are determined by future expectations.

With no help from economic theorists, accountants met the challenge pragmatically by becoming wedded to the principles of "historic cost" and "matching." The former is used as the foundation for asset values which are adjusted through time by systematic depreciation charges. There is also a caveat that total depreciation for any asset must never exceed historic cost. Depreciation charges conform to the matching principle, which states that costs should be matched with the revenues they helped to generate. Applied appropriately across the board these two principles (along with others) produce a net income figure which supposedly reflects both managerial efficiency and investment worth. Before exploring some of the deficiencies of current financial statements and the implications for regulated industries, it is worth pausing to explore briefly how historic costing and matching came into vogue.

There is persuasive evidence that the use of historic costs received enormous impetus while Robert H. Healy was chief counsel to the Federal Trade Commission. He was earlier responsible for an authoritative 95-volume study of the history of public utility holding companies. He concluded that anything that was not original cost was original sin and testified forcibly on this point before the newly formed Securities and Exchange Commission (SEC). He later became a member of the SEC and saw to it that historic cost was a required element for adequate financial disclosure.

Practicing accountants accepted this position for a variety of excellent reasons. Bitter experience had recently demonstrated the possibilities of fraud via stock watering. This was only too easy when management could revalue assets upward at will on the left-hand side of the balance sheet and plug in a corresponding increase in equity on the right-hand side. Similarly, the matching principle also introduced some needed safeguards against deliberate attempts to work the "Ponzy trick," whereby capital repayments are concealed as earned income. In short, historic costing combined with matching provided both a degree of objectivity and conservatism that the immediate post-1929 era demanded.

The deficiencies of the new accounting model soon began to

surface. The matching principle allows maximum latitude for reasonable experts to differ regarding how major expenditures should be prorated against revenues. As a result, the same set of basic data can often be compiled according to generally accepted accounting principles in several different ways to produce markedly different net income figures. This area of confusion is considerably narrowed for regulated industries due to the introduction of standard systems of accounts. Even so, substantive issues can still arise, as evidenced by the debate over flowing-through or normalizing accelerated depreciation.

As far as historic costing is concerned it was never pretended that net book values are equal to market values. This lack of equality causes little concern when prices are relatively stable. Since World War II, dissatisfaction with historic costing has understandably been correlated with the rate of inflation. It is during these periods that current prices shoot ahead of historic costs. As a result, "underdepreciation" occurs so that companies must spend much more than book depreciation to replace worn out plant and equipment just to maintain current levels of operation. This deficiency of conventional financial reporting is especially acute for capital-intensive industries (such as electric utilities) that have long-lived property.

Inadequate book depreciation means that reported profits are overstated. A similar process is at work creating fictitious inventory profits which evaporate when cash generated by sales is needed to replenish inventory levels at progressively higher prices. As this sequence of events unfolds, financial statements tend to give increasingly misleading signals which (it is alleged) result in injurious social and private policies. In summary, inflation has the following impact: (1) It overstates reported profits resulting in a much higher effective tax rate than is apparent; (2) it results in confusing capital with income and encourages stockholders to expect higher dividends than should be paid; (3) higher reported profits encourage excessive union demands, imperiling corporate liquidity; (4) investors and creditors are misled, causing poor investment decisions and misallocations of resources; (5) higher reported profits tend to mislead government regarding the level of public expenditures society can afford; (6) capital consumption forces businesses unduly into the capital markets while also encouraging excessive debt financing; (7) the general public is misled about the economic profitability of business enterprises, helping to stimulate antibusiness political action; and (8) managements are misled about the true financial health of their own operations.

We will evaluate these eight factors in more detail later as a means of putting the problem of financial reporting into better perspective. First, it is necessary to review briefly the response of professionals to the probability of continuing significant inflation. In the opinion of many, business must find a better way of keeping track of economic reality in financial reporting. Many proposals have come to the fore with the ebb and flow of price changes, but these usually fall into two categories: general price level adjustments and current values.

In December 1974 the Financial Accounting Standards Board (FASB) proposed retaining conventional statements but supplementing them with a second full set restated in "units of general purchasing power." The FASB Exposure Draft classifies all balance sheet items into monetary or nonmonetary ones and gives detailed instructions on how the Gross National Product Implicit Price Deflator should be used to arrive at price level adjusted statements. Monetary items are those such as cash and claims to cash that are fixed in terms of the number of dollars regardless of changes in prices. Similarly, monetary liabilities are defined as those for which the amount owed is fixed in terms of the numbers of dollars regardless of changes in prices. All other items are classified as nonmonetary. Clearly, holders of monetary assets suffer a loss of general purchasing power during inflation, whereas holders of monetary liabilities gain because the debt will be paid in dollars having less general purchasing power than the money originally borrowed. The Exposure Draft proposes that monetary gains and losses be included in determining current net income as they occur. On the other hand, depreciation of restated assets should be charged to income over the life of the assets.

Professors Sidney Davidson and Roman Weil (and others) have applied the Exposure Draft recommendations to conventional reports published by investor-owned utilities. One of their studies covers the 24 utilities in the Dow Jones and Standard and Poor's indexes.[1] The authors highlight the differences between the 1973 reported income and estimated general price level adjusted income. Among other things they show that adjusted net income *before* gain

[1]Sidney Davidson and Roman Weil, "Inflation Accounting: Public Utilities," *Financial Analysts Journal* 31 (May-June 1975): 30–34.

on monetary items for all firms was substantially *less* than the net income reported in the conventional financial statements. This reflects the sharply higher depreciation charges on a price level adjusted basis. When gain on monetary items is included to obtain total adjusted net income, all but two gas companies show adjusted net income more than 50 percent higher than in their conventional statements.

Needless to say, this type of solution has enormous implications for regulated industries because of the many peculiarities of the rate-making process. It is difficult enough to secure a badly needed rate increase when conventional statements report, say, a 10 percent rate of return on book equity. One can well imagine the public response for a rate increase in the face of a 50 percent jump in reported income! The situation reminds one of the hard-working man who recently recomputed his net worth in terms of purchasing power units and proudly told his wife they were worth $100,000 more than originally imagined. Next day, he returned from work and was astounded to find a new Cadillac in his driveway. His wife quickly explained that since they were $100,000 richer it was only fitting they should enjoy some of this windfall wealth. The poor fellow then sat down to explain why they could not spend any of the $100,000. After an exasperating hour of tiring discussion he concluded it would have been much better if he had just kept his mouth shut!

Obviously, the FASB proposal could easily be modified to distinguish between holding gains and operating income. Even so, an important public relations problem would always remain because some interested parties can be depended upon to do their own brand of arithmetic. The temptation to consolidate net price level gains or losses and transfer them to conventionally reported net income will prove irresistible. We must also remember that restating asset values will not necessarily induce original cost jurisdictions to change the way they arrive at rate base. In fact, price level accounting or replacement costing could very well set the opposite movement in motion, so that fair value jurisdictions switch to some form of original cost method.

As it turns out the FASB proposal has been shelved, and professional opinion seems to be moving strongly toward current value accounting. This has now found expression in the SEC Accounting Series Release No. 190, requiring companies with inventories and gross plant aggregating more than $100 million and amounting to more than 10 percent of total assets to disclose current replacement cost data for inventories, productive capacity, and cost of sales. These firms must also recalculate depreciation, depletion, and amortization expense on the basis of average current replacement cost of productive capacity, and they must describe the methods used in determining replacement cost amounts and the related effects on other costs. The SEC believes these disclosures will enable investors better to understand the current cost of operations as a prerequisite to making investment decisions. Significantly, there is no attempt in this partial restatement of conventionally derived figures to consider holding gains on nonmonetary items. Clearly, ASR 190 is a significant step toward trying to make financial statements more closely attuned to current market values. It remains an open question whether or not the ambiguities and expenses involved in implementing the new system are worth the expected private and social benefits. This is the key issue in the debate over historic versus any form of current cost accounting. An evaluation of this vigorous debate can be conducted on various levels, but we must be content here with some selected comments designed to put the key issue in proper perspective. I will conclude by recommending a much simpler, quicker, cheaper, less ambiguous, and readily feasible solution that will substantially improve financial reporting under any economic circumstances.

It is important to recognize that although the replacement cost requirements demanded by ASR 190 are limited, it will still take considerable judgment to develop the new figures. There are many unanswered conceptual and mechanical problems offering opportunities for alternative approaches. There is no one indisputable correct number which can be calculated in a given situation for each item of replacement cost information needed. At best, practicing accountants, aided by skilled personnel in their management consulting departments, will be able to set up zones of reasonableness in which experts will have plenty of room to differ. A simple example will suffice to demonstrate this point. ASR 190 calls for *net* replacement cost of productive capacity as well as gross replacement cost. The really tricky question is how to calculate the accumulated depreciation applicable to gross replacement cost. Most utilities do not maintain their property records on an item-by-item basis, so the computations would have to be made by vintage years. This makes the computation of an adequate reserve complex and subject to fairly wide margins of possible dispute. In any case, net replacement cost may not be particularly informative because it contradicts the basic assumption that existing capacity is replaced by new plant. Another uncertainty is introduced if the depreciation life is changed. Assume a piece of equipment has a 20-year life and is now 10 years old so that a 50 percent book depreciation reserve is needed. If the replacement cost is determined using similar equipment, a 50 percent replacement cost reserve will be required. But suppose it is to be replaced by equipment having a 40-year life. We now have at least four possible reserve ratios: (1) 50 percent, the book reserve ratio of the replaced equipment; (2) 25 percent, the ratio of the expired life (10 years) of existing equipment to the total life (40 years) of the replacement; (3) 75 percent, which assumes the remaining 10-year life of the replaced equipment is also the remaining life of the replacement property; and (4) some other percentage reflecting the additional features and revenue producing capacity of the new as contrasted with the replaced equipment.

In due course (after sizeable expenditures on professional fees) firms will acquire expertise in handling the jungle of technical problems posed by replacement cost accounting. The accounting profession, the SEC, and security analysts will also play an old game in a brand-new framework. It might be called the establishment of Generally Accepted Replacement Cost Accounting Principles (GARCAP). Unfortunately, the new game promises to be even more complicated than the one involving historic cost accounting, not to mention the additional public relations problems surrounding rate making noted earlier. This leads us into the assertions that replacement cost accounting is badly needed to improve public understanding about the dangers of capital consumption, excessive effective tax rates on business, and the dangers of excessive government spending.

The case of capital consumption is an uneven one. Looking at the entire economy it is evident our total supply of real capital continues to increase. This conclusion confirms Lord Keynes's injunction that economists must look through the veil of money. Many would argue that firms in the unregulated sector increase their prices to match or even exceed the pace of inflation sufficient to offset inadequate book depreciation. Regulated firms are obviously in a much more vulnerable position. Whether or not replacement cost accounting alleviates this problem will depend upon how the presumably new information about capital consumption influences the rate-making process as already discussed in connection with price level accounting.

It may also be true that historic cost accounting underreports the effective tax rates paid by all businesses. The implication is that replacement cost accounting will highlight this fact and induce individual taxpayers either to (1) reduce their demands for government expenditures or (2) stand ready to carry a bigger share of the burden themselves. This line of thinking in its turn assumes that those who read financial statements are woefully misinformed about what is really occurring. This is a very dubious assumption that pervades most of the reasons advanced for scrapping historic cost accounting. We can best evaluate the assumption by taking a look at the major audiences using published financial data.

Some years ago I investigated the way common stock investors react to flow-through versus normalizing electric utilities. My conclusions were that investors look behind the published accounting data to the underlying economic realities. Subsequently, these conclusions have been tested by other researchers using increasingly more polished statistical techniques. To the best of my knowledge all these studies have come to the same conclusion that I established. Today, there exists a voluminous academic literature exploring many aspects of the connections between accounting data and security prices. The overwhelming burden of evidence points toward a highly competitive, intelligent securities market that can be misled by outright fraud but is not significantly fooled by differences in accounting techniques as such. This should not be construed as an argument against disclosure, but rather as a warning regarding the kinds of information financial statement users are really seeking.

Modern financial theory teaches that existing and potential equity investors are motivated by the same aspiration. They seek the highest rate of return on cash committed relative to the risks borne. The required rate of return is that discount rate which will equate total cash benefits to the original outlay. *Cash benefits* are defined as cash dividends paid during any investment holding period plus cash received when the security is sold. Since sale price at any moment is also determined by expected cash dividends, it follows that the latter are the reward of ownership and the determinant of current stock prices. The logical conclusion is that an intelligent investor is continually trying to discover what portion of reported net income is in fact net free cash available for cash dividend payments. Stated differently, the investor is continually faced with the problem of trying to decipher the connection between accrual accounting techniques and their impact on cash flows. One example of this continuous hide-and-seek game is the interpretation of Allowance for Funds Used during Construction (AFC). For many utilities AFC accounts for a significant share of reported net income. Security analysts have characterized this trend as a decline in what they call "the quality of earnings." In more precise terms they mean that the increasing share of reported net income attributable to AFC makes net income a deteriorating index of the ability to pay cash dividends. In other words, the quality of earnings is governed by how closely they approximate free net cash flows.

Creditors, like investors, also have a keen interest in corporate earnings, which again translates more precisely into a concern about cash flows. The degree of safety enjoyed by any creditor is a direct function of the timing and size of the debtor's expected cash receipts as compared with expected cash outflows. The wider the margin between these two variables, the more secure the debt will be and vice versa. These considerations determine corporate debt capacity regardless of whether one is considering short-, intermediate-, or long-term situations.

The problem is that in the absence of direct information corporate outsiders must resort to using surrogate measures of liquidity such as the current ratio and variants of interest coverage, all derived from accrual accounting figures. Professional lenders understand this when they are evaluating a loan application. They place most reliance on cash statements for revealing the historic pattern of cash flows and on cash budgets for assessing the likelihood of future liquidity problems. Of course, this type of vital information is not directly available to most corporate outsiders, who must therefore develop considerable skill at being cash flow detectives.

Before leaving the question of how corporate outsiders view financial statements we must comment upon the inadequacies of published funds flow statements. These documents are a valuable aid in tracing changes in net working capital, but at best they represent a good opportunity lost when it comes to cash flow analysis. Unfortunately, funds flow statements are inextricably bound up with accrual concepts that only too often seem to be presented in a fashion designed to conceal rather than reveal dangerous trends in corporate liquidity.

As far as internal management of the firm is concerned there is little evidence that published financial statements are used at all for making important financial decisions. Effective management is essentially cash flow management. For example, capital budgeting decisions are made according to the same principles as those governing investments in the securities markets which were outlined earlier. Similarly, the ability to sustain or expand operations comes down to the issue of how much free cash is available after all other cash commitments have been satisfied.

Day-to-day financial operations revolve around working capital management, which is synonymous with controlling liquidity. Obviously, the necessary tools for all these jobs are once again cash flow statements and projected cash budgets.

There is no need to labor the point further. All audiences that read conventional financial statements are interested in the firm's historic cash flow patterns as a necessary foundation for making estimates about future cash flows. This information is vital because expected cash flows set the parameters within which most financial decisions must be made. In contrast, accrual accounting appropriately attempts to differentiate capital from income by measuring income as a flow of value which will eventually materialize as cash over an indefinite time horizon. Switching the valuation basis of assets from historic to replacement cost may result in better published estimates of economic income, but this is not the most pressing need. Those who use financial statements and other economic data are not as naïve as some would have us think. These audiences both inside and outside the corporation seem to know what is occurring. Inflation compounds their estimating difficulties because, among other things, it takes an increasing amount of cash to finance operations at a time when cash flows tend to get out of phase from their familiar patterns. In a nutshell, inflation aggravates liquidity problems that are best understood and remedied in those terms. By the same token, the lay public does not understand accounting techniques or the concept of economic income as currently employed. It is highly improbable that such neophytes will be any more enlightened by valuing assets at current replacement cost. On the other hand, the general public does understand that when cash outflows exceed inflows an acute fiscal problem is at hand. This is the central message that regulated industries are trying to get across to their rate-paying constituents.

The impact of inflation on regulated industries is well understood by anyone who studies the problem. Starting around 1965 cash expenses rose substantially more than cash generated by operations. Even so, the rules of accrual accounting managed to sustain book earnings. This meant that dividend payout ratios became much higher when related to net cash available for distribution than book figures indicated. As a result, cash left over to cover interest charges and finance growth declined. This unpleasant reality also made increased borrowing necessary until, in some cases, debt capacity limits were reached and lenders withdrew from the market. The problem was, and continues to be, one of explaining this sequence of events to a lay public in an understandable fashion.

At this point the solution suggests itself. Regulated industries should lead the way by supplementing published financial statements with some form of cash flow reporting. These reports should conform to at least two fundamental criteria. First, the reported cash flows must be completely divorced from accrual accounting concepts. The only items recorded must be actual cash receipts and payments made during the period covered. Any half-way house approach that mixes cash flow accounting with accrual concepts will defeat the purpose of the exercise. Second, the cash flow statements should be made public at relatively short (say, quarterly) intervals. This will make it easier for analysts to evaluate such things as seasonal and cyclical swings, the size and efficiency of major investment projects, and trends in the relationships between cash revenues and outlays. The latter is especially useful when the general price level undergoes rapid change. During inflation, for example, cash flow statements in effect provide a form of current price accounting which quickly reveals what is happening to cash operating costs relative to cash income.

The type of cash flow statement envisioned is much more than a summary of the firm's bank account. It should be designed as a cash model of the firm linking the past with the present and facilitating estimates of future cash flow trends. Thus we could have an operating cash flow statement showing cash income less all the major items of operating expense producing the net operating cash flow. The latter would then be transferred to a cash flow statement, where changes in the bank balance and other nonoperating cash receipts and payments would be shown. Finally, the item "net cash flow available" would indicate what was available for dividends and reinvestment.

The above information, evaluated in conjunction with conventional statements, would mark a significant step forward in helping both regulators and utility managements explain economic realities to a skeptical public. Equally important, it would make the job of professional analysts much easier by supplying them with the information they spend so much time trying to develop.

It is also worth noting that the private and social benefits to be gained from publishing cash flow statements are not conditional on the way assets are valued or the way economic income is defined. The case for a regular disclosure of cash flows stands on its own merits regardless of what happens to ASR 190 and all other proposals for adapting conventional financial reports to the changing value of money.

Rate of Return Regulation in the Current Economic Environment

Myron J. Gordon

Here I propose to review the current state of knowledge and of ignorance in the area of rate of return regulation of public utility companies. This will include the following: (1) an evaluation of the adequacy of the theory and its implementation under standard conditions; (2) an examination of the problems created by two departures from standard conditions: inflation and the application of the theory to a nontraded division of a firm; and (3) the desirability of a different approach to regulation than control of rate of return.

Measuring the Cost of Capital

The theory on the cost of capital may be stated quite briefly. A utility should be allowed a rate of return that permits it to raise capital to meet the demand for service without cost to the existing shareholders. This rate of return is the appropriately weighted average of the imbedded rate on the debt and preferred stock, a zero rate on the deferred tax reserve, and a return on the common equity equal to the yield at which the common stock is selling. This view of the problem has been widely accepted by practitioners in the field,

---

NOTE: An earlier version of this essay was given at the Federal Communication Commission's Future Planning Conference, 12–13 July 1976. The author has benefited considerably from discussions with E. J. Elton, David Fewings, L. I. Gould, and Paul J. Halpern. These discussions did not always end in agreement on the controversial issues examined below.

although a small number frequently consulted by companies use methods that are fifteen or more years out of date. They still employ return on book for allegedly comparable firms, earnings price yields for allegedly comparable firms, and subjective judgment after reviewing a wide range of data that are for the most part irrelevant.

Only two problems in implementing this theory in practice are of any consequence. One is the determination of the appropriately weighted average of the cost rates for each source of capital, that is, the problem of the correct capital structure. The other is the problem of measuring the yield at which the common stock is selling.

With regard to capital structure the problem is to balance the cost to the consumer of a low debt ratio against the risk to the stockholder and management of a high debt ratio. For a well-regulated utility the tax savings and capital cost savings of a high debt ratio are passed on to the consumer, and the regulatory agency is the only force that exerts an upward pressure on the debt ratio.[1] The debt ratio that provides a reasonable balance between the two legitimate concerns just raised is a matter on which we have little scientific knowledge. Interest coverage data and debt ratios for otherwise comparable firms that have satisfactory bond ratings appear to be the best approach to the problem. Space does not permit detailed discussion of this subject here.

The yield at which a common stock is selling is its dividend yield plus the *expected* rate of growth in the price of the stock. The latter is difficult to measure, and it is estimated by reference to past rates of growth in earnings, dividends, book value, and price of the stock. Given a choice among these four variables, a choice with regard to the number of prior years that is used to obtain an average, and a choice among the statistical techniques used to infer an average from the data, an expert witness can arrive at any figure his client wants.

There is another method for estimating the expected rate of growth in a utility stock's price which I believe is far superior to using past rates of growth in earnings, dividend, book value, or price. That method is the use of past data for the company's return on book and fraction of earnings retained to estimate br, the product of the expected retention and return rates.

I have shown elsewhere that if a firm is expected to retain the fraction b of its earnings and earn a return of r on common equity

[1]Conversely, if the regulator is ineffective or simply resists changes in consumer charges, a utility will find it profitable or necessary to push its debt ratio to the limit.

investment, its earnings, dividends, book value, and price are expected to grow at the rate br.[2] Why does the use of past values of b and r provide better estimates of future growth in earnings, price, and so forth, than the past growth rates in these variables?

The answer quite simply is that the past rate of growth in a variable such as earnings reflects changes in the underlying relevant variables that cannot reasonably be expected to continue in the future. I can illustrate the point by reference to a Canadian rate case with which I am familiar. The company had a dividend yield of 7 percent, a zero rate of growth in the price of its stock over the prior five years, and an 11 percent rate of growth in its earnings per share over the same five years. Was the expected growth rate zero or 11 percent? Obviously, neither of the two. The rise in the cost of capital over the five years had forced the regulator to increase the allowed rate of return on common. This explains the exceptionally high growth rate in earnings. Unless the cost of capital and allowed return on common are expected to continue to rise, this 11 percent overstates the expected rate of growth in earnings for the future. The price of the stock had not gone up over the five-year period because the allowed return on common had not risen as fast as the yield investors required.

An analysis of the past values of b and r for the company produced an estimated growth rate of 6.5 percent and a cost of equity capital of 13.5 percent. However, a simple average of b and r over the past five years does not always produce the best estimate of b and r. Rather, an analysis of that data plus other relevant information may produce estimates of br that depart somewhat from a simple average of past values.

The ideas just presented are demonstrated in greater detail in my testimony in the *New York Telephone* case.[3] Two of the exhibits presented there are reproduced here. Exhibit III shows what happens to the rate of growth in earnings when the return on common is increased. With a 4 percent rate of growth in earnings before period 4 and a 6 percent rate of growth after period 4, the arithmetic mean rate of growth over the five years is 18 percent. This is due to the rise in the return on common from 10 to 15 percent and the 56 percent rate of growth in earnings in period 4. Extrapolation of the 18 percent

---

[2]M. J. Gordon, *The Cost of Capital to a Public Utility* (East Lansing: Division of Research, Michigan State University, 1974), chapter 2.

[3]New York State Public Service Commission, Case 26755.

growth rate over this five-year period would seem to be quite unreasonable.

Exhibit IV presents financial statement data for AT&T for the period 1968 – 1974 and the values of *b* and *r* derived therefrom. The geometric mean rate of growth in earnings over this period was 6.3 percent. However, to forecast that rate of growth in earnings in the future one would have to believe that the allowed return on common will increase by about 1.3 percent every six years. The average value of *r* over the seven years was 9.5 percent, but to use this figure would ignore the fact that the rise in *r* over the prior few years was in response to a rise in the cost of capital. My conclusion from the data was that investors at the time expected a return on common equity of about 10.5 percent and a retention rate equal to the seven-year average of 38 percent. The product is an expected growth rate of 4 percent.

EXHIBIT III

Illustration of Influence of Change in Rate of Return on Rate of Growth in Earnings

Year	*SOY book value*[1]	*Share earnings*[2]	*Share dividends*[3]	*Retained earnings*[4]	*Growth rate of earnings*
1	$10.00	$1.00	$ .60	$.40	
2	10.40	1.04	.624	.416	.04
3	10.816	1.082	.649	.433	.04
4	11.249	1.687	1.012	.675	.56
5	11.924	1.789	1.073	.716	.06
6	12.640	1.896	1.138	.758	.06

[1]Value for previous year plus retained earnings in previous year.
[2]10 percent of book value in first three years and 15 percent of book value in last three years.
[3]60 percent of earnings.
[4]40 percent of earnings.

My reading of the evidence in this and other rate cases leads me to conclude that with the proper approach to the data the range of reasonable differences in arriving at a public utility's cost of equity capital under normal conditions is at most one percent. This conclusion, of course, does not hold for a utility that is experiencing ex-

EXHIBIT IV

AT&T Common Equity, Earnings, Dividends, and Related Statistics, 1968 – 1974, in Millions of Dollars

	1974[1]	*1973*	*1972*	*1971*	*1970*	*1969*	*1968*	*Average*
1 Common equity EOY	$28,556	$27,425	$26,147	$25,065	$24,295	$23,529	$22,682	
2 Common equity SOY	27,200	26,147	25,065	24,295	23,529	22,683	21,555	
3 Common equity average	27,878	26,782	25,606	24,685	23,912	23,106	22,118	
4 Earnings on common	2,970	2,761	2,386	2,191	2,189	2,199	2,052	
5 Dividends on common	1,758	1,591	1,483	1,428	1,428	1,346	1,312	
6 Dividend rate Line 5 ÷ Line 4	.592	.576	.621	.651	.652	.612	.639	.620
7 Retention Rate 1 — Line 6	.408	.424	.379	.349	.348	.388	.361	.380
8 Return on common Line 4 ÷ Line 3	.106	.103	.093	.089	.091	.095	.093	.095

[1]Year ending 30 November 1974.

traordinary difficulties, such as Consolidated Edison in the recent past or many railroads over their recent history. However, it is questionable whether a utility in such circumstances should be given a return on the book value of its existing capital equal to the return investors require on the company's stock. It is also questionable whether it is economically possible for a regulator to do so.

Cost of Capital for a Nontraded Operation

A problem I encounter with increasing frequency is arriving at the cost of capital for a nontraded subsidiary or division of a corporation. The Long Lines Division of AT&T and the New York Telephone Company are examples. The presence of Western Electric in AT&T makes it somewhat riskier than Long Lines or New York Telephone. In these particular cases the risk and other attributes of the division or subsidiary may differ so little from AT&T as a whole as to permit using the capital structure and cost rates for AT&T. However, there are other situations in which a publicly traded corporation owns one or more regulated utility companies and other companies in nonregulated and unrelated lines of business. In this situation risk may vary significantly among the subsidiaries, and the company's overall cost of capital is a poor approximation of the figure for a public utility subsidiary.

A similar situation arises when the problem is to arrive at the cost of capital for different classes of utility service that may differ in risk. For example, residential local exchange service and vertical business services may differ radically in risk and cost of capital. Costing these services on the basis of the company's overall cost of capital may result in substantial error.

In both of the previous situations capital asset pricing theory (CAPT) and Beta type statistics may be useful. This approach may be explained as follows. The yield on a company's common stock and hence its cost of equity capital may be decomposed into the risk-free interest rate and a risk premium. The latter is the product of the yield on a portfolio of all stocks and the shares' Beta statistic. The value of Beta is the covariance between the return on the stock and the return on a portfolio of all stocks divided by the variance in the return on all stocks. The Beta factor for a stock is easily estimated. Hence, given the risk-free interest rate and the yield on the portfolio of all stocks, the share yield and cost of equity capital for a company may be arrived at via capital asset pricing theory.

However, the CAPT approach to arriving at a utility's cost of equity capital is considerably less accurate than the discounted cash flow (DCF) approach described earlier. For the overall cost of capital of a publicly traded corporation where both approaches may be used, CAPT should be used with considerable caution and then only to supplement the DCF approach.

Assume, however, that we are interested in the cost of capital for a nontraded firm or a division of a firm. Here, neither DCF nor CAPT can be used directly since they both rely on market price data for the company's common stock. The earnings data for the company or division may be used to compute an earnings Beta. It has been found that for publicly traded companies earnings Betas and conventional Betas are correlated.[4] The relation between these two sets of Betas derived from a sample of publicly traded companies may be used to estimate the conventional Beta from the earnings Beta for the nontraded company or division. The derived conventional Beta combined with the interest rate and the yield on the market portfolio produce an estimate of the cost of equity capital. The estimate is subject to a wide margin of error, but it may nonetheless be the best possible estimate.

There are circumstances under which it is not even possible to obtain earnings data for the operation in question. The only data available are physical, such as number of calls or kilowatt-hours consumed. If certain conditions are satisfied, it is possible to use such data to arrive at an earnings Beta and estimate therefrom a conventional Beta. This approach to the problem is described in greater detail elsewhere, and it was used in testimony I prepared for the Canadian Commission on the Cost of Transporting Grain by Rail.[5]

Price Level Adjusted Rate Base

Let us now turn to the problems raised by inflation. Of course, regulatory lag is a serious problem, but let us assume that fuel adjustment clauses, interim rate increases, future test periods, and

[4]See M. J. Gordon and Paul Halpern, "The Cost of Capital to a Division of a Firm," *Journal of Finance* 29 (September 1974): 1153 – 63; and Donald J. Thompson, "Sources of Systematic Risk in Common Stocks," *Journal of Business* (April 1976): 173 – 88.

[5]See Gordon and Halpern, "Cost of Capital"; and Submission and Rebuttal Submission to the Commission on the Costs of Transporting Grain by Rail, by Robert L. Banks et al. on Behalf of the Provinces of Alberta, Manitoba, and Saskatchewan, 1976.

the many other changes in regulatory practice that have taken place adequately deal with regulatory lag. Is rate of return regulation based on historical cost a formula for bankrupting investor owned utilities, as some have charged? The proposals that have been advanced for dealing with the problem are price level adjustment to the depreciation charge and price level adjustment to the rate base. A theoretical analysis of the latter problem reveals that the investor is no better or worse off and the utility is no more or less able to raise the capital required to meet the demand for service under price level adjusted cost than under historical cost rate base regulation, when both are properly applied.[6]

This conclusion may be explained briefly as follows. Regardless of whether historical cost or general price level adjusted cost (GPLAC) is used to measure the rate base, the yield investors require on the utility's stock will include a premium over the noninflation yield insofar as the current interest rate and the yield on nonregulated stocks carry the premium.

The only difference between the two rate bases is in how the return is earned over time. The difference is illustrated in Figure 1, which assumes that all earnings are paid in dividends and the investment in the company by the present stockholders does not change.

Under GPLAC the rate base grows with the inflation rate, and the firm's earnings grow with the rate base. Under historical cost the rate base and earnings do not grow over time. Instead, the earnings immediately rise to and remain at a higher level that reflects the inflation adjusted return.[7] The initial level of earnings under GPLAC is what the historical cost earnings would be without inflation. It can be shown that the investor is indifferent between the growing GPLAC earnings and the initially higher but level historical cost earnings.

However, this analysis is based on a number of simplifying assumptions which ignore three questions: What do we do about the difference between the historical and price level adjusted cost rate base at the time the latter is adopted? What do we do about the depreciation charge? If it is price level adjusted, the financing as well as the cost of the excess of the GPLAC over the historical cost

[6]M. J. Gordon, "Comparison of Historical Cost and General Price Level Adjusted Cost Rate Base Regulation," *Journal of Finance* (forthcoming).

[7]If the company retains and invests part of the earnings, the rate base and earnings will grow on that account under either method of valuation for the rate base.

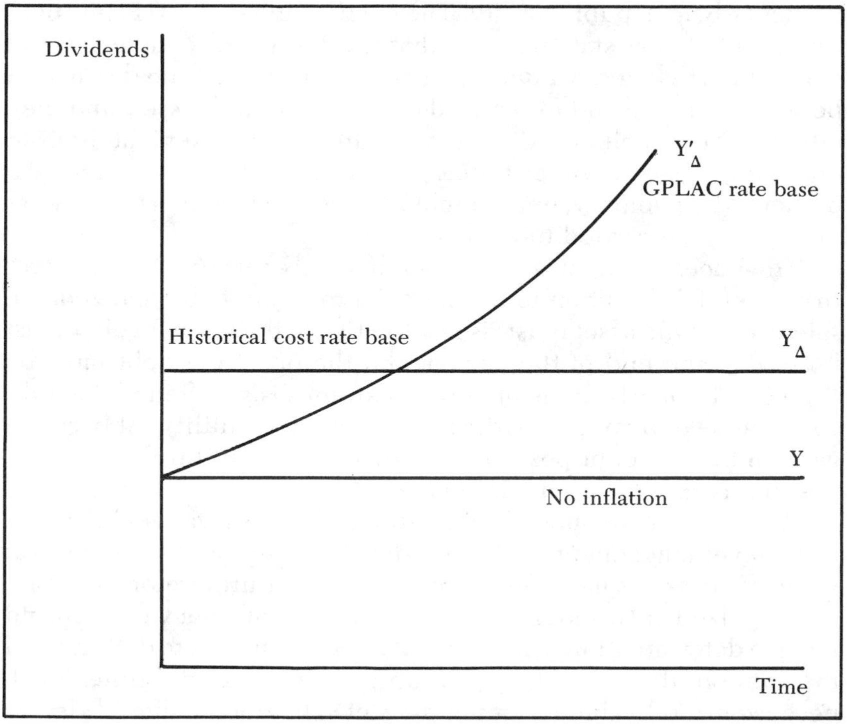

Figure 1. ***Comparative Dividend Streams under Inflation with Historical Cost and GPLAC Rate Base Regulation***

depreciation are transferred from the investor to the consumer. The latter bears the cost under either method. Finally, what do we do about debt in the capital structure? The solution that logically follows from allowing the utility only the imbedded interest rate on its debt is to price level adjust only that fraction of the assets which is equity financed. The other extreme, which provides something of a windfall to the common stockholders, is to price level adjust the entire plant account and carry the entire offsetting adjustment to the ownership equity account. There is no sense in adjusting the bond account unless the principal on the bonds is linked to the price level.

The solution proposed by the AICPA and by academic accountants who have advocated GPLAC financial statements is to carry the so-called gain (loss) on a company's net debt (monetary) position to the net worth account via the income statement. It is difficult to see an accounting or an economic rationale for this course of action, particularly for a public utility. The chief argument for GPLAC over replacement cost statements is that the former recognizes capital gains when realized. Under replacement cost there is no distinction between realized and unrealized capital gains and losses, and they either are not included in income or are reported separately from operating income. Under GPLAC, changes in the value of assets, particularly inventory, unaccounted for by the change in the general price level are carried to income.

How does the realization principle justify carrying the gain on a firm's net debt position to income? For this gain to be realized, the sale value of the asset must rise by the rise in the price level; it must be sold at the end of the period, and the offsetting debt must be liquidated. Clearly, none of these conditions is satisfied in the ordinary course of business, particularly by a public utility. At best, the gain on the net debt position is realized when and if the net debt position is reduced — a LIFO concept.

Turning to economic considerations, there is a gain equal to the price level adjustment to the net debt position only if the market value of the assets has risen correspondingly. Furthermore, the gain is recognized only under a market value basis of asset valuation and income determination. Under GPLAC there is no test to determine if the value of the assets has gone up by the rise in the price level, because market value is not the basis of valuation. It should also be noted that economic theory does not require the use of market value as the basis of measurement. There is ample precedent in economic theory, for example, the national income accounts, for excluding changes in the market value of assets from income and including therein only a firm's going concern operating income. That certainly is the appropriate concept in arriving at what the firm can pay in dividends and invest in additional facilities.

Including the so-called gain or loss on a public utility's net debt position in income is highly questionable when it is regulated on a GPLAC rate base. Doing so with historical cost regulation produces the ridiculous results confirmed by the empirical work of Sidney Davidson and R. L. Weil.[8]

There is a considerable literature on the comparative merits of historical and replacement cost depreciation that I will not review here. The argument in support of replacement cost that has been

---

[8]Sidney Davidson and R. L. Weil, "Inflation Accounting for Utilities," *Financial Analysts Journal* 31 (May/June 1975): 30 – 34.

raised recently is that under inflation the internally generated funds become too small a fraction of capital requirements to permit raising the remainder from external sources. A less dramatic statement of the problem is that the cost of external funds becomes prohibitively high.

From the consumer's point of view the problem may be stated as follows. Going to replacement cost depreciation forces the consumer to invest in the firm to earn a return on his capital equal to the firm's cost of capital. Is the reduction in the firm's cost of capital as a consequence of these internally generated funds sufficiently large to make it profitable for the consumer to provide this fraction of the firm's capital?

Problem with Rate of Return Regulation

I would now like to raise what may well be the most serious limitation of rate of return regulation. Does it fail to provide an effective control over the aggregate level of capital expenditures by a public utility?

Harvey Averch and Leland Johnson have shown that when a utility's allowed return exceeds its cost of capital, the company has an incentive to increase the capital employed by raising the capital-labor ratio. The theorem is true notwithstanding the confusion on the subject engendered by the numerous subsequent articles that have been devoted to qualifying the theory. Another means of realizing the same end noted by Averch and Johnson, and one that has not been adequately recognized in the subsequent literature, is the use of rate design to raise prices on inelastic demand services in order to reduce prices and even cross-subsidize elastic demand services. Capital requirements are increased by this use of rate design to increase the rate of growth in demand.

The Averch-Johnson theorem assumes that the objective of a utility management is to maximize the wealth of the company's stockholders. With the allowed return above the cost of capital, raising the capital employed increases the value of the company's outstanding stock. However, when the allowed return is equal to the cost of capital, the stockholders are indifferent to the firm's investment decision, and one might hope that the firm's investment decision is then made to benefit the consumer, for lack of any other decision objective.

The above reasoning assumes that stockholder welfare is the sole concern of a utility management, and it would be most foolish to argue that management is indifferent to that welfare. In fact, concern for stockholders is in all likelihood second only to management's concern for its own welfare, and there is ample evidence that this latter concern exists. The proposition has even forced its way into the literature of theoretical economics. There is also evidence that the welfare of a corporate management is positively correlated with the growth of the firm. Therefore, an allowed rate of return equal to the cost of capital will not deter a management from using capital intensity and rate design to justify a capital expenditure program that is excessive.

The events of the past few years have made this problem of great practical importance, not merely a theoretical possibility. Clearly, in energy related utility industries and in all likelihood in the telecommunications industry, rate design is stimulating demand at a time when long-run marginal cost is in excess of price for elastic demand services.

There has been a good deal of talk about peak load and usage sensitivity pricing. I am not familiar with what has been accomplished, but I have serious doubts about the ability of a regulatory commission to deal with the problem directly. My experience with the regulatory process leads me to conclude that regulatory agencies have a difficult enough time with the comparatively simple problems of rate base and rate of return determination. Limited regulatory staff, infrequent appearances of expert witnesses on behalf of the consumer, and the abundance of expensive supportive talent employed by the companies make the contest very uneven.

Rate design presents an even more formidable problem. The great body of cost and demand information by type of service required to arrive at conclusions reaches the commission staff only through a filter — the company staff. This information is of questionable value, and analyzing it is expensive. Thus, I am not optimistic that desirable changes in rate design will take place very rapidly as long as they are limited to those changes that are found to be desirable through the regulatory process. With a rate of return equal to or greater than the cost of capital, the company has no motive to cooperate, and what the regulatory staff discovers and pushes through the regulatory process is not likely to be impressive.

My impression is that the cutbacks in capital expenditure plans and changes in rate design that have taken place over the last few years have rarely been due to direct decisions by regulatory agencies on these matters. Rather, actions have been forced on the companies by a fall in the rate of return below the cost of capital and by the legal roadblocks thrown up by the environmentalists. If these motives for economizing disappear with a rise in the allowed return to the cost of capital and by the exhaustion of the environmentalists, the progress that has taken place may come to an end. In that event, the extraordinary, uneconomic, and burdensome growth in the size of public utility companies will continue unabated. Not only the unemployed but also the low income fraction of the working population will be priced out of the market for utility services. It will be necessary to subsidize the use of the basic services by this section of the population, nationalize the companies, or live with the divisive social tension of further increase in the inequality in the distribution of real income.

Perhaps regulators should try to estimate the overall rate of growth in capital expenditures that is required to meet the demand for service and allow the return on capital to fall below the cost of capital as a company's actual expenditures plan goes above this growth rate. This policy has its limitations, both legal and economic, but I have not been able to find a superior alternative.

Comment

William H. Fletcher

The papers by John O'Donnell and Myron Gordon indicate difficulties arising from inflation as well as from regulation. Accordingly, my first recommendation would be to stop inflating and, second, to stop regulating. Neither of these remarks seems to arouse any interest. This may be much too simple a solution, but it deserves serious thought.

Pricing and Competition

One of the participants has mentioned cross subsidy. This is the process by which one class of user is charged more than the cost of the service rendered to that user, and the excess revenue is then used to reduce the cost of another class of user. It has been the intention of regulators over the years to charge business more for the same service than is charged to households. Justification for this inequity has been based upon a theory called "value of service." The effect of cross subsidy is to encourage demand in the less profitable area and to discourage demand in the more profitable area. The natural result of this form of rate structure is to cause the utility to invest in ways which are not naturally responsive to the market. Accordingly, competition enters the market against the utility in the area in which prices are disproportionately high, namely, the business sector. This leaves the utility with the ever-increasing low margin business and forces the prices to rise in that sector as business volume is drained off by the competition. Parenthetically, the belief that utilities are not exposed to competition is an illusion.

Debt

Myron Gordon has commented that the gain on debt, according to the proposal by the Financial Accounting Standards Board (FASB), is illusory unless the amount of that gain can be charged to, and collected from, users of the utility. Commercial companies have varying ability to raise prices in time of inflation to permit them to collect a profit from the holding of debt. Utilities, on the other hand, have their prices fixed by a regulator, and unless the regulator allows that price to advance, the utility will never realize the "gain on debt."

It seems to me that the holding of debt of itself cannot give rise to gain. I would agree with Gordon that any gain must come from the use of the proceeds of the debt, either by selling inventory at advancing prices or by selling fixed assets at advancing prices.

Price Level Device

The FASB proposed to adjust historical dollars by the use of a general price index. In the face of opposition and action from the Securities and Exchange Commission, the FASB shelved its proposal. It is questionable whether or not the proposal would have survived on its own because of the unsolved problems involving debt, as discussed above. The SEC, in its ASR-190, requires that certain specific items be adjusted for replacement cost. These values and methods would not be carried through the entire financial statements, but would be limited to specific information to be shown in the footnotes of the financial statements. Specific indexes continue to confuse the general price level with the action in a particular market. That tends to confuse the question of the return of invested purchasing power with reinvestment of realized purchasing power. There is an assumption in specific index procedures that a businessman is entitled to remain in a particular business by charging his customers currently for the additional capital required to stay in that business.

It is my observation that participants in this conference have little interest in price leveling; rather, their interest is more directed toward whether utilities would be well treated in a historical cost situation or in some form of current value accounting. Gordon expresses the thought that the company would be very little affected by the methods of regulation provided appropriate adjustments were made in changing the data from historical cost to current value, or vice versa. In other words, Indiana allows a 7 percent return on 140 percent of historical cost. The 140 percent of historical cost is said to be a fair value rate base. If this rate of return were translated into historical cost alone, the rate of return would need to be 9.80 percent.

To Whose Advantage Bonds?

There seems to be an assumption that bonds are risk free to stockholders of utilities and that all the advantages of bonded debt, untrammeled by any disadvantages, should be passed along to the utility customers. There is a clear unwillingness to recognize that the customer uses the property without regard to the source from which it arose — be it bonds or stock. The possibility that the stockholder would benefit from contracts with bondholders is thought to be unfair by many participants. Under one proposal all advantages of issuing bonds in an inflationary period would inure to the benefit of the customer. An intermediate proposal, not discussed at any length, is that the stockholders would be permitted any holding gains on the equity, but not on debt. It seems to me that the debt is the obligation of the stockholders, and the details of the contract are those arrived at by the stockholders; that there is no guarantee by the customers or a public service commission that the stockholders will be held harmless from the effects of the debt. Accordingly, it seems to me that the stockholders should have the benefits of the indebtedness.

Gordon at least implies, if he does not state it directly, that the pressure for debt arises from the public service commission. This is completely contrary to my experience. The pressure for debt has come from the *demands* of customers for increased service which could not be purchased with the capital of the stockholders — comprised of their original investments plus accumulations. Faced with the requirement for additional capital, the stockholders often have found that debt is a cheaper means of financing than additional stock. In short, debt has been used as a least cost means of financing capital investment demanded by customers.

Gordon finds the increasing use of capital by public utilities downright burdensome. He therefore appears perfectly willing to support legislation to restrict the capital used by utilities. At the same time, he openly professes to have a consumer bias. Since my experience tells me that additional capital has been demanded by consumers who want specific services, I must conclude that a restriction of the investment of capital by the utilities which render these services will prevent the consumers from getting that which they have demanded. I am at a loss to understand how consumers who want more telephone service, and are willing to pay for it, are better served by depriving them of it.

Efficient Market

Both O'Donnell and Gordon cite the theory of efficient markets as indicating that the facts become known to the investor despite the best efforts of the issuer of financial information to cover them up. There has, indeed, been a good deal of work done to show that markets are efficient, that investors do know more than we give them credit for, and that the prices of securities tend to be adjusted for the realities existing within the companies. Neither O'Donnell nor Gordon offers an explanation for the overnight debacle of Penn Central commercial paper. Commonwealth Edison has not been discussed, but I wonder why security holders did not discover the trouble of this company before it exploded upon the market. Furthermore, I wonder why New York banks — and others — got caught with New York City bonds. On the local scene in Indiana, I wonder why investors did not tumble to Dolly Madison before it went bankrupt. In short, my very small and inadequate empirical studies lead me to doubt very seriously the efficient market theory. If, in fact, my doubts are not well founded and the efficient market works, I then ask why the method of accounting or the amount of information furnished to investors makes any difference, since somehow or other investors are going to discover all they need to know about a company without being told?

Cash Flow Statement

O'Donnell recommends as a solution to the problems of inflation a cash flow statement unsullied by accrual accounting concepts. I find this startlingly naïve. In my own experience I recall several situations where cash information was being used and where the facts were being covered up. For example, it has been a source of considerable difficulty in at least one bank of which I have knowledge. I also remember Zechendorf and Webb & Knapp. Zechendorf was peddling cash flows publicly in the Copley Plaza Hotel in Boston, Massachusettts, as being the only suitable measure on which to buy Webb & Knapp's buildings. When questioned about depreciation — and accrual concepts — he waved us all away and let us know what small minds we had. Nonetheless, within a few years he had managed to bankrupt Webb & Knapp, partly because he did not keep track of accrual concepts.

Nationalization

Both O'Donnell and Gordon see nationalization as a cure for such things as the investment of excessive amounts of capital in the utility business. There is at least the implication that pricing would be more satisfactory and the service equal, or superior, to present service. It may be that O'Donnell, from the United Kingdom, and Gordon, from Canada, are unfamiliar with the U.S. postal system, or TVA, or Amtrak. There are numerous examples, both within and without the United States, but there is in my opinion very little evidence that our federal government will give us honest pricing, lower pricing, less cost, minimum capital, or decent service. It is for all these reasons, which may be demonstrated by empirical studies, that I would reject nationalization and plead mightily for deregulation.

Wealth Distribution

Gordon abhors the imagined inequality of maldistribution of wealth, and, of course, his recommendations concerning nationalization and regulation indicate a strong socialist bias. Needless to say, I belong to those "predators" who believe that the producer should eat better than the nonproducer, especially when the nonproducer is voluntarily so. I am reminded, by Gordon's remarks, of an example which was given at an Athens, Ohio, conference directed by Svetozar Pejovich. The discussion brought up the subject of wealth distribution. At the two poles of the idea, all wealth would be in one person — that pole might be numbered 100. At the other pole, all wealth would be distributed with absolute equality — that pole numbered 0. If I remember the statistics recited, the USSR has a quotient of 27 and the United States 33. The thought was also expressed by some in that meeting, who apparently had personal knowledge, that the differences between the wealthy and the poor in the Soviet Union were much greater than those between the wealthy and the poor in the United States. With different legal systems with respect to property, it is probably difficult to make measurements of dispersion of this sort with any accuracy, but if the quotients of 27 and 33 are realistic, the wealth distribution in the two countries is not far apart. In short, socialism and communism do not offer a substantial improvement in the distribution of wealth to those who believe that equal distribution of wealth is a *sine qua non.*

Cost of Capital

Gordon extensively discusses the cost of capital. Some of the terms he defines and some he does not. Two which he does define are "BO" and "Beta sector." Nonetheless, struggling mightily with the information furnished, I understand that he would find the rate of return equal to the embedded cost of borrowed money, plus a zero rate on deferred income taxes, plus the actual yield rate on stock. It is not clear when he speaks of yield whether or not he is referring to earnings — whether or not distributed — or to dividends. It would seem to me that the cost of capital should properly be the current cost at the margin. It would be appropriate here to include a remark from Benjamin Rogge concerning the cost to raise the capital for this company in the existing marketplace: Embedded cost is universally obsolete.

Comment

Richard Walker

The papers by John O'Donnell and Myron Gordon on financial reporting and rate of return regulation during inflation go to the most significant matters facing the utility industry today. I compliment them on their work and the attention that they have focused on these issues.

I would also like to express my admiration for their courage, which they demonstrate by their willingness and even enthusiasm to take on the chore of lifting the veil on the future. The comments by Professor Gordon and Professor O'Donnell and their approach to determining rate of return by reference to future values is indeed as bold as it is difficult. I think all would agree that estimating the growth in the market price of a share of a company is a not inconsiderable task.

Gordon, in his approach to a more reliable method of determining rate of return by reference to dividend yield and future growth in the market price of stock, suggests a simplification in the means of estimating this growth in market price. He prefers to estimate the future return on common and the expected fraction of those future earnings to be retained, and he would consider that the product of these two numbers would produce the approximate growth in the market value of the common stock. As I understand him, he thinks this will produce a more reliable answer than the individual estimation of the factors affecting the growth in market value and dividend yield. I personally believe his method may be more internally consistent than some others that have been used in this regard, but I believe that he is still in the position of estimating the future returns to be allowed and earned on common stock — which is the very function of the regulatory process for which the data would be prepared. And it appears that he also assumes a constant relationship between future market price and the expected future dividends times the product of the return on common and the percentage of earnings retained. This seems to be circular and largely dependent on the proposition that things will be in the future as they have been in the past.

On the matter of general price level adjusted cost (GPLAC) as a rate base, I think that Gordon has made significant contributions. I agree that whatever can be done through the rate base theoretically can be done through rate of return. However, for the correct accounting for the effect of price level to occur through the rate of return, I think it will be necessary for the rate of return to vary instantaneously with the inflation rate so that the full impacts of the change in the price level are entered into the pricing formula immediately. This instantaneous change in rate of return, however, has not happened, and in my opinion will not and cannot happen in the future. Therefore, I at least question Gordon's conclusion that the investor is no better or worse off under GPLAC than under historical cost. His theory is nonetheless interesting.

If you can visualize a one-time 10 percent change in the price level, and if the rate of return for that one year were to be increased by 10 percent, it is true that the investor would be no better or worse off than under a GPLAC rate base. But quite aside from the fact that that type of rate of return regulation does not and cannot happen, such a charge in utility rates for the full impact in the year of change would be an improper price apportionment among the various vintages of customers. Therefore, as a matter of customer fairness, as I believe was pointed out by James Bonbright some 15 years ago, accounting for inflation impacts should be made through the rate base and through the depreciation allowances if it is to be made at all.

Should GPLAC be applied to rate base and therefore to depreciation? I agree with Gordon that it is not feasible to apply the adjustment to the debt-financed portion of the historic cost rate base. Therefore, there should be a weighting between the common equity portion and that portion financed by preferred in debt. As I am sure many realize, this theory has been advanced in rate case after rate case throughout this country with little acceptance.

To the best of my knowledge, this is the first view of the matter that has been taken by an eminent scholar such as Gordon, other than Bonbright, and I am very pleased to see his interest in this subject and the work that he is doing. I agree that if such a form of GPLAC were adopted as a regulatory system in which both customers and investors could rely, then the overall cost of capital would likely be lower than it otherwise would be. The risk and uncertainty in the investor's mind are huge, and unanticipated inflation losses undoubtedly require large amounts of risk compensation. Any plan which would tend to minimize this cost would be a most desirable regulatory step.

A GPLAC system was advanced by the Financial Accounting Standards Board (FASB). Unfortunately, the FASB in effect foolishly proposed to apply the index to the long-term debt outstanding to determine a "profit" which would be included in income in the year of the price level change. This particular concept of the impact of inflation together with the advancement of replacement costs by the SEC have caused the FASB to set aside its GPLAC supplemental financial statement requirements for the moment. Gordon has ably analyzed the notion that the price level changes as applied to debt produce current income. Should the FASB reconsider GPLAC along these more correct lines, it is possible that GPLAC may yet find a proper place in the financial reporting and price setting mechanisms that pertain to the utility industry.

Why should GPLAC financial statements be applied only to the common equity portion and not the portion financed with debt and preferred stock? The answer is that the regulatory process effectively treats the rate base to the extent it is financed with debt and preferred as though it were a "monetary asset." This is true in almost all states with perhaps the exception of a few which use fair value. Therefore, I think it is quite clear that if there is a gain on debt as proposed by the FASB, there is a corresponding loss on the holding of the utility plant which is tantamount to a monetary asset to the same extent. If it is appropriate to include in income the gain from the debt, it is also appropriate to include the loss in the holding of the monetary asset in the form of utility plant priced at original cost, with the return allowed at the embedded debt rates and the embedded preferred stock rates.

In the United Kingdom, the accounting standards committee has discussed the basis on which replacement costs are to be computed. These are (1) suppliers' official price lists, catalogues, and so forth, with appropriate deductions for trade discounts; (2) the company's own replacement cost estimates, based on expert opinion; (3) an index compiled by the company from its own purchasing experience; (4) authorized external price indices analyzed by asset type; and (5) authorized external price indices analyzed by using industry.

As I read those criteria, I thought for a moment I had slipped back into the 1920s and was reading from the appraiser's reports that were the basis in those days of writing up the assets and the capital structure of utility companies in this country. The writing down of these assets to cost involved a great deal of my time at one point in my career.

As you know, the thesis underlying original cost pricing is that a single body of economic data is accepted by and made known to customers, investors, and the public which serves as a basis not only of financial reporting but also for pricing and therefore of balancing these interests. In a period of relatively stable prices, this system, while not without limitations, was not too bad. Today, with rapidly changing prices, it is inadequate unless compensation occurs in the rate of return. If an adjustment for inflation is to be made, why should it not be done overtly and explicitly rather than relying on the notion that the market knows something that would have to be inferred from unpublished or even nonexistent data?

But will replacement costs be able to provide data which can be relied upon by investors, customers, and the public for financial reporting purposes and for pricing purposes? The SEC, I think, has answered the question in part by referring to the "subjective" nature of replacement costs. The extensive rate regulatory history in this country involving the use of replacement cost and other current value estimates, lack of objectivity in the preparation of such amounts, and indeed the circularity that is involved between the results that are obtained from showing financial information on replacement cost basis and the act of making the replacement itself, all seem to make the likelihood of any substantial reliance on replacement cost in utility regulation remote.

Thus, there seems to be a need for additional research and documentation along the lines of Gordon's consideration of GPLAC as a rate-making device and as a means of financial reporting. It would appear that in GPLAC the utility industry has the best chance for a system which would operate in the overall public interest.

I understand that one of the proposals in conjunction with the British Sandilands Report is that historic original cost data will no longer be recorded. I cannot conceive of this situation and feel that there are grave risks attached to it. I would hope that if the British companies are to be shot into outer space in that fashion that they have some form of a reentry system laid out before the blast-off. Or, as in the case of original cost, perhaps we in the accounting profession can look forward to a huge new wave of work in the future when the need for historic original cost economic data becomes evident and the public demand forces companies back to it. In any event, I think it would be a mistake to even contemplate an accounting-financial reporting system in the United States which would not provide for the accumulation of historic cost data.

It is clear that many business people do not understand the purpose behind inclusion of replacement cost data. Apparently, sponsors of the concept must do a substantial job of educating the business public. O'Donnell makes a point that informed investors do examine published data to make their adjustments. He cites, in this regard, a study he made years ago of investor's reactions to flow-through versus normalizing for the income tax benefits of accelerated depreciation. While this conclusion appears to me correct, there is a serious question that this would apply to price level adjustments for the simple reason that they are extensive and complex to make, and until they are made and presented to investors, the investor has grossly inadequate information upon which to act. This was not true in the case of accelerated depreciation flow-through, as there were advisory services that widely reported current and accumulated effects of the flow-through practice with full adjustment to retained earnings, and so forth. Therefore, it would appear that O'Donnell's analogy would apply only after GPLAC's effects have become familiar and the investing and other publics are educated as to their significance. O'Donnell's suggestion for the publication of more extensive cash flow information is indeed interesting. He puts forth the proposition that, to be more useful, such statements should be completely disassociated from accrual accounting concepts. While creditors, particularly short-term creditors, obviously have a substantial need for this kind of information, is it necessary and desirable for the long-term equity and debt investors? This is a subject that definitely needs further exploration.

Anyone with experience of financial statements on a cash basis realizes the tremendous swings in cash flows that result from accident, holiday schedules, and even the control of cash flows by a management. It is difficult to see how additional cash flow data, at least any other than that shown in the funds statements, would be helpful to most investors in the usual, healthy company situation. In any event, I doubt that a cash flow statement is going to indicate more than the conventional accrual financial statements as to the cash that will be available for cash dividends — an overall objective suggested by O'Donnell.

The Automatic Adjustment Clause as a Regulatory Tool

The New Mexico Regulatory Response to Inflation

Stanley Bazant, Jr.

This essay centers on what has been dubbed "cost of service indexing," in particular, its origins, philosophy, mechanics, and consequences thus far.

The method was conceived, designed, and recommended by Charles D. Olmsted, Commission Special Counsel, and myself, as case director, in a rate proceeding initiated by Public Service Company of New Mexico in fall 1974.

Unfortunately, our recommendation, which met with a warm reception from the company, was rejected by the New Mexico Public Service Commission when first offered. Instead, the commission issued a traditional order based on a historical test year authorizing new base service rates designed to generate a 14 percent return on average common equity (at book value) after payment of all other costs of service. As predicted, the market price of the company's stock, which then stood at 55 percent of book value, scarcely fibrillated when the October 1974 order was entered, and the company was still effectively prohibited from attracting greatly increased amounts of urgently needed new capital under reasonable terms and conditions. Early in 1975, however, Public Service Company, joined by its most vigorous opponents in the earlier proceeding — several environmental and consumer protection organizations convinced of the new method's effectiveness — petitioned the commission for allowance of the rate indexing method of regulation. After a short hearing in March 1975 concerned solely with the problems rate indexing is designed to solve and with the advantages and consequences of the solution, the commission announced its decision to grant the request on 7 March. A lengthy Decision and Order followed on 22 April.

The problems confronting the commission, the Public Service Company, and its customers and which inspired rate indexing were those with which we are all too familiar: (1) ever increasing costs of generating, transmitting, and distributing electric energy occasioned by inflation, the machinations of OPEC, and environmental restraints; (2) growth in electric power and energy demand; (3) the need to move toward more capital-intensive energy generating systems in an effort to reduce petroleum fuel dependency and ultimately to achieve comparatively lower energy costs; (4) the compounding consequences of regulatory lag upon the increasing cost of capital; and (5) the near total preoccupation of the regulators with service rate proceedings to virtual exclusion of all other important regulatory considerations and efforts.

As we perceived the dismal prospects, the traditional method of periodically fixing relatively inflexible rates for each class of service, following expensive and lengthy adversary hearings, simply did not help to solve the problems. To the contrary, the traditional methods seemed to compound the difficulties in some respects and, at best, served only the short-range interest of the consumer. And even this seemed largely illusory.

Our objectives in designing and implementing rate indexing were manifold. First, we sought to restore or establish earnings stability and reliability and, by reducing investor risk, to reduce the cost and facilitate the attraction of necessary new capital to the company. Second, we sought to encourage and enable the company to do what it must in the public interest, that is, provide for demand growth, improved system reliability, and comparatively lower energy costs to the consumer in the future. Third, we sought to establish and preserve strong management incentives to resist cost increases and to effect economies without sacrificing the incentive or ability to plan and prepare for the future. Fourth, we sought to moderate the magnitude of inevitable rate increases and to more exactly time and correlate service rate changes to the company's current net service cost fluctuations; our intention was to provide for automatic and relatively immediate benefits to consumers where net service costs savings are achieved and, similarly, for relief to the company where irresistible cost increases are incurred. Fifth, we sought to achieve a more equitable and realistic allocation of the capital costs attendant upon construction work in progress between the current and future ratepayer. Sixth, we sought to reduce the inordinate and largely wasteful demands upon the time, energies, and other resources of the company, the commission, and its staff involved in traditional rate proceedings and, thus, to enable them to concentrate on more promising areas such as generating resource planning, efficient load management, demand forecasting, new rate structures, and so forth.

The method devised and implemented by the New Mexico Public Service Commission's order of 22 April 1975 to achieve the foregoing objectives is direct and simple. First, it established a set of base rates for the several types of retail electric service furnished by the company in New Mexico. These rates had been justified earlier by the company's annualized 1973 test year, long-run incremental cost study and had been designed to result in a net rate of return on allocated common equity capital (at book value) of 14 percent per year, after payment of all other cost of service. This 14 percent rate of return was lower by one to 1.5 percentage points than that which the company had sought in a 1974 rate proceeding; however, it was anticipated by all concerned that a stable and reliable average 14 percent rate would ultimately achieve and maintain a market price for the company's stock at a modest level above its book value and, thus, enable the company to attract needed new capital on reasonable conditions and terms in order to satisfy its statutory service mandated in the future.

Second, in order to achieve and thereafter maintain this net rate of return, the 22 April order provides for automatic, quarterly adjustments in all base service rates in response to experienced increases or decreases in the company's earned rate of return on average allocated common equity capital in relation to an allowed range of return on either side of 14 percent. The range is from 13.5 to 14.5 percent, and so long as the accounting reports of the company, which are independently verified by experienced public utility accountants retained by the commission (Touche Ross & Company), indicate at the end of each quarter that its earned rate of return for the preceding accounting period is within the allowed range or band, no adjustment in the then current level of service rate is allowed during the succeeding quarter. The exception is for monthly cost of fuel and purchased power adjustments pursuant to the commission's earlier general order. Should it be indicated that the rate of return exceeded the upper limit of the range, all service rates are to be adjusted downward by application of a decremental amount per kilowatt-hour of consumption designed to restore the company's rate of return during the accounting period ending with the next calendar quarter to 14.5 percent. Conversely, if a rate of return below 13.5 percent is demonstrated, the company's service rates are adjusted upward on the same basis to restore it to the lower limit of the allowed range. The same decremental or incremental adjustment per kilowatt-hour of energy consumption, as the case may be, is applied to the energy charge for each class of service.

It should be noted that each automatic adjustment in rates is designed to restore net earnings to the nearest edge of the allowed range of return, not to the middle. This device is calculated to encourage the company to resist cost increases and to effect economies whenever possible, for the net difference to the common stockholders of the company in this one percent range is currently about $840,000 per year, which the company may achieve and keep through the application of effective management. By the same token, the consumers derive the benefit of larger economies which would otherwise result in net earnings above 14.5 percent by automatic, quarterly reductions in service rates.

The competing requirements of prohibiting recovery of past revenue deficiencies and of moderating the magnitude of service rate adjustments made necessary by below "band" earnings in the second quarter of 1975 and by seasonal fluctuations in kilowatt-hour sales was resolved by providing for an initial reporting period. This consists of the quarter ending 30 June 1975, and a quarter was added to each reporting period thereafter until the full 12 months ending with the quarter immediately preceding the service rate adjustment was reached (which is delayed for 30 days after the end of each quarter to allow time for preparation and verification of the necessary accounting reports and calculations) and by averaging the allocated common equity capital denominator of the earnings rate calculation. Also, in order to dampen and further moderate rate adjustments, as well as to account for the one-month delay in their application, the method provides for calculation of the rate of return on a simulated or pro forma, as distinguished from an actual, basis. That is, in making each quarterly calculation of jurisdictional electric operating revenues, it is assumed that the last preceding cost of service index was in effect during the entire reporting period and not just for the last two months of the preceding quarter.

Insofar as possible, the quarterly account reports submitted by the company and verified by the independent accountants are keyed to the Federal Power Commission's uniform system of accounts in order to provide a check against the company's annual report to that agency. Empirically derived allocation factors for "jurisdictional electric investment" and for "jurisdictional expense allocation" are required to be determined by the company and verified by the New Mexico commission's staff each year.

As a final feature, the new method includes in the denominator with which the rate of return is determined all capital invested in current transmission, distribution, and miscellaneous construction work in progress (CWIP), as well as that invested in environmental CWIP on existing generating plant, and excludes from the numerator any offsetting allowance for funds used during construction (AFDC) on such capital as a revenue item. Naturally, it also prohibits capitalization of AFDC in the cost of these plant items. The formula also includes in the denominator all capital invested in new generating plant CWIP, but requires the inclusion of AFDC on all such CWIP in the numerator and permits capitalization of such AFDC unless the commission otherwise directs at the time the new generating plant is certified for construction by the commission. This is deemed the appropriate time to make the determination as to what portion of the costs of capital invested in new generating plant construction the current rate payer should pay. At present, Public Service Company is allowed an AFDC rate of 6.5 percent on such capital; accordingly, under the formula the current rate payer is paying the difference between the company's weighted cost of total capital and the 6.5 percent rate.

You may note that this method does not concern itself with the value of utility plant and other rate base items, except for purposes of determining the jurisdictional electric investment factor. Since we are concerned with a market cost of capital, it obviously makes more sense to concern ourselves with capital values than with asset or property values. Moreover, the device avoids the frustrating and circular exercise of determining what is a fair return on the fair value of property. Obviously, however, service rates can be indexed to rate base values, whether original cost or fair value, if this is desired or required by law.

By itself, the rate indexing method does not attempt to regulate or to impose normal capital ratios. To the extent that a regulatory authority, as distinguished from management and the marketplace, should seek to control this feature, the appropriate time to do so is in proceedings to approve the issuance of securities, not service rate proceedings. The commission in New Mexico has rather comprehensive power to control permanent financing by the company.

Service rate adjustment dates are set by the commission's order on the first day of February, May, August, and November of each year. At least ten days before each adjustment date, the company is obliged to prepare and file an attested "cost of service index report form" with the commission. An example is provided in Figure 1. This one-page document consists of 66 line items of financial information developed during the accounting period ending with the last day of the preceding calendar quarter. There are two "bottom line" calculations. One is pro forma calculation of the company's percentage rate of return on average jurisdictional common equity capital during the preceding accounting period, which now consists of a full 12 months. The other is a calculation of a "current cost of service index," expressed in dollars per kilowatt-hour, designed to restore the company's return on equity during the accounting period ending with the last day of the next calendar quarter to the nearest edge of the allowed band or range of return, that is, 13.5 to 14.5 percent. Assuming that the commission's independent accountants, who have at least ten days to verify each quarterly report against the company's books, have no serious quarrel with the calculation, implementation of service rate adjustments is automatic and requires no formal proceeding or approval by the commission. Such hearings and official approvals are now reserved for changes in the midpoint and the limits of the allowed range of return and for changes in base service rate design.

Obviously, the method of service rate regulation I have described is designed to achieve for Public Service Company, and thereafter maintain, a level of service revenue sufficient to cover its actual costs of debt and preferred stock capital, as well as its operation, amortization, and tax costs, and to provide a stable and reliable rate of return on average allocated electric common equity capital at a level calculated to restore the market price of its stock to or slightly above its book value. Admittedly, the method tends to eliminate clear distinctions between common stocks and the bonds of an electric utility, and I for one regret the necessity of this, but I see no other way at the moment to enable Public Service Company and others like it to solve the problems confronting them or to reduce their costs of capital. And if it is necessary to do so by placing a floor under the earnings of a utility, the symmetry of a law and of common concepts of fairness oblige the regulatory authority to prescribe a ceiling as well.

To date, three cost of service index adjustments have been applied to Public Service Company's base service rates. The one implemented 1 August 1975 was based on second quarter 1975 revenues and costs, that implemented 1 November 1975 was based upon second and third quarter revenues and costs, and that implemented 1 February 1976 was based upon second, third, and fourth quarter revenues and costs. The 1 August adjustment was 2.688 mills per kilowatt-hour and resulted in an approximate 9 percent increase in the average cost of electric energy (and in Public Service Company's jurisdictional electric revenues) *above base rates*. The 1 November adjustment was 1.997 mills per kilowatt-hour, or an approximate 6.6 percent increase above base rates. Thus, the average cost of electric energy in effect was reduced during August, September, and October 1975. The 1 February 1976 cost of service index adjustment was 1.974 mills per kilowatt-hour above base rates. Accordingly, a small reduction in rates again occurred.

Unfortunately, the situation was somewhat muddy when the New Mexico Public Service Commission granted rate indexing to Public Service Company in March 1975. Shortly after the commission's order of the preceding October, which granted only 44 percent of the requested increase, the company appealed the order and put its full proposed rates into effect. Since it continued to charge these full rates from November 1974 through April 1975, when the rates were substantially reduced for the remaining two months of the second quarter (as well as for the first month of the third quarter) by the commission's 22 April 1976 order, the company's earnings on average common equity capital during the first and second quarters of 1975 were 12.45 and 7.74 percent, respectively. This unfortunate circumstance, coupled with the fact that the company's first quarter earnings were not considered in calculating the 1 August 1975 cost of service index factor, resulted in the substantial increase in rates on that date. A decided improvement in the company's load factor and an increase in its kilowatt-hour sales during the third and fourth quarters of 1975 apparently caused the slight reductions in the index

Figure 1. ***Public Service Company of New Mexico, Electric Department, Integrated System: Cost of Service Index Report Form, 30 September 1975, Revised***

	Column A	Column B	Notes
Part I – Jurisdictional Electric Investment	*Total PNM*	*Total Electric*	
1. Acct. (101-106, 114, 116, 120.1-120.4) utility plant	$ 300,430,237	$ 275,615,269	Form #1*, p. 113, 351
2. Acct. (103, 111, 115, 120.5) accumulated depreciation & amortization	(65,684,464)	(62,576,382)	Form #1, p. 113, 351
3. Acct. (107) construction work in progress (CWIP)	76,463,224	74,875,308	Form #1, p. 113
4. Net utility plant (line 1+2+3)	$ 311,213,997	$ 287,914,195	Net plant ratio — 92.5133%
5. Acct. (121-128) other property and investments (nonutility)	4,740,829	-0-	Form #1, p. 110
6. Acct. (131-136) cash and special deposits	2,110,793	1,952,769	Net plant ratio 92.5133%
7. Acct. (141-146) notes and receivables	11,528,994	10,665,853	Net plant ratio
8. Acct. (151-157) materials and supplies	8,961,247	8,657,562	Form #1, p. 207
9. Acct. (163) stores expense undistributed	127,068	122,762	Materials & supplies ratio
10. Acct. (165) prepayments	1,607,300	1,449,248	Detailed classification
11. Acct. (171-174) interest and rents receivable & deferred fuel expense	1,118,705	1,123,375	Detailed classification
12. Total current assets (line 6+7+8+9+10+11)	$ 25,454,112	$ 23,971,569	
13. Acct. (181) Unamortized debt expense	2,528,605	2,339,296	Net plant ratio
14. Acct. (183) preliminary surveys	472,984	468,269	Detailed classific., p. 212
15. Acct. (184) clearing accounts	287,101	265,607	Net plant ratio
16. Acct. (186) miscellaneous deferred debits	1,455,790	1,394,383	Detailed classific., p. 214
17. Acct. (182, 185, 187-189) other deferred debits	-0-	-0-	Detailed classification
18. Total deferred debits (line 13+14+15+16+17)	$ 4,744,480	$ 4,467,560	
19. Total assets and other debits (line 4+5+12+18)	346,153,418	316,353,324	

Deductions:			
20. Acct. (232-242) current and accrued liabilities	15,814,038	14,630,088	Net plant ratio
21. Acct. (252) customer advances	3,210,365	2,326,197	Form #1, p. 224
22. Acct. (255) accumulated deferred investment tax credits	5,621,180	5,020,275	Form #1, p. 229
23. Acct. (253, 256, 257) other deferred credits	346,999	332,197	Detailed classific., p. 225
24. Acct. (261-265) operating reserves	(48,170)	(44,564)	Net plant ratio
25. Acct. (281-283) accumulated deferred income taxes	14,801,785	14,241, 511	Form #1, p. 227
26. Total deductions (line 20+21+22+23+24+25)	$ 39,746,197	$ 36,505,704	
27. Total investment (line 19-26)	306,407,221	279,847,620	
28. Jurisdictional electric investment allocation factor		.89631	
29. Jurisdictional electric investment (line 27B × 28)		250,830,220	

Part II – Jurisdictional Electric Common Equity	*Total PNM*	*Jurisdictional Electric*	
30. Acct. (201-217) capital stock and surplus (monthly average)	$ 136,479,221		Form #1, p. 111
31. Acct. (204-214) preferred stock, preferred stock expense (monthly average)	39,430,434		Form #1, p. 111, 218
32. Common equity (line 30 – 31) (monthly average)	$ 97,048,787		
33. Jurisdictional capital allocation factor ((line 29) ÷ (line 27A-5A))	.83148		
34. Jurisdictional electric common equity investment ((line 32-5A) × 33)		$ 76,752,221	
35. First preceding jurisdictional electric common equity investment		72,415,848	
36. Second preceding jurisdictional electric common equity investment		-0-	Previous reports
37. Third preceding jurisdictional electric common equity investment		-0-	
38. Average jurisdictional electric common equity investment ((line 34+35+36+37) ÷ 2.0)		$ 74,584,035	

Figure 1. – *Continued*

	Column A	Column B	Notes
Part III – Jurisdictional Electric Net Income Available for Common Equity	*Total Electric*	*Jurisdictional Electric*	
39. Acct. (400) electric operating revenue	$ 41,655,744		Form #1, p. 409
40. Jurisdictional electric operating revenue		$ 36,952,132	Form #1, p. 409, 412, 416
Electric Expenses:			
41. Acct. (401, 402) electric operation and maintenance expenses	19,464,877		Form #1, p. 114
42. Acct. (403-407) electric depreciation and amortization expense	4,163,010		Form #1, p. 114
43. Acct. (408.1) taxes other than income taxes	2,604,960		Form #1, p. 114
44. Electric expenses other than income taxes (line 41+42+43)	$ 26,232,847		
45. Net income before income taxes (line 39–44)	15,422,897		
46. Acct. (409-411) income taxes	4,588,153		Form #1, p. 114, 229
47. Jurisdictional expense allocation factor	.88043		
48. Jurisdictional expenses other than income taxes (line 44×47)		23,096,185	
49. Jurisdictional net income before income taxes (line 40–48)		$ 13,855,947	
50. Jurisdictional income taxes ((line 49+45)×46)		4,122,002	
51. Net jurisdictional electric operating income (line 49–50)		$ 9,733,945	
52. Electric allowance for funds used during construction (AFDC)	1,164,523		Electric only
53. Jurisdictional electric AFDC (line 52 × 28)		1,043,774	
54. Income adjustment for preceding calculations		1,190,181	

Interest Expense and Preferred Dividends:			
55. Acct. (427-431) interest expense	$ 5,755,262		Form #1, p. 116A
56. Acct. (437) preferred dividends	1,577,300		Form #1, p. 117
57. Total interest expense and preferred dividends (line 55+56)	$ 7,332,562		
58. Jurisdictional interest expense and preferred dividends (line 57×33)		$ 6,096,879	
59. Jurisdictional net income available for common equity (line 51+53+54−58)		5,871,021	
Part IV – Return on Jurisdictional Common Equity			
60. Annual return on jurisdictional common equity (ROE) ((line 59÷38)×100%)×2.0		15.743%	
61. Percentage difference between current ROE and 13.5%-14.5% range		(1.243%)	
62. Revenue differential ((line 38×61)÷48.59%)÷ 2.0		(953,982)	
63. Jurisdictional kwh sales during period		1,381,356,115 kwh	Form #1, p. 409
64. Incremental index factor (line 62÷63)		(.000691/ kwh)	
65. Previous index factor		.002688/ kwh	
66. Current cost of service index (line 64+65)		$ .001997 kwh	

ATTESTATION: B.D. Luckey certifies that he is Controller of PUBLIC SERVICE COMPANY OF NEW MEXICO; that he has examined the foregoing report; that to the best of his knowledge, information, and belief, all statements of fact contained in the said report are true and the said report is a correct statement of the business and affairs of the above-named respondent in respect to each and every matter set forth therein during the period from and including April 1, 1975, to and including September 30, 1975. *Signature of Attester.*

*Form #1 means Federal Power Commission Form #1.

for those quarters. (In this connection, it is interesting to note that during 1975 Public Service Company's peak load increased only 0.4 percent, but its kilowatt-hour sales increased 13.9 percent over those of 1974.)

More significant perhaps than its effect on service rates are the effects of rate indexing on Public Service Company's cost of capital. As stated earlier, the commission's public announcement that it intended to grant the company's request for rate indexing occurred on Friday, 7 March 1975. At that time, Moody and Standard & Poor's had both indicated that they intended to downgrade the company's bond rating from double-A to single-A and its preferred stock rating correspondingly, due primarily to its very low coverage ratios. However, owing entirely to the commission's action and despite the fact that the company's service rates were to be reduced in the ensuing months, as explained earlier, this downrating did not occur. Accordingly, Public Service Company was able to sell $25 million in 30-year bonds at a double-A yield of 9.125 percent and $10 million of preferred stock at a single-A yield of 10.6 percent on 12 March 1975. Comparison of these issues with reasonably contemporaneous issues of single-A bonds and triple-B preferred stocks by comparable companies indicates that rate indexing saved Public Service Company approximately 85 basis points on its bond yield and 50 basis points on its preferred stock yield. Rate indexing, therefore, saved the company and its customers approximately a quarter of a million dollars per year, or $8 million over the next 30 years on these two modest issues alone.

The calculated effect of rate indexing on Public Service Company's cost of common equity capital and related tax costs is even more impressive. In a recent preliminary study made by Herman G. Roseman of National Economic Research Associates, Inc., in which he compared the performance of the company's stock since March 1975 with that of the other 94 electric utilities listed on the New York Stock Exchange, Roseman definitely concluded that the company's "cost of equity capital has declined relative to that of other utilities"; that, "absent indexing, Public Service Company stock would sell for 10% less than the actual market price"; that "it takes roughly a 1-percentage-point decrease in the cost of equity to raise the price of a utility stock by 10%"; and that "it may be concluded that the adoption of cost indexing has reduced Public Service Company's cost of equity by roughly 1 percentage point." Roseman's preliminary study, dated 15 March 1976, concludes with the following observations:

> There are two postscripts to this analysis which may be of interest. First, the Commission appears to have reduced PNM's allowable return on equity by 1 percentage point at the time it adopted cost indexing. This has already resulted in savings to consumers at the rate of about $2 million per year. Second, despite the increase in earnings which PNM has enjoyed over the past year, despite the general rise in utility stock prices, and despite cost indexing, PNM's market price is still about 5 to 10 percent below book value per share. Were the price of the stock 10 percent lower, the diluting effect of sales of stock would be much greater than it has been. Given the extraordinary growth rate of PNM, it must sell large amounts of new stock if it is to finance the necessary construction. The cost indexing, by very substantially reducing the dilution from sale of new stock, has greatly reduced the likelihood that dilution will render PNM unable to finance needed construction expenditures.

Since the company achieved a market-to-book price ratio of approximately 0.95 by the end of the year on 1975 average net book earnings of slightly less than 12 percent, and since indexing must raise its earnings to between 13 and 13.5 percent in 1976, its stock should soon achieve a market price modestly above its book value and enable the company to attract needed new common equity capital under favorable terms and conditions.

In closing I do not wish to convey the thought that cost of service indexing is *the* answer to our regulatory problems. It is certainly experimental, and after another year of close surveillence of its operation and effectiveness we will be in a better position critically to evaluate this unique regulatory technique. From hindsight, we do believe that a management study should have preceded the implementation of the cost of service indexing, but such a study is now under consideration.

The Case against Automatic Adjustment Clauses as a Means for Improving Regulation

Sylvia M. Siegel

While the inordinate increases under fuel adjustment procedures granted gas and electric utilities during 1974 and 1975 prompted some regulatory commissions to tighten or abandon the operation of the clauses, the majority of state regulatory commissions continue to pass through fuel costs without hearings for investor-owned utilities. Nor do Federal Power Commission procedures reassure hard-pressed consumers that the costs for electricity sales under its jurisdiction receive the thorough scrutiny required to ensure just and reasonable rates.

Histories of automatic adjustment clauses covering a specific factor such as fuel, wages, taxes, or other identifiable cost items have been noted in the literature. Studies by the National Association of Regulatory Utility Commissioners,[1] the Environmental Action Foundation,[2] the Congressional Research Service,[3] and the U.S.

---

[1]National Association of Regulatory Utility Commissioners, "Automatic Adjustment Clauses Revisted," Economic Paper No. 1R, 8 July 1974; and Paul Rogers, J. Edward Smith, Jr., and R. J. Profozich, "Current Issues in Electric Utility Rate Setting," report prepared for the National Association of Regulatory Utility Commissioners, 13 April 1976.

[2]The Environmental Action Foundation, "A Citizens Guide to the Fuel Adjustment Clause." Washington, D.C., 1975.

[3]D. N. Jones and Susan Dovell, "Electric and Gas Utility Rate and Fuel Adjustment Clause Increases, 1974," prepared for the Subcommittee on Intergovernmental

House of Representatives Subcommittee on Oversight and Investigation,[4] in addition to utility texts and essays in the periodical literature, all recite the origin and development of automatic adjustment clauses.

The avowed purpose of such clauses, particularly during periods of inflation, is to pass through increased costs and allow the company to maintain its financial status quo. The volatility of oil prices during 1974 found previously reluctant regulatory commissions eager to allow automatic price increases to pass through at frequent intervals — monthly or quarterly — ostensibly to keep companies whole. Thus, rate increases via fuel adjustments were four times as large in 1974 as in 1973.[5] By 1975, fuel adjustment clause (FAC) increases rose $2 billion more, to a staggering $8.5 billion.

According to the Congressional Research Service 1976 study, of the $9.2 billion electric utilities received in 1975 rate adjustments, $5.9 billion was issued through FACs. FAC adjustments of $2.6 billion were granted investor-owned gas utilities in the same period. Only $3.3 billion for electric and $800 million for gas utilities in 1975 were issued through formal rate cases of the total $12.6 billion 1975 rate adjustments.[6] In some areas the multimillion-dollar rate increases were due entirely to fuel pass throughs.

Not all regulatory commissions have contracted the FAC fever: Six states disallow FACs entirely, eight others require prior approval of fuel adjustments, and one, Nevada, excludes residential customers from its application of FACs; a number of other states are closely scrutinizing the FAC procedure and effect. California's recently

---

Relations and the Subcommittee on Reports, Accounting, and Management of the Committee on Government Operations, U.S. Senate, 94th Cong., 1st sess., 27 March 1975; and D. N. Jones and A. Lancaster, "Electric and Gas Utility Rate and Fuel Adjustment Clause Increases, 1975," prepared for the Subcommittee on Intergovernmental Relations and the Subcommittee on Government Operations, U.S. Senate, 94th Cong., 2d sess., September 1976.

[4]"Electric Utility Problems: Fuel Adjustment Clauses," Hearings on Utility Fuel Adjustment Clauses before the Subcommittee on Oversight and Investigations of the Committee on Interstate and Foreign Commerce, House of Representatives, 94th Cong., 1st sess., 1, 2, and 5 May 1975; and "Electric Utility Automatic Fuel Adjustment Clauses," report by the Subcommittee on Oversight and Investigations of the Committee on Interstate and Foreign Commerce, House of Representatives, 94th Cong., 1st sess., October 1975.

[5]Jones and Dovell, "Adjustment Clause Increases, 1974," p. vi.

[6]Jones and Lancaster, "Adjustment Clause Increases, 1975," p. vii.

revised fuel procedure is currently on appeal to the California Supreme Court.[7]

Pros and Cons

Proponents argue that automatic adjustment clauses not only allow for rapid recovery of escalating prices but also enhance the position of the utility in the financial community and make it easier to raise capital. In addition, such procedures eliminate the need for lengthy and costly general rate cases.

Critics attack FAC offsets for one specific cost item, since relationships to other cost items may be distorted, and offsetting efficiencies are ignored. Without the benefit of a full and thorough hearing to examine all facts behind the substantial fuel hikes that occurred in 1974 and 1975, there is good cause to question the justness and reasonableness of the rates that resulted. Especially is this important where oil and gas costs constitute from 50 to 85 percent of the total fuel costs and/or operating costs of the company.

Generally, when offset rate increases are processed, the adjustment requested to cover the one cost factor follows closely a general rate case where presumably all cost factors and offsetting efficiencies were considered. But with FACs, the individual and/or aggregate adjustment can far exceed the revenues produced from general rate increases. Thus, 88 percent of the increases passed through to customers of Southern California Edison Company from May 1972 through November 1974 were the result of FAC quarterly collections. The enormous sum of $622,900,000 represented fuel revenues during this period, with an additional $89,138,000 resulting from the October 1973 general rate increase.[8] Although Edison's FAC was established to eliminate the need for general rate increases, the record for Edison as well as other utilities indicates the companies are successful in obtaining both special and general rate relief.

In more comprehensive adjustment clauses, such as that adopted by the New Jersey Board of Utility Commissioners for telephone companies it regulates, four components are included, but, for example, offsetting productivity increases are not among them.

---

[7]In the Supreme Court of the State of California, *Southern California Edison Company* v. *Public Utilities Commission of the State of California*, filed 4 August 1976.

[8]Hearings, "Electric UtilityProblems: Fuel Adjustment Clauses," p. 637.

With inflation factors considered in test year projections where rates are set prospectively, as they are in some jurisdictions, the excuse to ignore compensating economies is not present.

Even more comprehensive adjustment clauses, such as those proposed by John W. Kendrick, are faulted because they tend to reduce efficiency incentives. Where such comprehensive formulas include a productivity factor as part of the cost adjustment clause, the advantages are questionable, since the operation of such clauses presupposes "continued day-to-day surveillance and less frequent, but still relied upon conventional rate procedures."[9] Supposedly, regulatory supervision will not be diminished, and one of the justifications for establishing FACs is removed. In practice this just is not so.

Overcharges

That FACs operate to remove incentives for bargaining has been cited in the investigative hearings of the House Oversight Committee as well as revealed in individual state investigations.

Incidents of accepting blatant price gouging, fraudulent layer-loading of coal, tying prices of less costly fuel to oil prices, questionable bargaining practices between affiliates, and interlocking directorates between utilities, banks, and suppliers all operate to increase fuel prices to the ultimate rate payer and pass on without much or any scrutiny inflated prices that add fuel to the inflationary fires of our economy.[10]

Thus, FEA has reported that utilities did little to protect themselves from price gouging during the Arab embargo, with the result that customers of Virginia Electric and Power Co. paid $2 million more than necessary for oil. Since costs can be passed through to customers, TVA authorities were slow to correct fraudulent layer-loading of coal trucks and paid at least $1.5 million for slag instead of the premium priced coal contracted for. The Canadian subsidiaries of Pacific Gas and Electric (PG&E), presided over by the same individual, are supposed to bargain with each other for gas produced in Alberta — a case of the right hand shaking the left, with the resulting high costs picked up by customers of the parent who were not protected by on-the-spot investigations by the regulators. Now

---

[9]John W. Kendrick, "Efficiency Incentives and Cost Factors in Public Utility Automatic Revenue Adjustment Clauses," *Bell Journal of Economics and Management Science* 6 (Spring 1975): 312.

[10]"A Citizens Guide to the Fuel Adjustment Clause," pp. 5–19.

the question of Canadian affiliates bargaining with each other to supply their U.S. parent may be moot since export prices are dictated by the Canadian government. However, when prices could have been influenced by toughness it was not until public pressure was exerted on the California Public Utility Commission to seek Department of State intervention and congressional help in international trade exchanges that any attempt to explore this avenue was made.

Computations for the large amounts of fossil fuel used by gas and electric utilities are especially liable to error in an escalating price market unless very close supervision is exercised over the operation of FACs. This is particularly true where prospective rate setting methods are used by the regulators, and estimates of test year quantities and prices are submitted in justification for increased revenue requirements.

As I testified before the House Oversight and Investigations Committee on 5 May 1975: "As a result of the combination of excellent hydro production, overestimated sales, underestimated gas available and FiFo accounting, Edison overcollected $145.8 million in fuel adjustment revenues over expenses actually incurred by the end of 1974. Indeed, Edison's Annual Report and Prospectus glowingly report record high revenues, earnings and dividends and attribute the $70 million net income to the above factors."[11]

The same overcollection problem occurred with PG&E, whose collected revenues exceeded fuel expenses by $108 million as of January 1975.

The embarrassment caused by such monumental increased profits (48 percent for Southern California Edison) prompted the California commission to halt further quarterly fuel adjustments for any of the California utilities on 29 April 1975 and to schedule an investigation into the procedure as well as recovery of customer overpayments.[12] Even though new quarterly increments were halted during 1975, both large California companies continued to overcollect on an escalating basis; the Case No. 9886 record reveals Edison excess collections of $177.1 million and PG&E overcollections of $147.2 million as of October 1975.[13]

Commissioner D. W. Holmes of the California Commission pre-

[11]"Electric Utility Problems: Fuel Adjustment Clauses," p. 339.
[12]*San Francisco Chronicle,* 30 April 1975.
[13]California Public Utility Commission, Case No. 9886 record.

dicted accurately in his dissent to Decision No. 79838, the 21 March 1972 Southern California Edison Company fuel clause precedent:

> One of the criticisms of the so-called "fuel clause" listed on page 10 of the majority opinion is particularly cogent in its suggestion that the quick and frequent increases portended by the "fuel clause" will act as a disincentive to economical acquisition of fuel supplies by Edison. Edison, one of the largest utilities in our Nation, should be given every reason and motivation to make the most effective use of its bargaining strength and managerial and technical expertise, to the end that the ratepayers will receive good service at the least possible cost.
>
> The other real problem that is involved in establishing this procedure is that it precludes public hearings in situations that have had and will have an extremely significant impact on the ratepayers of California.

Since the steep escalation of oil prices in 1974, prices have moved less precipitously. In fact, in both Southern California Edison Company Application No. 55424 for fuel cost adjustments and Case No. 9886, the California Public Utility Commission's investigation into fuel adjustment procedures, evidence on lower oil prices was introduced. Edison testified it would not accept unsolicited bids for spot purchases even though prices were lower and one-year contracts offered by some of the bidders were considered a long-term contract by the company. Hearings in these proceedings produced evidence used to reopen FPC wholesale price applications by Edison in Docket No. E-8570.

The oil price softness continues, with at least one shipping company receiving the benefit of lower prices through special discounts for the same product used by utilities. The predicted West Coast oil glut should have some effect on prices, but how utility buyers will press this advantage in current bargaining remains to be seen.

Automatic pass-throughs permit utility buyers to accede to price tie-ins for low priced fuels based on higher costed alternates. Thus, PG&E could sign a contract with Union Oil, supplier of both oil and geothermal generated steam, based on the price of oil rather than the cost to produce geothermal energy. In the case of Southern California Edison Company, negotiators agreed to contract provisions that bar the use of other cheaper fuels when available.[14]

Contract Enforcement

With too few exceptions utilities do not seek to enforce contract

[14] "Electric Utility Automatic Fuel Adjustment Clauses," p. 14.

provisions of supply or price requirements. The Consolidated Edison Company and Long Island Lighting Company are among the few utilities to charge suppliers with violations of antitrust laws in conspiracy to raise fuel prices.

The revelations of uranium cartel pricing, first broken by Jim Harding, caused California Energy Commissioner Ronald Doctor and Public Utilities Commissioner Leonard Ross and Harding to call for Department of Justice investigations. These must have prompted various utilities, including Virginia Electric and Power Company, to sue their uranium suppliers for failure to perform their contract in regard to supply requirements. According to the *Washington Post,* Westinghouse Electric Corporation then sued 29 major U.S. and foreign companies for increasing uranium prices 500 percent as a result of price fixing and alleged conspiracy to divide world markets.[15] Westinghouse asserted "commercial impracticability" as a legal excuse in failing to deliver the promised uranium supplies to utilities.

It is noted that none of the utility companies sought to invoke contract clauses for failure to deliver contracted natural gas quantities. Following congressional investigation, the Federal Power Commission, in the first order of its kind, ordered Gulf Oil Company to deliver contract amounts to its pipeline customer on 15 October 1976. The House Commerce Committee in August 1976 accused the FPC of willful disregard of its obligations under law because it had not acted for five years on the known failure of several major producers to fulfill supply contracts with interstate pipelines.[16]

The utility buyers of pipeline gas in turn fail to invoke their contract privileges or, at least, combat attempts to escalate price. The existence of purchase gas adjustment (PGA) clauses automatically passing through price hikes no doubt gives utility managements security of prompt recovery of increases but fails to protect customers through avoidance of higher costs.

For example, Southern California Gas Company recently petitioned the California commission to extend its PGA to 1 December 1976 in order to track additional price hikes requested by El Paso Natural Gas Company as a result of FPC Order No. 770.[17]

---

[15]*Washington Post,* 16 October 1976.

[16]Ibid.

[17]"Petition for Extension of Purchased Gas Rate Authority Granted by Decisions Nos. 86048 and 86425," Application No. 56540, Southern California Gas Company, filed 25 October 1976.

However, Southern California Gas was noticeably absent from the coalition of public interveners (20 parties) opposing the Opinion No. 770 tripling of natural gas prices to $1.42 per mcf without evidentiary hearings. The impact of the $1.42 national gas rate will increase rates an estimated $4 billion annually.

Procedural Adjustments

Because of the substantial overcollections under fuel adjustment procedures, the California commission, after hearings and review of evidence (see above), revised its formula and procedure for full cost reimbursement.

In a decision on 27 April 1976 the California commission revised the fuel procedure to an Energy Cost Adjustment Clause (ECAC) that includes all energy sources, with amortization prospectively of any differences in revenues over expenses from the inception of the clauses. Currently, the ECAC is based on a twelve-month moving recorded basis for sales and quantities of energy, with costs of energy computed on an end-of-period basis for all energy except oil, which is computed on a weighted average of the existing inventory costs.

Since April 1976 PG&E has received its first six-month fuel adjustment of approximately $73 million, which included an amortized deduction of $20 million from the balancing account to cover one-third of the excess of existing financial inequities due to past performance.[18]

Currently, PG&E is before the California commission seeking a 1 January 1977 adjustment of $144.4 million because of an extraordinarily dry year that reduced average hydroelectric generation and required higher fossil fuel use. In addition, higher natural gas prices, which became effective with the June 1976 adjustment, are to be recovered.

As mentioned above, Edison is appealing the ECAC formula but in the meantime has submitted a request for a downward adjustment of $75 million because of more natural gas availability than estimated previously. The enormous dollar advantages of underestimating gas availability and overestimating sales are somewhat curtailed with the revised procedures, although it is impossible to scrutinize the evidence since the reduction will be accomplished by ex parte action to forestall any delay in refunds. In the meantime, many

[18]California Public Utility Commission, Application No. 56160, Pacific Gas and Electric Company. A $73.4 million net increase was authorized 15 June 1976 in Decision No. 85968.

questions that would have been raised in public hearings will have to await the next rate case or the next six-month adjustment, whichever comes first. Obviously, there will be no opportunity to test the evidence without cross-examination of witnesses, since the new ECAC procedure does not require a hearing for rate decreases "if no special circumstances exist."

The fact that the California commission staff reviews these procedures is not necessarily reassuring. Even the most competent staff cannot cope with excessive work loads and accomplish detailed and exacting review. One engineer given a total of four weeks to investigate and prepare testimony for the PG&E anticipated hearings, as well as the San Diego Gas and Electric Company fuel filing, cannot hope to do detailed research on invoices, contract negotiations, account records, heat rates, and the like, even though the commission has called for close staff review.

In our opinion more appropriate action on the documented overcharges should have required reparations within a short period of three months. Toward Utility Rate Normalization (TURN) submitted that such immediate correction of overpayments would not be contrary to retroactive ratemaking prohibitions. Although a close reading of *Pacific Tel. and Tel.* v. *Public Utilities Commission,* 62 Cal. 2d 634 (1965) precludes the commission from rolling back "general" rates already approved, the court's reference to "general" rates does not apply to the extraordinary and separately stated fuel clause charges. Therefore, adjustments to fuel charges should not be construed as retroactive ratemaking.

Fuel clauses had been rejected by the California commission in previous years and were adopted only because of the emergency nature of pricing in a volatile oil market. The fuel clause is subject to modification or removal without damage to the rate structure developed as a result of a general rate case review.

In agreeing with this contention, Decision No. 85731 states (at page 12, mimeographed decision) that, "had the amount of overcollection occurring to date been an equal amount of undercollection, we believe the utilities would have been before this Commission forthwith with applications for rate relief to assist them in keeping their operations viable. Now it is of academic interest since the shoe is on the other foot; we think the shoes on both feet should match."

Regulatory Lag

Commissions assert the need for pass-through procedures during inflationary periods to save time and prevent the need for lengthy hearings that characterize general rate proceedings. But in all cases, utilities in California have had fuel adjustments and, at the same time, pursued general rate increases. The quarterly fuel filings of the several California utilities have not reduced the number of filings but provided utilities with a means of manipulating the regulatory process for their own benefit by this process of "pancaking applications." Edison's fuel revenues now constitute 50 percent of total costs.

PG&E similarly has benefitted from the pancaking of fuel cost adjustments, tracking increases for gas rates, offset increases, and general rate requests so that within a two-year period PG&E had some rate relief on the average of once every 16 weeks. Considering the total number of rate applications processed annually for each company, regulatory lag is a myth. The facts show utilities in other states similarly benefit from all types of rate adjustments.

Of the states responding to the questionnaires sent out by the Congressional Research Service (CRS) in 1975, only Montana and Mississippi failed to issue any electric general rate increases during 1975, although both had pending applications not yet acted upon.[19] Mississippi had issued $70 million through FAC procedures in 1975, however.[20]

Eight of the states reporting general rate increases during 1975 totally disallow FACs.[21] The others, with exceptions noted, granted FACs.

Generally, then, while two-thirds of the 1975 revenue production for electric companies came from FACs, the additional one-third ($3.3 billion) resulted from formal rate cases, so the pattern is for electrics to seek both special and general rate adjustments. Thus, the practice of pancaking applications is not peculiar to California.

And as CRS authors D. N. Jones and A. Lancaster state in the 1975 rate study, "clearly, the general increases ratepayers experienced in 1974 were not of the 'one shot' variety, as the 35 states responding to the 1975 questionnaire reported the same amount granted as did 37 states in 1974."[22]

Based on the amount of general applications pending at the end of 1975, CRS authors predict higher total general rate increases for 1976, a reasonable conclusion.

[19]Jones and Lancaster, "Adjustment Clause Increases, 1975," p. 4.
[20]Ibid., p. 7.
[21]Ibid., p. 17.
[22]Ibid., p. 6.

With FACs prevailing practice among the investor-owned utilities and general increases the pattern for 1975 and 1976, proponents can no longer claim regulatory lag, since rate relief appears to be issued frequently in all jurisdictions. In fact, utilities themselves contribute to regulatory lag by purposely swamping regulatory commissions with several filings in one year. Planning schedules of the investor-owned utilities, furthermore, indicate general filings at the rate of one a year in order to coincide with planning for plant additions. None can dispute that general rate applications of far greater magnitude than several years ago now involve far more complex issues than was the case in former years. These recent applications simply require more time for scrutiny.

This leads to the conclusion that it would be far more appropriate where volatility of prices constituting a significant proportion of costs has tapered off to consider fuel costs as part of a general rate case. Given relative stability of prices, it is far better to consider total costs, including fuel, once a year but very thoroughly, along with all other factors, than to act in piecemeal fashion on rates that have the same aggregated impact in amount but with thin supporting justifications.

Indeed, some 16 regulatory commissions allow roll-ins of electric or gas rates, according to Douglas and Lancaster. While it may be more difficult to reflect declines in fuel costs if fuel is included in base rates, the duty of the regulatory commission is to maintain vigilance and call the utilities in where rate reductions are indicated. Allowing rates to pass through automatically is an abdication of regulatory responsibility. Should prices begin moving up precipitously after fuel costs are rolled in to base rates, again, commissions have procedures for emergency relief; upon an adequate showing, an expedited proceeding can remedy the problem.

Conclusions and Alternatives

There are advantages to stating fuel costs separately, whether authorized as a separate fuel procedure or through a general rate proceeding, especially where fuel costs are such a large portion of total costs. However, there is no reason why a full-scale general rate proceeding, without the costly and frequent separately considered offset procedures, cannot result in the preferred statement of fuel costs on customer bills.

In regard to the more comprehensive types of adjustment clauses, including the guarantees provided by the New Mexico

Public Service Commission, innovations to protect the economic viability of the monopoly utility are very laudable, but not when they are at the expense of the consumer who underwrites the now riskless corporation without any voice in its management. How else to interpret authorization to index and pass costs of operation and maintenance, depreciation and amortization, taxes and capital?

We would be shocked if the financiers did not respond to this guaranteed rate of return with less than an AAA rating. This is not regulation but corporate socialism.

It is because the New Mexico indexing and other comprehensive adjustment clauses prevent a new look that is required for utility operation in the future that we express strong views on the shortcomings of such methods.

What is not permitted with any of the above are the following questions, let alone opportunities to provide answers. (1) What incentives are there to reduce costs, fuel and others, when a cost-plus operation is sanctioned? (2) Are regulatory commissions ordering adoptions of appliance and building standards to encourage more efficient use of energy? (3) Are utilities engaged in vigorous conservation programs to reduce demands on their system and eliminate waste? (4) Are utilities wedded to the historical growth rate in the face of reduced growth rates possible without detriment to the economy? (5) Since high fossil and nuclear fuel costs can be passed through to customers, what chance will the development of solar generating power, a feasible technology already available, really have? Or is it necessary to have a solar fuel factor included in FACs before the industry supports solar strategies in a meaningful way? (6) If bond ratings depend, in part, on removal or reduction of risks as provided by FACs, what investigations are conducted by regulatory authorities of the practices and policies of the rating agencies? Or will the regulators fall, like sitting ducks, to the demands for CWIP, FAC, and other company benefits before AAA ratings are issued? Do regulators actually measure the cost of maintaining AAA or AA ratings compared with issuing irrevocable multimillion-dollar rate increases? (7) What assurances do captive customers have of maximum efficiencies in operating practices? The recent NARUC report and other studies are of importance in determining whether or not all reported costs should be passed through in any form, whether by extraordinary fuel adjustments, escalator clauses, or general or offset rate increases. (8) With domestic and imported natural gas prices soaring, what assurances do customers have that gas utilities and electrics that still burn gas will act individually or in concert with the industry to forestall such increases? (9) Does the existence of PGAs mean that we must accept a price of about $4.00 per mcf for liquified natural gas or a price probably double that extraordinary figure for gas resulting from current ERDA coal gasification demonstration projects? Indeed, will California customers be forced to accept the Alaskan gas price, already announced to be the highest prevailing at the time the flow begins, on top of an astronomical transportation cost estimated to be $22.50 per 100 therms delivered to California? With approximately 90 percent of Southern California gas costs passed through PGAs, does Southern California Gas Company's quest for supply at any price override the public interest concern about economic impacts and requirements for innovative solutions to meet demands? (10) How can rate design problems that arise from implementation of staggering price increases be considered in automatic adjustments? The thoroughgoing scrutiny of the facts presented in justification for rate changes, whether caused by fuel price changes or other cost changes not considered part of a general rate case, and the impacts on various classes of customers as well as the system as a whole, are absent when costs are passed through without a hearing. Thus, considerations of application of fuel cost increases that could and should be assessed to larger users in recognition of lifetime principles may not be given in the course of automatic adjustments. With fuel adjustments larger in magnitude (and preceding in time general rate applications), the special adjustments may be the first opportunity, in many jurisdictions, to even consider rate design applications.

These are basic issues that require close and specific action now to develop, in the absence of any political leadership, a sound economic energy policy within which sound regulation can operate.

The Oversight Subcommittee's recommendation that "fuel clauses, in any form, are unwise, unnecessary, unworkable and unfair" says it all. The effect on regulation, according to the subcommittee, "may be the forerunner of a campaign to undermine utility regulation by means of a full range of automatic adjustment clauses that will render utility commissions virtually powerless while reducing utility management to the not so fine art of adjusting monthly consumer electric bills to reflect the industry's unchecked cost increases."[23]

Regulation of utilities is a difficult task. The possibility of easing the burden with automatic adjustments is tempting. But, it just does not work!

[23]"Electric Utility Automatic Fuel Adjustment Clauses," p. 1.

Automatic Adjustment Clauses as a Means for Improving Regulation

William W. Lindsay

It has been said of public utility rate regulation that its primary objective should be to assure that the prices charged are those that would prevail in the absence of regulation if the services were rendered under conditions of competition. In the words of James Bonbright, "rate regulation must necessarily try to accomplish the major objectives that unregulated competition is designed to accomplish; and the similarity of purpose calls for a considerable degree of similarity of price behavior."[1] One of the principal attributes of a competitive market is that price is brought into equality with cost of production,[2] and to the extent that regulation results in a lack of equality between price and cost, it brings about results that differ from those of the competitive market. If, for example, the regulated price exceeds the competitive price, some consumers are prevented from obtaining the service even though they are willing to pay the cost of the resources necessary to produce the service; resources such as labor are "wasted" in the sense of either being idled or used to produce services having less social value than the public utility

[1]James Bonbright, *Principles of Public Utility Rates* (New York: Columbia University Press, 1961), p. 107.

[2]Specifically, it is brought into equality, into equilibrium, with marginal cost.

NOTE: The views expressed in this essay are those of the author and do not necessarily represent the views of the Federal Power Commission or any of its members.

service. Conversely, if the regulated price is below the competitive price, resources are "wasted" in the sense that consumers are able to obtain them at less than cost of production so that they are drawn away from uses for which consumers would be willing to pay the cost of production.

Partly in recognition of these principles, the courts have long held that a public utility is entitled to charge prices that will enable it to pay all of its costs, including cost of capital, but not so high as to enable it to earn "windfall" profits. Although there may be considerable disagreement over what kinds of costs are being sought or what is to count as a cost, most regulatory commissions have little trouble with the notion that in a rate proceeding their object is to set rates equal to costs.

One of the difficulties with the process of rate regulation stems from the need for these rate proceedings. A proceeding begins when a utility files an application with a regulatory agency for a rate increase; it ends when the commission issues its decision concerning the application, or when court review has been completed. Typically, such proceedings require a substantial amount of time even without court review,[3] and they constitute the principal source of regulatory lag. For our purposes, the latter may be said to be the delay between the time the earnings of the enterprise became so high or so low as to justify the change and the point at which a rate change is permitted to become effective by the regulatory authority. To the extent that regulatory lag creates a mismatch between rates and costs, it interferes with the ability of rates to perform their essential functions, which include demand control as well as providing the enterprise with sufficient revenue to enable it to attract capital. Thus, it is not surprising that during the recent period of rapidly changing costs there have been efforts to find ways of eliminating or at least reducing regulatory lag.

One of the principal devices for accomplishing this purpose is the automatic adjustment clause. Essentially, this is a provision in a rate schedule that allows a utility to raise or lower its rates in response to changes in one or more elements of cost without the necessity of a full rate proceeding. These can be designed in such a way that regulatory lag is eliminated wholly or partially, but they also have

[3]Currently, a fully litigated electric rate proceeding at the FPC generally requires two or three years.

certain disadvantages and create side effects that some consider so serious as to warrant their complete elimination.[4]

Fuel Cost Adjustment Clause

The most common form of automatic adjustment clause for electric utilities is the fuel cost adjustment clause, which allows the pass through of changes in fuel costs to customers without the delay attendant upon full rate proceedings. Since much of the recent controversy has centered on this type of automatic adjustment clause, it shall be considered first.[5]

Fuel represents the largest element of cost for the great majority of electric utilities. Nationwide, fuel costs accounted for about one-third of total revenues of Class A & B electric utilities in 1975. For many individual utilities, the percentage was much higher.

Fuel is also the most volatile cost element for most electric utilities. An extreme example occurred in 1974. During that year the fuel costs of Class A & B electric utilities increased about 75 percent, from $6.7 billion in 1973 to $11.8 billion in 1974. For many individual utilities the cost increased much more sharply. For the typical East Coast electric utility, the cost of fuel more than doubled.

Without fuel clauses in their rate schedules in 1974, the electric utilities would have had to absorb most of these cost increases, since it is doubtful that the cumbersome process of contested rate proceedings would have permitted a significant proportion to have been passed along to customers by way of higher rates until 1975. The severity of the financial impact can be gauged from the fact that even after taking full account of the income tax effect, the net cost increase exceeded the entire common stock equity earnings of the industry for 1974.

---

[4]See, for example, Subcommittee on Oversight and Investigations, Committee on Interstate and Foreign Commerce, House of Representatives, 94th Cong., 1st sess., *Electric Utility Automatic Fuel Adjustment Clauses* (Washington, D.C.: U.S. Government Printing Office, October 1975).

[5]While the fuel cost clause is by far the most common form of automatic adjustment clause in electric rate schedules, other types may be found, of which the most prominent are various forms of tax adjustment clauses. In addition, there have been recent proposals for other kinds, including a debt interest cost escalation clause, a revenue maintenance clause, and a clause designed to recover costs related to facilities installed for environmental protection. Although the FPC has permitted tax adjustment clauses to be included in rate schedules, it has required that in each instance in which the clause is triggered, it must be filed as a proposed rate change. No action has been taken to permit any of the other types of clauses mentioned above.

From the standpoint of many individual utilities the impact would, of course, have been considerably more severe than is reflected in the national totals. Table 1 presents relevant data for three large East Coast utilities for 1974. It shows the effect on net income and net cash flow of each utility on the assumption that it was unable to recover any of its increased fuel costs before the end of the year.[6] As indicated in the table, in all three cases failure to collect the increased fuel costs would have wiped out net income for each company and would have resulted in a substantial reduction in earned surplus even if no dividends on common or preferred stock were paid. The table also shows that the fuel cost increases would have absorbed the entire net cash flow from operations for two of the companies, so that even if no common or preferred dividends were paid, no cash flow would have been available for interest payments. These numbers indicate that in the absence of fuel adjustment clauses, each of these utilities might well have experienced serious financial difficulties.

Table 1. ***Fuel Cost Increases for Three Electric Utilities as Compared with Net Income and Net Cash Flow, 1974, in Millions of Dollars***

	Company A	*Company* B	*Company* C
(1) Increase in fuel cost	74	368	160
(2) Income taxes (total)	3	-0-	17
(3) Net increase in fuel cost	71	368	143
(4) Net income	30	195	129
(5) Excess net fuel cost	41	173	14
(6) Net income	30	195	129
(7) Plus depreciation	35	144	77
(8) provision for deferred taxes	12	31	49
(9) Net cash income	77	370	255
(10) Less AFUDC and other noncash credits	10	31	72
(11) Net cash flow from operations	67	339	183
(12) Excess net fuel cost: (3)-(11)	4	29	(40)

SOURCE: Federal Power Commission, *Statistics of Privately Owned Electric Utilities in the United States* (Washington, D.C.: U.S. Government Printing Office, 1974).

[6]More precisely, it is assumed that each utility actually recovered its increased fuel costs by way of fuel cost adjustment clauses during 1974, and the table shows what the results would have been had they been unable to do so as a result of the exigencies of the regulatory process.

While the rise in fuel costs during 1974 was exceedingly unusual when compared with previous years, there is no guarantee that a comparable increase may not occur in the future. Elimination of fuel adjustment clauses would therefore materially increase the risk of investment in electric utility securities and thereby increase capital costs and rates. In addition, it might well lead to windfall profits for utilities should average fuel costs begin to fall either as a result of changes in fuel prices or changes in the mix of generation.

Elimination of fuel adjustment clauses would have the effect of multiplying the magnitude and frequency of general rate cases. If the electric utilities subject to FPC rate regulation had no fuel adjustment clauses, it is reasonable to suppose that they would have had to seek rate increases at least twice per year during 1974 and 1975. This would have meant roughly 300 electric rate cases initiated annually at the FPC, which would have placed an intolerable burden on its already overstrained staff resources. The impact at the state level is likely to have been at least as serious. The deleterious effect on the quality of regulation is likely to have been severe. In addition, the attendant delays would have resulted in grossly improper price signals to consumers. Rates would not have risen as rapidly as they did, so that load growth would not have been retarded, and the strain on fuel resources and fuel prices would have been magnified. Admittedly, these are only more or less likely possibilities, but they serve to illustrate that fuel adjustment clauses perform an important function, and their elimination is likely to be disadvantageous to consumers of electricity as well as to the electric utilities.

Disadvantages of Fuel Adjustment Clauses

While it is generally recognized that the fuel adjustment clause can be an effective method of reducing regulatory lag and thereby maintaining rates in a closer relationship to costs, there is no doubt that it has certain disadvantages. Four principal ones have been suggested.

First, the fuel clause represents an abdication of the regulatory function to assure that charges to customers do not exceed the cost of rendering the service. One form of the argument asserts that fuel clauses, since they operate automatically, are particularly susceptible to manipulation in such a way as to overcharge customers. The other form of the argument emphasizes the fact that many existing fuel clauses are designed to result in fuel adjustment charges that exceed the costs of fuel properly collectible by this means.

Second, the fuel clause reduces the incentive of the utility to minimize its cost of fuel.

Third, such a clause may result in rates increasing while most costs (other than fuel) are decreasing.

Finally, the fuel clause could introduce a bias in the selection of production methods.

The first of these arguments makes a case not so much against the fuel clause in principle as against the laxity and unsophistication of regulation in practice. There is no doubt that many fuel clauses have not been designed to pass on to consumers changes in costs which closely approximate the actual changes. But this is not to say that a fuel clause cannot be designed to achieve this objective.

In 1974 the Federal Power Commission promulgated an amendment to its regulations under the Federal Power Act which established a form of fuel clause to be used by all jurisdictional electric utilities.[7] There are five principal characteristics of this amendment.

First, it is a "variable efficiency" clause, that is, it adjusts for changes in total fuel costs per kilowatt-hour, whether occasioned by changes in fuel prices or by changes in generation mix. If, for example, a utility generates more or less energy by way of hydro in the current period than in the base period, that would be reflected in the current adjustment.

Second, all fuel costs, fossil as well as nuclear, are included. Many utilities strongly objected to the inclusion of nuclear fuel on the ground that when a nuclear plant goes into service the fuel clause adjustment would go down at the very time costs of plant in service are going up as a result of the higher capital costs associated with nuclear generation. The FPC responded that this should be no problem when utilities can file for changes in basic rates on the basis of estimated costs for a projected test year, since this allows the basic rates to be adjusted at the same time the fuel clause is triggered.

Third, all energy purchases are included. For energy associated with firm power purchases, the recovery is limited to the specifically identifiable fuel costs associated with those purchases. For energy associated with energy purchased on an economic dispatch basis, the net energy cost (exclusive of capacity charges) may be recovered. The reason for this departure from strict adherence to fuel costs only is to give the buyer an incentive to purchase energy when the total

[7]Order No. 517, Docket No. R-479, issued 13 November 1974.

energy charge is less than the cost of his own generation. Otherwise, he would only have an incentive to buy when the seller's loading factor (system lambda less fuel cost) is less than the buyer's loading factor.

Fourth, fuel costs are limited to those items included in Account No. 151 for fossil fuel and Account No. 518 for nuclear fuel, thereby excluding labor and other costs related to such functions as fuel handling.

Fifth, specific provision is made for treatment of fuel costs from utility owned or controlled sources.[8]

Fuel clauses designed in accordance with these requirements of the commission's regulations will, if properly administered, maintain a very close relationship between changes in total fuel costs and changes in charges resulting from the operation of the fuel clause.

Emphasis on the susceptibility of fuel clauses to manipulation appears to be more a commentary on the manner in which such clauses are administered by the utilities and the lack of close regulatory surveillance than an indictment of the fuel clause as such. In mid-1975 the Federal Power Commission initiated a program of special audits of about 15 major electric utilities related to charges to customers for wholesale electric service under the provisions of fuel adjustment clauses. One purpose of these audits was to determine whether wholesale customers were being properly billed for changes in fuel costs in accordance with their filed fuel adjustment clauses. The reports, issued between October 1975 and July1976, indicated that, in general, the utilities were billing their customers in accordance with the provisions of their fuel adjustment clauses as filed with the FPC. While there were a few instances of possible overcharges, these were generally quite small and apparently inadvertent. The audit results and other fuel clause investigations at the state level do not reveal any widespread effort to cheat consumers of electricity by way of improper administration of fuel clauses.

The second argument, that the fuel clause reduces the incentive of utilities to minimize fuel costs, cannot be lightly dismissed. It does certainly appear that, other things being equal, a utility having a fuel clause in its rate schedule is less likely to seek every possible means of reducing fuel costs than a utility with no way of automatically recovering its fuel cost increases. While it is true that the lag

[8]The requirements of this section are somewhat obscure and are probably more in need of further consideration than any other part of the regulations dealing with fuel clauses.

between fuel cost changes and the triggering of the fuel clause provides some incentive to minimize fuel costs, that lag has been reduced in recent years — to one or two months for most utilities. For some it has been eliminated altogether. Nevertheless, hard evidence that electric utilities with fuel clauses lack incentive to minimize fuel costs has been generally absent. Another purpose of the FPC's special fuel clause audits mentioned earlier was to determine whether utilities were seeking to keep fuel costs down. In general, the conclusion was that procurement policies and procedures were adequate to ensure that fuel costs were prudently incurred. It is clear that there is a need for careful, comprehensive regulatory surveillance to assure that fuel clauses are being properly administered and that reasonable efforts are being made to minimize fuel costs. If evidence becomes available that utilities are failing to make such reasonable efforts, then consideration should at least be given to reducing the proportion of fuel cost change to be passed through to consumers to something less than 100 percent. Absent such evidence, however, reduction in the proportion below 100 percent, or elimination of fuel clauses altogether, would not be in the public interest.

The remaining arguments against the fuel clause listed above derive from the fact that the fuel clause adjusts for changes in only one element of cost. Some critics claim the fuel clause may result in charges increasing while most costs are decreasing. While such a situation is possible, it has occurred infrequently. Furthermore, should it occur, a regulatory agency could take action to suspend the operation of the fuel clause and limit increases in charges to net increases in costs. Finally, other critics maintain that the fuel clause could bias the selection of production methods, presumably by creating an incentive to utilize methods involving minimum capital intensity. Again, it is difficult to find evidence that fuel clauses are in fact having this effect. While some utilities may, for example, have chosen to ship low sulfur fuel long distances rather than install scrubbers, it does not follow that scrubbers would have been installed in the absence of a fuel clause. But if it can be shown that fuel clauses are biasing selection of production methods in such a way as to affect efficiency seriously, consideration should be given to modification of the fuel clause or to other methods of eliminating this kind of bias.

House Subcommittee Recommendations

The House Subcommittee on Oversight and Investigations has recommended that fuel adjustment clauses be abolished (except during limited emergency periods) and that utility commissions consider interim rate relief, subject to final commission review, and refund as an alternative to fuel adjustment clauses.[9] The Report of the House Subcommittee is a thoughtful document that deserves careful consideration, but its recommendations have several defects.

First, the report nowhere explains its concept of allowing fuel clauses during limited emergency periods. It is not at all clear why consumers should be asked to pay rapidly rising fuel costs during some limited period only to have the clause withdrawn or rendered inoperative when the emergency subsides — presumably when fuel costs cease to rise or when their ascent tapers off materially.

Second, interim rate relief is not an acceptable substitute for automatic adjustment. It takes time and money to prepare an application for interim rate relief, and it takes time and effort for a regulatory agency to reach a considered judgment on the extent to which such relief should be granted. If costs are moving rapidly, the delay occasioned by the need to examine the application carefully could be costly to either the utility or the rate payers. If fuel costs are rising steadily, a whole series of interim actions may be necessary before the ultimate commission decision can be issued, with a consequent compounding of complexity and delay. This would be especially true if the public were to demand full participation and full processing of each proposed interim increase, as it would have every right to do. In addition to these difficulties, the interim rate technique during a period of rapidly rising costs means that the utility will be collecting a large amount of its revenue subject to refund, with the attendant uncertainty and adverse impact on capital costs that this entails. Finally, if fuel costs move downward rapidly, many regulatory agencies would be unable to assure that such cost decreases could be promptly passed along to customers. At the Federal Power Commission, for example, a proceeding to initiate a rate reduction could only be brought under Section 206 of the Federal Power Act. This means that no rate reduction could be effected by the commission except after notice and opportunity for hearing and the issuance of a final commission order, all of which could require years. For these reasons, the interim rate technique does not constitute a viable substitute for the automatic fuel adjustment clause.

Comprehensive Automatic Adjustment Clause

The most extreme form of automatic adjustment clause would adjust charges to customers for changes in all costs, including return

[9]Subcommittee on Oversight and Investigations, *Fuel Adjustment Clauses*, p. III.

on investment. The New Mexico Public Service Commission[10] is the only state regulatory commission that is permitting the use of such a comprehensive clause for retail electric business at the present time.[11] Although there are a number of rate schedules of this sort on file with the FPC, they are limited in general to highly specialized services provided among affiliated companies.

A comprehensive adjustment clause does not have two of the disadvantages of a fuel clause, namely, the possibility that the clause could adjust rates in one direction while most costs are moving in the other, or the possibility of bias in the selection of production methods. Yet, the other two disadvantages of a fuel clause seem to apply with greater force to a comprehensive clause. Clearly, a comprehensive clause can be viewed as a more complete abdication of the regulatory functions than a fuel clause, and the fuel clause problem of reduced incentive to minimize fuel cost becomes a problem of reduction in incentive to minimize all costs.

These difficulties may, however, be more apparent than real. Whether a comprehensive clause can be viewed as an abdication of the regulatory function depends on the character and degree of sophistication of the regulatory surveillance of utility operations, procurement policies and practices, and construction programs that accompany permission to use such a clause. Certainly, a regulatory agency would be able to devote more resources to a surveillance program aimed at securing maximum efficiency and productivity if it were freed from the necessity of providing a forum for the endless and costly litigation of rate schedule changes.

With respect to incentives to maximize efficiency, the provision of a neutral range for rate of return on common stock equity as provided for in the New Mexico Public Service Company clause may be expected partially to accomplish this purpose. That ability might be improved in the New Mexico case if the lower limit of the range were reduced somewhat below the 13.5 percent rate now contained in the clause. In fact, the range of 13.5 to 14.5 percent seems to be

---

[10]New Mexico Public Service Commission, *Re: Public Service Company of New Mexico*, Case No. 1196, 22 April 1975. Reprinted in *Public Utilities Reports*, 4th Series, vol. 8, 1975, pp. 113–39.

[11]It is reported that the Houston City Council has authorized automatic adjustment to reflect changes in labor and depreciation costs and in bond interest and preferred stock dividend requirements in addition to fuel costs. See American Bar Association, *Public Utility Law* (Chicago: the Association, 1976), p. 28. An adjustment clause covering wages, taxes, and depreciation for a telephone company was recently approved by the New Jersey Board of Public Utility Commissioners. See *Re New Jersey Bell Telephone Co.* (1974), 3 PUR 4th, 298.

based on a midpoint of 14 percent authorized in a previous rate proceeding and does not seem to give any effect to the reduction in capital cost that should be expected to accompany a comprehensive adjustment clause.[12] In any event, the New Mexico commission has provided the opportunity to observe the operation of a comprehensive clause so that we can determine the extent to which clauses of this sort may be workable under current inflationary conditions.[13]

The need to assure that a comprehensive adjustment does not unduly dissipate incentives to maximize efficiency and minimize costs has prompted several recent proposals for clauses specifically designed to avoid this disadvantage. In general, these would incorporate into the comprehensive adjustment clause a factor that would limit upward adjustment to that part of an actual cost increase that reflects an efficiency improvement target. One form of this kind of clause was filed by Illinois Bell Telephone Company before the Illinois Commerce Commission in 1974 in Docket No. 58916.[14] The general formula contained in this clause was:

$$CEA\ (\$) = (aX + bY) \text{ or } Z,$$

whichever is less, where

X = aggregate dollar value of change in unit costs, excluding equity capital cost changes;

Y = aggregate dollar value associated with change in efficiency; and

Z = aggregate revenue dollar change necessary to meet the ceiling rate of return specified by the regulatory authority.

The first factor (aX) would adjust rates in accordance with a part of the change in unit costs and would thereby compensate the utility (in the case of an upward adjustment) for the proportion of the effect of inflation represented by a. The second factor (bY) would be

[12] This may help to explain the dramatic effect of the New Mexico commission's decision on the market price of the company's stock. See National Association of Regulatory Utility Commissioners, *Current Issues in Electric Rate Setting*, 13 April 1976, pp. 43–44.

[13] The New Mexico commission in its order authorizing the comprehensive adjustment clause stated: "At this stage, we view the method as an experimental innovation having application only to a vertically integrated energy utility which is subject to our jurisdiction in all phases of its operations."

[14] Described in H. A. Latimer, "The Cost and Efficiency Revenue Adjustment Clause," *Public Utilities Fortnightly* 94 (18 August 1974): 19–24.

specified in such a way that if productivity increases were more than those of the past, this part of the adjustment would recover more than the balance of the inflation effect; if productivity increases were less than those of the past, it would recover less than the balance of the inflation effect. The Z factor ensures that the utility will earn no more than a specified return on equity, presumably that established in the last rate case.

It should be evident that a clause of this sort could maintain incentive on the part of the utility to improve productivity, while providing some protection to consumers against excessive charges. This is not to say that this particular clause could not be improved.[15] Rather, it is to say that the problem of maintaining incentives in the context of automatic rate adjustment is not necessarily insurmountable.

Summary and Conclusions

Because fuel costs are the largest and most volatile element of total costs for most electric utilities, fuel adjustment clauses are essential features of rate schedules if rates are to be maintained in reasonable relation to costs during periods of rapid change in fuel costs. While such clauses have certain disadvantages, these appear to be more than offset by the enhancement of financial stability and reduced capital costs that result from their use as well as the reduced necessity for the lengthy and costly litigation that is generally a prerequisite to a change in basic rates, particularly a reduction in basic rates. The recommendation by the House Subcommittee on Oversight and Investigations that fuel clauses be abolished and replaced by provisions for interim rate relief appears to be defective and may well work to the disadvantage of consumers of electricity.

Several of the disadvantages of a fuel clause can be eliminated by a comprehensive cost adjustment clause. Such a clause constitutes a viable method for reducing regulatory lag during periods in which costs are changing rapidly if the clause is combined with a comprehensive program of regulatory surveillance and if it is designed in such a way as to maintain incentive to maximize efficiency.

---

[15]See, for example, Ralph E. Miller, "Commentary on 'The Application of a Productivity Measurement System to Public Utilities' by H. A. Latimer," in *Public Utility Productivity: Management and Measurement* (Albany: New York State Department of Public Service, August 1975), pp. 229 –38. Also see John W. Kendrick, "Efficiency Incentives and Cost Factors in Public Utility Automatic Revenue Adjustment Clauses," *Bell Journal of Economics and Management Science* 6 (Spring 1975): 299–313.

Comment

J. M. Quigley

Regulation of gas, electric, telephone, and other utility services acts as a substitute for direct uneconomic competition as William Lindsay so eloquently explained. But utilities have competition; there is no such thing as a complete monopoly.

One thing is certain: All businesses must compete with one another in the marketplace for new capital. Utilities are always in need of capital for additional plant necessary to serve new customers, for replacements which generally cost more than the plant being retired, and for costs incurred in meeting new safety requirements and environmental laws. These needs cannot be met from current cash flow for many reasons. One of the major factors, even in the absence of inflation, is that utilities are expected to pay out a substantial portion of current earnings in dividends. If they do not, the market quickly reflects the fact in the price of a company's common stock.

We all know what happened when a major utility cut out its dividend to conserve cash. It was disaster! The price of its stock dropped to about one-sixth of its book value, and there were severe reverberations for all other utility stock prices. None of us would have believed it was possible for the action of one utility to affect all of our stocks so adversely.

Many things affect a company's financial health. Since utilities have a high percentage of debt in their capitalization, the recent years' rise in debt costs has taken its toll. At the same time, the rate of return on common equity has remained about the same. Thus, there has been a sharp reduction in interest coverage. Some utilities' debt that was rated triple A just a few years ago has been downgraded to triple B — not investor grade for a number of potential buyers. As a matter of fact, triple A utilities, except for "Telephone," have practically disappeared. Consequently, all capital costs have become more expensive, resulting in greater costs to customers.

Let us look at specifics. In the mid-1960s the imbedded cost of long-term debt of utilities was less than 4 percent, and a typical utility's rate of return on common equity was about 12 percent. In the latter 1970s, debt costs are in excess of 7.5 percent, and the rate of return for common equity on average has slipped a bit.

Ten years ago the yield on a thirty-year government bond was just over 4 percent; it is now about 8 percent. The present differential between government securities and the earnings rate on utility common stocks is hardly worth the added risk for an investor. This makes selling utility common equity even more difficult, which is reflected in the market prices of its stock.

In an effort to offset high inflation rates, increased construction costs, and the higher cost of money, labor, taxes, fuel, and all the other expenses, utilities have had to seek regular rate increases. This is a shift from earlier years, when the order of the day was regular rate decreases. Furthermore, the usual regulatory lag has hamstrung the utilities and prevented them from maintaining anything resembling reasonable financial health.

It is no wonder that many utilities and commissions have been dismayed. Many knowledgeable financial people have stated that any change in this serious situation would have to be an improvement.

Gas and electric utilities in a number of states have had, for many years, adjustment clauses for their fuel costs. The companies with such clauses have fared much better than those which are forced to seek rate relief each time fuel costs increase. We all know that this expense is a substantial one for all electric and gas utilities. While Lindsay dwells on the adverse effects resulting from increases in electric fuel costs, particularly as a result of OPEC actions, gas costs have always been a substantial expense for gas distribution companies. Today, this cost is even more significant.

For example, in the case of Northern Illinois Gas Company, gas costs were typically in the area of 40 percent of revenues during the 1960s. Today, the percentage is over 60 percent and climbing. When one part of the operating expense is so significant, an adjustment clause makes a great deal of sense. Parenthetically, I should add that Northern Illinois Gas has had such a clause in its rate schedule since 1954, which has resulted in both decreases and increases in billings to our customers.

I have no basic problem with Lindsay's comments on the adequacy and proper design of fuel clauses. I agree with him that a fuel clause which results in overcollections is not fair to consumers. It is not right to attempt to justify such overcollections on the basis that a reasonable rate of return is not being earned. Any attempt to rationalize this result is utter nonsense. But, it does bother me that Lindsay, in discussing the problems with fuel adjustment clauses, said nothing about those which do not fully collect increases on a timely basis. This should be a concern of regulators.

I must take exception with Lindsay on a couple of points. He stated that "if evidence becomes available that utilities are failing to make such reasonable efforts [that is, to hold down fuel costs], then consideration should at least be given to reducing the proportion of fuel cost changes to be passed through to consumers to something less than 100 percent." He goes on to suggest that if other costs are going down more than fuel costs are going up, the regulatory agency could suspend the operation of the fuel clause. In my opinion, an up-to-date fuel clause will work and should be allowed to continue to function. If the rate of return goes beyond the zone of reasonableness on the upper end, a general rate reduction should be made on either a permanent basis or for a temporary period.

In my opinion, there are ways to develop fuel clauses so that they will work as intended to reflect fairly incremental changes in costs of fuel. It is up to utilities working with regulators to see that such clauses do so. To do otherwise would penalize some companies and continue to cast doubt on fuel clauses that work properly.

What about the possibility of a utility taking undue advantage of a poorly designed fuel adjustment clause? Those who think that good management would make such an unwise decision do not understand the flexibility and double-edged sword of regulation. Furthermore, if advantage were taken of a current regulatory gap, such rules would soon change, and that management might be forced to leave if the blunder were of sufficient consequence.

As to the thoughts of a committee of Congress that fuel clauses should be abolished, in my opinion this is an unadulterated appeal to voters on the part of congressmen and is thoroughly unobjective.

Turning to Sylvia Siegel's essay, it is difficult to comment on several aspects because they relate to specific company situations with which I am not fully familiar. There are many interesting points made, however, and we agree on a number of them. My comments will focus on those areas where we may disagree, or where I fail fully to understand the position taken.

First, I do not believe that the avowed purpose of fuel clauses is to pass through increased costs only. Rather, they are a means of keeping track of the major expense, both increases and decreases, in a reasonable fashion. Neither were they adopted to avoid rate cases. Yet, it has worked out that way for my company. Since 1954, when we were first allowed a gas adjustment clause, Northern Illinois Gas has had only one general formal rate case, although rates were reduced a number of times during the 1960s.

Whether or not the number of rate cases is roughly the same is not a reason to throw out fuel clauses. The point should be to correct fuel clause deficiencies if and when they arise. I am sure Siegel does not mean to infer either that all fuel clauses result in blatant price gouging or any of the other things quoted from a booklet entitled "A Citizen's Guide to the Fuel Adjustment Clause."

Fuel clauses recently have received much attention because such costs have escalated. Siegel and Lindsay gave some statistics on the amounts, which merely illustrates that the clauses work. What was not said is that such higher costs of fuel do not result in higher profits for utilities. I know of no clause that is free from lag or has a built-in profit factor. Assuredly, utilities were not in favor of the Arab embargo and the higher prices. What company would vote for higher prices without added profit?

In a few cases where fuel purchases are not from third parties, added profits may have resulted, even though probably reasonable. Even this is not a typical case.

I accept the criticism that perhaps not enough utilities challenged fuel price increases, but I am sure more challenges will occur in the future. I hope we have learned from the past — one of our best teachers. Northern Illinois Gas certainly does not want to pay one cent more than it needs to for anything. Our big problem, besides the price of gas, which is low compared to any other alternative, is how to obtain an adequate supply.

Moving from an adjustment clause for a major cost to full indexing of all expenses including a return, as was done in New Mexico, is, in my opinion, a different matter. However, I suppose that when things become bad enough, drastic action sometimes needs to be taken. I would like to believe that this type of regulation is acceptable only as a temporary cure.

The experiences of the late 1960s and 1970s have indeed been dramatic. Some companies have fared better than others. Has this been luck? Or could it be that these companies were more diligent than others in watching their capitalization ratios? Also, did some perhaps have their expenses under better control? Could it be, too, that regulation had something to do with it? In those jurisdictions where consistent, reasonable returns were allowed, utilities weathered the storm of the last few years fairly well. However, no business, utilities included, has shown that it can forever expect to have smooth sailing without any adversity.

Where does all of this lead? I, for one, would like to think that regulation could and should use a less heavy hand on those under regulation. This does not mean that commissioners should abdicate their duty. I think it has been proven, however, that steady, reasonable regulation will result in bringing out the best in utility management. If this is done, utility customers as well as stockholders will benefit.

My next few words should not be taken as being critical of any company's management and are stated as my beliefs on a theoretical basis. When lethargic utility management is allowed to earn for its stockholders the same rate of return as an aggressive, innovative management, something is wrong. Management will become dull not only if it is held down too much by regulators but also if it is rewarded for failures. We all know that the rate of return of utilities is limited on the upper end, as well it should be. However, if utilities are truly a part of the free enterprise system, and I think they are, should they not want to earn a good rate of return, have the best product or service possible, and at the same time have the lowest possible price for their product or service? This is true in other kinds of business. In my opinion, regulation should stimulate management to do the best possible job of meeting these challenges.

Siegel made the point that changes in fuel costs should be made only in general rate proceedings. Practically speaking, this has not worked when trying to collect fuel cost increases on a timely basis. Also, I do not believe that utilities, any more than commissions, delight in having rate cases. As a matter of fact, I think they waste a lot of valuable management time, although they are necessary for the regulation of the general rate terms.

Lindsay says that full indexing of costs might be made to work under proper conditions. At least this is the conclusion I draw from his words. This may be true from a theoretical viewpoint, but I firmly believe that utility management should be charged with managing and regulators should be charged with regulating. These obligations and responsibilities are separate and distinct. They cannot and should not be mixed. There is an obvious attraction to do so, but I think it is abhorrent even to consider it as a realistic alternative. Siegel would probably agree with me on this point.

If utilities are properly challenged, I do not believe that they should need a fixed formula for indexing the total income account down to the rate of return they are allowed to earn for the shareholders. In no case would I like to have a fixed formula to ensure that the price of my company's stock will be at a level which will permit it to be sold at just book value. This is the heart of the Public Service Company of New Mexico's rate order, at least as I read it.

Less than a month ago, the Office of Economics of the Federal Power Commission (where Lindsay is Assistant Chief) made a proposal in Docket No. RM 77-1 for the determination of the zone of reasonableness for the rate of return of electric and gas pipeline companies. Lindsay did not mention this fact, although the subject is relevant here. Without going into details about the proposal, my first impression of it is negative; since it, too, attempts to use a formula to establish a rate of return which will result in maintaining the utility's stock market value near, if not equal to, its book value.

It may be possible that these types of arrangements can result in good management. I do not know. But, I would not characterize such efforts as part of the free enterprise system.

In closing, let me reiterate that sometimes extreme actions are called for, as in the New Mexico situation. In the longer run, however, I would hope utilities can be creative enough so that there can be less regulation rather than more. Again, I repeat that this in no way means regulators should not be close overseers of the actions of utilities and ensure that management meets its customer needs in a responsible manner. If regulators and utility managements both do their jobs, utility customers should reap the benefits of good service at reasonable prices.

Comment

Douglas N. Jones

Unscholarly as it may sound, the automatic adjustment clause is one of those ideas about which one can fairly choose up sides and come down on one side or the other. In large part it really is a question of what you believe the true results of such clauses to be on the workings of public utility regulation. I view these clauses as a poor regulatory tool, perhaps better only than a comprehensive adjustment clause. The widespread use of automatic adjustment clauses I regard as a major step in the continuing decline, but I hope not fall, of commission regulation.

My remarks treat first the two papers that I received ahead of time and then offer some additional observations on the general proposition of automatic adjustment clauses in public utility regulation.

The Two Essays

The Lindsay essay surely presents a balanced assessment of the pleasures and uses of automatic adjustment clauses, with special reference to the fuel clause. In each case of acknowledged disadvantage of automatic adjustment clauses he does find some redeeming feature that brings him down in favor of them. He is a good deal more skeptical of comprehensive adjustment clauses such as the New Mexico one, but even here he concludes that their difficulties are "not necessarily insurmountable." Certain refinements and the

NOTE: The views expressed are those of the author and do not necessarily represent those of the Congressional Research Service or the Library of Congress.

grafting on of provisions for comprehensive surveillance and maximizing efficiency should do the trick, he feels. The problem, of course, is that regulatory abdication and uncorrected inefficiency are at least as likely an outcome of any such scheme.

To be more specific, the *tone* of the first third of Lindsay's essay troubled me some. His statement that "the need for . . . 'rate proceedings'" is "one of the difficulties with the process of rate regulation" seems strange in that many would say that full commission hearings on changes in the rates charged rate payers are the main *point* of regulation. There seemed to me an undue preoccupation in the early part of the essay with what was generally called "the financial plight" of the industry over the last few years. I feel the "plight" was largely overdrawn and in any event was the incorrect preoccupation for the period, the plight of the rate payer being a better focus. Lindsay's finding that utilities in 1974 in the absence of fuel adjustment clauses in their tariffs probably would have experienced serious financial difficulties does assume that commissions would have done nothing in the way of rate relief, an assumption that is surely questionable.

His definition of "regulatory lag" was defensible and avoided the notion sometimes advanced that regulatory lag begins the day a utility files a rate increase and somehow is an unwarranted delay until the moment it is granted.

Lindsay's dismissal of the problem of the susceptibility of fuel adjustment clauses to manipulation as merely "a commentary on the manner" of administration is a bit too casual if you feel that accounting mischief by the utilities and diminished commission surveillance are endemic to such clauses. He does say that the tendency for these clauses to reduce incentives for minimizing fuel costs may be real, but then concludes there is little "hard evidence" to prove it. One wonders what kind of evidence he would consider "hard," and in any event, should not the presumption on the part of the regulator be in the other direction?

Lindsay's cautious embracing of partial fuel adjustment clause pass-throughs under certain conditions is heartening, as is his emphasis on the need for netting out cost elements which move in different directions in arriving at allowable increases.

Finally, his criticisms of interim rate relief as a useful alternative to fuel adjustment clauses seemed much too harsh to me. The statements that such applications take "time and money," "compound complexity and delay," and encourage "full participation" by the public are peculiar objections if one believes that all of these are the necessary ingredients to good public interest regulation.

On the question of what else might have been included in the essay I would like to have seen a careful discussion of why the FPC came to adopt fuel adjustment clauses in recent years; why the FPC rejects certain automatic adjustment clauses and not others; and why the inclusion of nuclear fuel in fuel clauses came about. I have in mind here not the policy change *per se,* but the changing persuasiveness of the arguments themselves.

Bazant's essay is one I would like to have seen prepared and delivered at the end of the experimental period contemplated by the New Mexico commission's introduction of "cost-of-service indexing." The fact that we are only 18 months into the experiment precludes evaluation of its results and undoubtedly explains why Bazant had to limit his remarks mainly to a recitation of why New Mexico did what it did. Still, a number of comments come to mind.

Again, the tone is bothersome. Throughout the piece the emphasis is on "problems besetting the utilities," "restoring earnings stability," "reducing investor risk," and "a warm reception from the company," while full commission proceedings are described merely as "expensive and lengthy," "adversary" in nature, and as placing "inordinate and largely wasteful demands upon the time, energies, and other resources of the company." Regulators, according to Bazant, are reduced to "near total preoccupation with service rate proceedings to the virtual exclusion of all other important regulatory considerations and efforts." One wonders just what these "other considerations" might be that should come ahead of what the rate payer should properly pay. I am aware that comments about "tone" are rather subjective and perhaps even inappropriate, but it is a bit disturbing to find that the most positive thing to be said on the side of the public in a commission's placing a floor under utility earnings is that "the symmetry of law and of common concepts of 'fairness' oblige" a ceiling as well. This seems a far cry from the populist idea that a commission should not see itself as sitting halfway between the public and the company, but as actively on the side of the rate payers.

Turning to specific content, a rate of return on equity and not on the rate base is the focus of the New Mexico scheme, and this higher number seems high indeed. I note that *Fortune 500* shows an all industries median return on stockholders' equity for 1975 of 11.6 percent (down from 13.6 percent in 1974). I note also that Standard and Poor's average return on equity for the electric power industry in 1975 was 11.7 percent (up from 10.4 percent in 1974) and estimated to be 12.75 percent in 1976. While the translation from medians and averages to individual company needs and behavior is perilous, it would seem to me (as it did to Lindsay in his essay) that the New Mexico range is too high a band of earnings. Among other things, the certainty that the commission has now injected into company earnings should be worth a couple of points in investor evaluations. As I understand it, the 14 percent was arrived at in part by being the most recent figure granted *before* the institution of the assured earnings device.

With respect to changes in the ratio of market to book value for the stock of Public Service Company of New Mexico, Bazant reports that it went from 55 to 95 percent from 1974 to 1975. In preparing a comparison of market to book value for 27 major electric companies throughout the country, I note that the average in1974 was 56.7 percent, 70 percent in 1975, and 84 percent by mid-1976. This convergence of 28 percentage points was experienced without comprehensive automatic adjustment clauses, although certainly with major general rate increases and the operation of fuel adjustment clauses.

A better understanding of the New Mexico device on my part would perhaps obviate the question, but I do not readily see why the incremental or decremental adjustments in restoring returns to within the limits are done via the *energy* charge. Why not via the *demand* charge, which would seem to be more closely related to the provision of capital. I do not know just what the consequences would be, but presumably there would at least be some distributive differences.

I would be anxious about leaving verification of utility company books for purposes of triggering the adjustment mechanism in New Mexico to accounting firms under contract to the commission. A better arrangement would seem to be to have the commission staff have the capability and responsibility for the task — or at least rotate the contract from firm to firm. Public utility accounting firms, as do utility consulting firms generally, tend to take on the coloration of their industry clientele over time.

Finally, while no big point is made of it, I would be slow to conclude (as the author does) that a quarter of a million dollars per year has been "saved" already by rate indexing. That may be; but the complexities and dynamics of the diverse forces bearing on costs and pricing in this sector make definitive statements on savings tentative at best.

Some Further Considerations

Academic, journalistic, and public attention to utility regulation is inversely related to the performance of the economy at large. Bad times make for heightened interest in this technical field. This is a force for good. But a counterforce is now in operation, namely, that as numbers increase — numbers of court cases, commission hearings, dollars, large numbers of anything — the system response is to become more arbitrary. I view the movement toward automaticity in utility regulation and away from full and fair commission deliberations as a part of the latter phenomenon.

Surely, the strongest proponent of the fuel adjustment clause half a dozen years ago did not have in mind that in 1974 electric and gas utility bills would increase more than 1.5 times as much as all utility rate increases during the previous quarter century ($9.6 billion); and that the next year would see an additional $12.6 billion rise, two-thirds of which was attributable to fuel adjustment clauses. Understandably, this presents a series of major system shocks that will have to be worked out without, I hope, the abandonment of all perspective.

Some of the problems I have in mind are noted below.

First, failure on the part of commissions to protect consumer interest when the stakes are as high as they currently are encourages legislative intervention at both state and federal levels. Similarly, undue greediness on the part of utility companies in time of adversity serves to encourage public acquisition of private companies and expanded congressional interest in joint operations, such as public ownership in production facilities with an interface with price distribution systems.

Second, the decline of utility regulation in the public interest is not really a matter of inexpert personnel, or inadequate legal underpinnings, or a defective concept; rather, it is a matter of allowing the *process* to deteriorate to the point where the outcome is loaded against the rate payer and in favor of the regulated. It is not true that the interests of each party are coincident, and it is unfair to argue that somehow the short-term interests of the consumer in lower rates are illusory and should be supervened by the short-term interest of the companies in higher earnings, ultimately to be reconciled by some presumed benefit at some uncertain date. If higher returns to equity have rate payer benefits, then it is not a viable proposition to say that still higher returns must have still more benefits.

Third, there are times when the attraction of capital argument can be misplaced. If the risk utilities so often talk about really is high, then we would expect new finance capital to go elsewhere. Sometimes capital should be repelled, not attracted, as with undue expansion, or misjudgments of demand, or the pursuit of incorrect technologies. In any event, a time dimension is important here; capital shortages are often followed by capital gluts, and there is a temporary nature to much of industry adversity, where overcompensation by public bodies is a frequent danger.

Finally, against the larger backdrop of adapting reglation to a period of shortage, curtailment, and inflation, it seems to me that it is poor public policy to let local electric power rates be essentially set in the Persian Gulf instead of in the regulatory commissions. One can at least argue that the OPEC embargo was an external shock of the random variety, not aimed at utility companies or rate payers but at U.S. foreign trade and aid policies. As such, this (hopefully) one-shot affair presents a problem of *collective adversity* for the country as a whole; therefore, the costs should be collectively shared—some by stockholders, some by suppliers, some by rate payers, and some by the public at large through the treasury. But not *all* by the rate payer through automatic and other rate increases.

Foreign Experience with Inflation and Price Structure Reform

The Impact of Inflation on the Electricity Supply Industry in Great Britain

B. H. F. Johnson

In the context of adapting regulation in a period of inflation, it is of interest to compare the experience in Great Britain, where the electricity industry is state owned, with the U.S. regulatory system and to assess their relative success (or lack thereof) in coping with inflation and its insidious side effects. This essay discusses developments in Great Britain since 1968, the year when public, and hence political, concern about general inflation began to be reflected in regulatory influences upon electricity tariffs (rates). As the words *inflation* and *regulation* are the essence of the theme, it would be best to define them at the outset.

Inflation is here defined as it is by the general public: an upward spiral of costs and prices, regardless of cause. *Regulation* includes any form of government influence relevant to the context. It thus embraces three aspects in particular: (1) duties, obligations, and rights of the electricity industry imposed by statute or formal regulations made by government under statutory powers; (2) government influences other than those arising under statute, for example, published policy statements, appeals for voluntary cooperation, and government reactions to representations from pressure groups of one kind or another, in short, influences which are not statutory but could become so; and (3) price controls imposed by statute as part of general counter-inflationary measures which affect not only the electricity industry but also all trading organizations whether privately or state owned.

The effects of inflation are all-pervasive; directly or indirectly they permeate every facet of work in an electricity supply undertaking. Selecting the aspects for discussion and marshalling them into a coherent pattern, therefore, present problems stemming from an overabundance, rather than a dearth, of material. Any number of approaches is possible, and mine is but one.

The British Electricity Supply Industry

The British electricity supply industry was brought into full state ownership in 1948. In the 28 years since, there have been reorganizations (and rumors of reorganization), but none has materially altered the statutory obligations originally imposed with regard to those matters most pertinent to the subject of inflation. In short, we live in an inflationary clime never envisaged by our founding statutes. This produces complications, as will be seen later, but first I will explain our present constitution as briefly as possible.

I will deal only with England and Wales; there are differences elsewhere in Great Britain, but it would be too much of a digression to pursue them. In England and Wales one board is responsible for generation and transmission, and 12 area boards are responsible for distribution (132 kv and down). By statute each of these boards is autonomous, but their fortunes are interlinked because the Generating Board must provide bulk supplies to the area boards, and thus its costs form the greater part of theirs. There is thus a federal constitution. At its center stands the Electricity Council, which comprises a full-time chairman, three other central members, the chairmen of the 13 boards, and two additional Generating Board members. All of these are appointed by the appropriate cabinet minister (Secretary of State for Energy). The Electricity Council advises the minister on any electricity supply matter and in particular upon proposals by the boards for tariff changes and their programs for capital expenditure. It also borrows on behalf of the industry (in effect, it is the sole borrower) and is responsible for all negotiations on pay and conditions of service. It is also the spokesman for the federation, a forum for discussion, and is much involved in forward planning, in particular, corporate and financial planning. It must also produce consolidated accounts for the industry.

To return to the main theme, the following statutory obligations seem most pertinent to a discussion of inflation.

Tariffs (Rates)

The Generating Board and the area boards are required to consult the Electricity Council before fixing their tariffs. In practice, the Secretary of State for Energy is then provided with a general description of the changes and an estimate of their impact.

The effect of this requirement was not too marked in earlier years, but indirectly it has been among factors tending to promote rationalization both by government (which had to evolve criteria by which to judge proposals) and by the industry (with regard to tariff structure). Increasingly, however, and particularly since 1968, government has used this statutory process to intervene in pricing matters and to exert influence over and above the formal powers available to it under counter-inflationary legislation.

Also relevant is the statutory requirement that in fixing tariffs and making agreements for supplies of electricity, no undue preference or discrimination should be shown to any person or class of persons. This is significant partly as another factor which has tended to promote rationalization of tariff structures within the industry and partly because the development of that rationale proved significant when (under pressure from inflation) the government became concerned about energy prices to domestic users.

In summary, tariff regulations (using this expression in the broad sense described earlier) have, on the one hand, exposed the industry to more government intervention than the private sector in general, yet, on the other hand, they have been conducive to the evolution of a tariff rationale which has helped to stave off the worst that might have happened by way of arbitrary intervention.

Capital Outlay

It seems appropriate to consider various statutory requirements concerning capital outlay in parallel. First, there is the requirement that in carrying out capital development work each board shall act in accordance with a general program settled by the board after consulting the Electricity Council and after approval by the Secretary of State for Energy. Second, there is a set of statutory provisions (dating from before nationalization) requiring boards to afford supplies of electricity to persons who require them, to lay mains for and to connect new consumers in a variety of circumstances, and to maintain the frequency and voltage of the electricity they supply.

The power of the Secretary of State for Energy to approve capital programs has been used, under pressure of inflation, to impose annual cash limits (in effect, these attempt to restrict borrowings to amounts which are predetermined in advance but are based on estimates which include specified allowances for ongoing inflation). A danger here is that electricity supply (which is an inherent part of the nation's manufacturing processes) might be treated (simply by reason of nationalization) as a part of public expenditure, such as defense or social welfare, and in this way become subject to arbitrary intervention. However, the other aspects of statutory regulation (consumers' rights to supply and maintenance of frequency and voltage) act as a constraint, for capital outlay is needed to comply with law.

In short, there is a rough analogy to be drawn with the tariff situation just described, in the sense that the regulatory processes, on the one hand, increase risks of arbitrary intervention under pressure of inflation but, on the other hand, have aspects which have served to stave off the worst that might have happened by way of dislocating programs of capital development.

Financing Capital Requirements

In essence the nationalizing statutes provide that capital requirements can be met only from internal resources (depreciation, capital receipts, and profits) and borrowing. Over the years there have been various changes in regulations governing forms of borrowings, the general trend being toward flexibility tailored to the industry's requirements and cash flow patterns. To discuss all the variants would, however, be a digression; the following remarks are confined to borrowings from the National Loans Fund, which constitute the hard core of the loan portfolio.

Loans from the National Loans Fund are mainly (92 percent) 25-year loans repayable by half-yearly installments throughout that period. A small element (8 percent) is 10-year loans, also repayable by half-yearly installments. The two loan periods are intended to be a reflection of weighted asset lives. The interest rates are fixed. They are, in fact, established by a formula which, broadly speaking, reflects the market rate at the time the loan is taken for government securities with a redemption date of either 12.5 or 5 years ahead (that is, the full loan periods, halved to reflect the effect of repayments).

The implications, in a period of inflation, of these main features of the sources of finance are numerous and important. Whereas the industry had shown profits ever since nationalization in 1948, the picture began to change after 1968. Since then there have been, at best, minimal profits and, at worst, large losses. Moreover, inflation has progressively undermined the adequacy of depreciation provisions, the major element of internal resources. Traditionally, the industry's depreciation policies had been prudent by any standards, but after 1968 they became at first barely adequate and later, inadequate, for the effect of price regulations to date has been to prevent allowance in tariff increases for changes from a depreciation policy based on historic (original) cost of assets. The effect of inflation has thus been to worsen cash flow and increase borrowings. This tendency has been compounded by the high interest rates attendant on inflation; as of late 1976 the going rate for new 25-year money from the National Loans Fund exceeded 16 percent.

Electricity supply, being capital intensive and having a technology that demands long construction periods, requires stability in sources of finance if operational plans are to be pursued with confidence. To the extent that internal sources of finance are rendered unstable by the combined effects of inflation and regulation, it follows that there is heightened need for stability in sources of external finance. In this respect, there is much to be grateful for: From a purely "electricity" standpoint the system of borrowing from the National Loans Fund (which can look to taxation or national savings for its sustenance) provides the stability needed. There are, however, underlying problems, for inflation progressively reduces the real worth of debt installments repaid so that the state, as lender, suffers loss in real (constant money value) terms. Thus far, at least, high interest rates reflecting inflation only partly redress the balance.

In summary, the effects of regulations that influence sources of finance have, from an electricity standpoint, both good and bad features. As with tariffs and capital outlay discussed above, there are aspects of the regulatory system which have staved off the worst that might have happened; for example, construction of a power station has never had to be left in a partly finished state for lack of funds. Moreover, the effect of increasing electricity borrowing requirements from the state is, in itself, an inducement to government to refrain from imposing prolonged and extreme restraints on tariff increases in face of rising costs. On the bad side, price constraints have limited internal cash flow and have left the industry with a high interest burden.

Financial Performance

The statutory requirement is that each of the 13 boards should "secure that the revenues of the Board are not less than sufficient to meet the outgoings of the Board properly chargeable to revenue account, taking one year with another"; items so chargeable include "proper allocations to reserves, and proper provision for depreciation." The text is quoted because it is a characteristic of statute law that the words of the legislature have a status and life of their own which can persist, in practice, for quite a long time, quite independently of the realities of the day-to-day world. Areas of uncertainty were inherent in this statutory requirement from the outset, but these uncertainties have been increased still further by the confusions of thought occasioned by inflation.

There are three problem areas. First, if the object is to break even (making neither profit nor loss), how can reserves be created? Moreover, what is to be the philosophy and purpose underlying the creation of reserves? The statute was silent on the point, beyond saying that one of the purposes was equalization of tariffs, a concept that fits ill with inflation. Second, what is "proper depreciation"? Guidance on this was limited to a requirement elsewhere in the statute that accounts should conform with "best commercial practice." Until now, however, the consensus in private and public sector alike had been to keep to the historical cost convention, another concept that fits ill with inflation. Third, interest is, by normal conventions, a legitimate charge against profits, but when borrowings are the sole source of finance it is also the sole indicator of return on capital if the industry breaks even. Yet, it is a most imperfect criterion of financial performance. First, it relates only to externally financed capital and not to all capital employed. Second, interest rates are geared to transient market conditions, whereas scientific tariff structure and long-term financial planning require a stable criterion expressed in real, not money, terms, a distinction that grows more pronounced with inflation.

Successive governments sought to overcome these defects, not by statute, but by published policy statements, actually carried into effect from the early 1960s onward. Briefly, the aim was to earn a specified level of net return (7 percent) on capital employed over a five-year period, with "net return" comprised partly of interest on borrowings and partly of profit. In parallel, the government accepted the principle that tariff levels should normally be geared to long-run marginal costs (including return on capital employed). There were elements of pragmatism in all this, but the system worked and might have evolved further. However, the painfully erected edifice crumpled as inflation gathered pace after 1968. Governments arbitrarily restrained electricity prices but could not control costs, particularly fuel costs, interest rates soared, and any consensus as to real (net of inflation) rates of return on capital over the long term became lost in the confusion. The gap between historical and current cost depreciation destroyed any meaningful correlation between published accounting results and the realities underlying tariffs based on long-run marginal costs.

There is no combination of good and bad influences to record here, only disarray! However, for believers in financial discipline there are shafts of light. First, despite setbacks, the industry has never flagged in its efforts to evolve, and to be allowed to work within, a settled, logical financial framework. Second, there have of late been tangible signs of response within the regulatory system. It is to this process of rationalization that I now turn.

Commercial and Financial Objectives

It was mentioned earlier that the statutory requirement to refer tariff changes to the Secretary of State for Energy had given impetus to the rationalization of tariff structures within the industry. At times, as we have seen, this has been paralleled by government attempts to evolve a settled financial framework for electricity, and other nationalized industries, in the interests of national resource allocation and public accountability for performance. Our industry welcomes such moves, and the approach we favor is described below.[1]

The Aims of Pricing Policy

The aims of satisfactory pricing policies are threefold: (1) prices charged should bring in sufficient revenue to secure that the enter-

[1]The following paragraphs are based on a paper by myself and R. W. Orson, "The Relationship between Long-Run Marginal Cost and Accounting Practice, Especially during Periods of Inflation," UNIPEDE Tariffs Symposium, Madrid, Spain, 21–23 April 1975.

prise pays its way; (2) prices should be fair as between the different customers or classes of customers of the enterprise; and (3) prices should contribute toward the correct allocation of national resources as between the particular enterprise and all other uses of resources.

Taking the fairness objective first, this requires that prices charged to different customers should as closely as possible recover the costs of supplying them. Any other approach would involve charging some customers less than cost and other customers more than cost, that is, cross-subsidization, and it would appear to be intrinsically unfair to follow such a policy. Indeed, it would be difficult to interpret our statutory duty to avoid undue preference between consumers without a calculable basis such as this. Thus what in England and Wales are called "wider social considerations" are excluded from this concept of fairness. We believe governments, not public utilities, should determine such issues, and if they consider some customers more deserving than others, they should take the financial responsibility.

The definition of "costs of supply" is obviously crucial. It needs to be emphasized that costs include the cost of capital, that is, the return which needs to be achieved in order to make it worthwhile for national resources to be invested in electricity rather than in alternatives. This will be referred to later. It also needs to be emphasized that costs derive from investment appraisal, which requires, of course, comprehensive and often difficult assumptions about the capital cost of plant; its running costs over its lifetime; the future rate of technological change, as one factor influencing the life of the plant; the running costs of existing plant, so that any savings in running costs resulting from the new investment can be assessed; and the discount rate to be used, which, of course, is related to the return aimed for on the investment.

One output of the investment appraisal is the present value of the lifetime costs of the new plant. This corresponds with the present value over the life of the plant of meeting an increment of demand from today. If that increment of demand were postponed until next year, the same present value calculation could be made, allowing for the rate of technological change. This gives two present value calculations: one of the lifetime costs of meeting an increment of demand starting this year, and the second of the lifetime costs, at today's values, of meeting the increment if it were postponed to next year. The difference between these two present values is the marginal cost of meeting the demand increment in this year. This has been only a brief summary of the calculation of long-run marginal cost (LRMC). In our view, the prices charged for all customers should reflect this principle. The third aim of prices suggested earlier was to secure the correct allocation of national resources to electricity. There is no need to repeat the extensive material on the subject of marginal cost pricing and resource allocation here. However, the issue is particularly relevant in the context of energy conservation, for the best use is more likely to be made of energy, and indeed all other resources, if prices reflect costs.

The question remains whether the LRMC principle will satisfy the first objective, that is, bring in sufficient revenue. The proponents of marginal cost pricing have not always taken full account of the investment required to meet additional demand because of the optimism which has usually been associated with future estimates and because of the economies of scale and the technological progress which have been obtained in the past. Thus it has usually been believed that marginal costs are typically less than accounting costs, and considerable economic literature has been devoted to the problem of recovering the excess of accounting costs over prices equated to marginal costs. However, in our judgment, the scope for the economies of scale previously obtained by the electricity supply industry has been exhausted in the developed countries, and further technological progress is likely to be offset by increases in the real cost of primary fuel and the increased difficulty of obtaining sites for power plants.

In the absence of economies of scale, marginal costs should equal accounting costs if (1) depreciation schedules are calculated so that depreciation and the return on capital, taken together, match the expected future pattern of net earnings; (2) the net return on revalued assets is equal to the real return assumed for LRMC calculations; and (3) the expected pattern of net earnings proves correct.

If LRMC is calculated on the lines epitomized above and the principles governing depreciation policy and return on capital are on the lines described below, the enterprise will pay its way provided past expectations of future costs are fulfilled. Where expectations are falsified (for example, by the dramatic recent increases in oil prices), additional questions are raised, and these too are discussed later.

Pricing and Depreciation Policy

It is sometimes argued that while these LRMC calculations may be correct for charging new customers, they surely cannot be correct for existing customers, who may have appeared on the scene many years ago, when the costs of plant were completely different. There are three main points to be made in this connection. First, if there is an integrated network for generating and distributing electricity, then no item of plant is normally associated with any particular customer. If an existing customer reduced his demand for electricity, the industry's investment would be reduced so that the costs saved would be precisely the same as the LRMC calculations already described. If an existing customer were charged less than LRMC, then the industry would be financially better off without his business than with it. Second, the argument is confused by the effects of inflation. If inflation did not take place and assuming that there is technological progress, costs would clearly be seen to be falling over time. In these circumstances existing customers would prefer to be charged at the new LRMC levels. The third and fundamental point is that the whole argument revolves around the valuation put on historic assets. If assets are valued correctly, there is no difference between the cost today of continuing to use an existing asset and the cost of using a new asset.

The problems here are depreciation and return on capital. Depreciation has been exciting great controversy in England and Wales. Much of this centers, quite correctly, on the effects of inflation, but before considering the arithmetic needed to adjust for changing money values, it is essential to develop a sound basic depreciation philosophy. The approach evolved after prolonged collective deliberation and research under the aegis of the Electricity Council is that the value of an asset or group of assets rests upon its earning power and that depreciation should reflect the decline in earning power over time. More precisely, depreciation provisions should represent the annual decline in present (discounted) worth of the future operating margins earnable by the assets currently in use. "Operating margin" is defined below.

Depreciation is the mechanism by which the correct cost for the economic use of assets is charged in a profit and loss account before a profit is declared. As depreciation is the difference between the net book value of assets expressed in succeeding balance sheets, it is also the mechanism responsible for the balance sheet showing a realistic view of the net worth of a business. From the point of view of determining what the appropriate pattern of depreciation should be, therefore, one must first ask what are the major influences which determine the value of assets in the balance sheet and the way in which this changes over time.

Assuming that the balance sheet and accounts are prepared on a going-concern basis, the value that should be shown is the present value of the future cash flows that can be expected as a result of using the assets owned by the industry. In any one year these cash flows are represented by the margin between income and revenue expenditure, excluding depreciation, and this represents the "operating margin." The value of assets in a balance sheet then should be the present value of future operating margins, and in our view the test of an ideal depreciation policy is whether it satisfies this objective.

Consideration of what the future operating margins of existing assets are likely to be inevitably leads to the conclusion that depreciation is in large measure interrelated with investment appraisal and pricing policy; in our case this means assumptions used in developing a pricing policy based on LRMC. The main areas of judgment in developing such a depreciation policy are the pattern over time of future operating margins, the economic life of the assets concerned, and the rate of return to be expected.

Return on Capital Employed

The question of return on capital has been mentioned above in two ways: as an element in the revenue needed to secure the financial viability of the enterprise and the determinant of resource allocations, and as a factor affecting operating margins and hence depreciation provisions.

The determination of the appropriate return on capital is subject to the following considerations: (1) Electricity being a semimonopoly in the sense of having a statutory monopoly to afford public supplies, the rate of return must be influenced by conscious decision and policy rather than sole reliance on market forces; (2) since allocation of national resources is involved, decision must ultimately rest with the government, although the industry would naturally expect to have a voice in decisions; and (3) considerations of resource allocation lead to the conclusion that an important factor in determining an appropriate rate of return is the real rate of return expected by investors in industry generally.

The figure resulting from these considerations is somewhat controversial. Periodic investigations at the Electricity Council between 1968 and 1973 suggested that investors in industry, taking all forms of investment into consideration, obtained a real (net of inflation) return no greater than 5 percent on revalued net assets. This judgment was based to some extent upon the results of very large companies in the private sector but was cross-checked by reference to various sets of data. Nonetheless, this is a matter on which it is difficult to come to firm conclusions, and it is accepted that the rate inevitably has to be fixed after consultation with the government.

The initial processes of evolving the depreciation policy outlined above are admittedly complex, but it has been found possible to evolve simplified formulas compatible with basic theory but capable of practical application in the field. An integral part of those processes would be adjustment of the basic calculations to reflect the effects of inflation.

Only fleeting reference has been made to cash flow and the level of internal financing. This is not because these are thought unimportant, but because the considerations involved are separate from the main theme. There is, however, one important point to be made: If electricity tariffs covered costs, including proper provision for depreciation and a reasonable real return on capital, the problems of financing electricity supply investment (widely experienced in Europe and in the United States, I believe) would be considerably alleviated.

Effect of Changed Circumstances

Both the rational pricing policy and the interrelated depreciation policy described above depend on a number of judgments about the future. However, it needs to be borne in mind that even conventional depreciation formulas involve such an implicit judgment in order to arrive at depreciation charges. Provided past judgments turn out to have been reasonably correct, revenue from prices equated to LRMC will reasonably match costs, including depreciation and an adequate return on investment.

If past judgments turn out to have erred badly, then prices equated to LRMC may yield too much or too little revenue, that is, assets may now be more valuable than expected, and should be written up, or assets may now be less valuable than expected, and should be written down. It could be argued that the dramatic increase in world oil prices has made nuclear power so much more competitive than oil-fired power stations that the LRMC of electricity from nuclear power is much less than the present accounting costs of oil-fired power stations. This is debatable, but even if the argument were correct it would be correct not only to concentrate new investment on nuclear power, but also to write down the asset value of present oil-fired power stations so as to match their accounting costs to the LRMC of nuclear power.

Putting the Approach into Effect

The approach described is an ideal, a hypothesis to be adapted to the real world. How near are we to attaining a real-life approximation to the theoretical model? Inevitably, this is a game of patience. Much thought and research is needed within the industry to evolve and update a body of logic which embraces a range of activities, beginning with sophisticated techniques for appraising new investment projects and ending with a retail tariff structure with its attendant complexities of subdivision between consumer classes with differing load characteristics and between fixed and running charge components. Moreover, government must be persuaded. This is vital for three reasons. First, financial objectives set by government for nationalized industries must conform to some policy pattern; ground rules cannot be settled unilaterally by any one industry. This is true generally, but true of the energy sector particularly. Second, not only the form of financial objectives has to be settled but also the rate of return to be expected. This is material — a percentage point of return on revalued net assets is equivalent to about 3 percentage points on retail tariffs. The target rate must also be reflected in the discount rate used for capital appraisal purposes. Finally, depreciation ground rules must for various reasons (company law, taxation, price regulations, and so forth) be broadly common to all trading organizations whether in the private or public sector.

The task may appear daunting, but in fact there has been material progress on several fronts. Thought within the industry is well advanced, and we have long been in touch with government about our ideas. Also, the gap between present tariff levels and LRMC is not unbridgeable. Furthermore, government has recently given tangible evidence of willingness to move toward realistic pricing and of its intention to grasp the depreciation nettle. The most slow-moving front is the establishment of a system of financial objectives embracing a real rate of return, for although dialogue continues, it is bedevilled by the statutorily imposed capital structure (fixed interest borrowings) and the confusing effect of changing money values. Inflation also impedes progress because government, in attempting to control it, must have regard to short-run implications as well as the longer term considerations that predominate in industry thinking.

In short, inflation and regulatory influences impede progress, but the aims remain attainable.

The Impact of Inflation and Counter-Inflationary Regulations

We now consider the extent to which inflation and regulation have affected financial performance as measured by the statutory obligation to break even on revenue account after charging interest on borrowings and depreciation based on historic cost and by the criteria described above, that is, prices reflecting LRMC and so embracing a real (net of inflation) return on capital employed and realistic depreciation. It is useful to begin by giving the rates of inflation actually experienced and epitomizing the main counter-inflationary regulations.

Rates of inflation experienced since 1968, as measured by the official Retail Prices Index (RPI), are shown in Table 1. There has been an abatement in the rate of inflation in 1976, but the government does not expect the annual rate to fall to single figures until late in 1977. Our problems are worse than yours!

Table 1. ***Retail Price Index***

Calendar year	*Index*
1968	100
1969	105
1970	112
1971	123
1972	131
1973	144
1974	167
1975	207

Increasingly as inflation gathered pace there were attempts by government to hold down electricity tariffs. At first these were informal and unilateral in nature, but fairly early on there was a government call to the Confederation of British Industry (to which we belong) to exercise voluntary price restraint. The trouble was that, in effect, "voluntary" meant "compulsory" in the case of nationalized industries. For a time, then, electricity was among the "loss-leaders" in government counter-inflationary plans, but more rational measures ensued. In 1973 a generally applicable Price Code was enforced. This allowed price increases only when specified criteria of costs and profitability were satisfied. Manufacturing organizations, such as ourselves, must satisfy a specially created Price Commission that cost increases per unit of product justify the increase. Moreover, the basic rule is that organizations must not exceed a level of profitability (expressed in terms of percentage of turnover) achieved in a standardly specified past period. There is one exception: Those with low profits in the past can increase profits to 2 percent of turnover. Broadly, electricity has been in the latter category because of being a "voluntary/compulsory" loss-leader in the initial period.

For nationalized industries there is provision in the Price Code for the relevant government minister to intervene to reduce the price increases to a level at which the industry would break even. He does this under powers which enable him to have regard to the general level of prices in the economy, and it is a power that has been exercised. In addition to the need to notify price increases, there is a procedure for the quarterly reporting to the Price Commission of the level of profitability.

Until very recently, the Price Code rules involved using accounts based on historic cost depreciation. In August 1976, however, a change was made enabling organizations seeking increases to allow for the recovery of historic cost depreciation multiplied by a factor of 1.4. This is one of the tangible steps toward realism to which I referred earlier.

Turning now to the impact of inflation and counter-inflationary regulations on financial performance, Table 2 indicates how increases in the costs of the electricity supply industry have compared with the general rise in the cost of living shown in Table 1 and how increases in the average retail price per unit of electricity compare with both.

There are five main points brought out by Table 2. First, electricity cost indexes rose faster than the general retail price index. Second, notwithstanding this adverse trend in "electricity" indexes, increases in average price per kwh sold lagged behind the general retail price index over most of the period. In other words, they fell in real terms. Only in the last year did electricity prices overtake the general retail price index and then by only a slight margin, certainly

Table 2. ***Comparisons of Price Indexes***

Year	*Retail price index (calendar year)*	*Electricity supply industry's cost indexes*[a] *(year commencing April 1)* *Fuel*[b]	*Capital equipment*[c]	*Salaries and related costs*[d]	*Average price of electricity per kwh sold (year commencing April 1)*
	(1)	*(2)*	*(3)*	*(4)*	*(5)*
1968	100	100	100	100	100
1969	105	103	106	109	99
1970	112	124	118	125	100
1971	123	136	129	147	110
1972	131	138	143	168	113
1973	144	164	154	189	118
1974	167	280	193	239	156
1975	207	362	240	306	215

NOTE: Retail Price Index from Table 1.

[a]Fuel, capital charges (depreciation and interest), and salaries together constitute 85 percent of costs chargeable to revenue account (more than 85 percent if capital charges fully reflect current costs). Hence, the above indicators of electricity supply cost charges are reasonably comprehensive. Other costs (miscellaneous goods and services and local taxation) have moved with inflation, and their inclusion would not materially alter the picture.

[b]National delivered fuel cost — pence/tonne.

[c]Gross Fixed Capital Formation (Electricity Supply) Index, compiled by the Government Central Statistical Office.

[d]Salary and related costs per employee.

Table 3. ***Electricity Council and Electricity Boards in England and Wales***

Year	*Profit/loss after interest and historic cost depreciation (millions of £)*	*Apparent net return on capital employed*[a] *(in percentage)*
	(1)	*(2)*
1968–69	101	7.0
1969–70	65	6.5
1970–71	(–) 56	4.0
1971–72	(–) 23	5.0
1972–73	2	6.0
1973–74	(–) 184	3.0
1974–75	(–) 265	2.0
1975–76	9	7.5

[a]Profit/loss before charging interest, expressed as a percentage of average net capital employed during year, calculated on the historic cost convention. Both columns (1) and (2) include the results of selling appliances in shops and work on consumers' premises, but the effect on the overall figures is minimal.

by a very much smaller margin than appears to be justified by the excess of the "electricity" cost indexes over the general index. Third, on the face of things, electricity did well, an impression seemingly strengthened if one takes into account the fact that the industry made a slight profit in that last year (see Table 3). To an extent the impression is true; there have, for example, been savings in labor costs due to improved productivity, and thermal efficiency has improved. But the harsh truth is that no industry could absorb the swinging cost increases shown by means of savings (unless it was inefficient to start with!). Fourth, the answer lies in the distorting effects of inflation. The profit in the last year existed only on the basis of the historic cost convention of depreciation and because interest chargeable to revenue account reflected loans advanced at outdated money values and hence outdated interest rates. Finally, there is a separate aspect to comparison between columns (1) and (5) in Table 2, namely that, measured over the last three years only, electricity prices increased faster than prices in general and, indeed, earnings. I return to this later.

Table 3 shows aspects of financial performance based on the conventional published accounts; it relates, that is, to performance against the statutory requirement to break even.

Two points emerge from Table 3. First, between October 1967 and April 1971 there were no general price increases in electricity, hence the deterioration up to 1970 – 1971. The increases introduced in April 1971 were limited in deference to government views, so that they were not such as to put the industry back in the black in 1971 – 1972. Then came the period of "voluntary" price restraint referred to earlier. As a result, 1972 –1973 showed an inadequate level of profit. A "price freeze" was introduced nationally in November 1972, and although this was succeeded by the formal Price Code which permitted price increases, the industry was restricted to below the rules of this code in its price increases, hence the large loss in 1973 –1974. By this time massive fuel cost increases were being experienced, so that our overall financial position became worse. The industry has been "compensated" by government for published account losses incurred as a result of restraining price increases, albeit at a cost to the taxpayer. With relaxation of the Price Code rules, deficits are no longer expected and compensation payments have now ceased. Second, on the face of it, return on capital employed stayed positive. This was partly due to the effect of interest costs but mainly to the fact that the asset base stayed relatively static. The effect is wholly misleading, for had the calculations reflected the real (current cost) value of assets, the returns shown from 1972 onward at least (we did not begin calculations until then) would have been either nil or negative.

Table 4 is a resource analysis of costs showing the change in the proportions represented by the main elements between the first and last years of the period under review, on a published account basis. The table brings out another misleading aspect of inflation. On the face of things the proportion of costs represented by fuel has increased, and the proportion attributable to capital expenditure has fallen. There would be some who, conscious of the recent explosion in world fuel costs, would accept this and possibly orient tariff decisions accordingly, but a basis of accounting which took proper account of inflation would show a different picture. The depreciation element (reflecting increasing capital intensity) would be appreciably higher and other items (including fuel) correspondingly lower, in fact, closer to the 1968–1969 picture.

Table 4. ***Electricity Council and Electricity Boards in England and Wales***

Costs	*Percentages of total costs chargeable to revenue account*			
	1968–69		*1975–76*	
Fuel (at delivered cost)		32		45
Other materials, goods and services, rents, and local taxation		12		15
Salaries and related costs		17		16
Depreciation	21		11	
Interest	18	39	13	24
		100		100
Total costs	£1,203m		£ 3,268m	

Obviously, inflation and arbitrarily imposed price restraint have played havoc with the statutory objective of breaking even. Moreover, they have rendered the underlying conventions of calculation meaningless. Tables 1–4 show that the distortions of inflation have made traditional criteria misleading as a guide to performance in keeping down prices by absorbing costs (true achievements are concealed by the magnitude of the effect of changing money values); misleading as a guide to profitability (profits and returns on capital are shown where there are none); and misleading in terms of composition of internal costs. Inflation, compounded by a regulatory system which ignores its effects, distorts national resource allocation and runs counter to energy conservation by concealing the extent of underpricing.

Arbitrary price restraint played havoc not only with historic cost criteria, but also with criteria of the kind discussed earlier. Fortunately, as the tables show, the restraint has been eased; there was a small profit in 1975–1976 and results for 1976–1977 will be distinctly better. As indicated earlier, prices reflecting LRMC are therefore seemingly attainable within a reasonable time. The considerations involved are too complex to quantify in the present context, but as a rough approximation, a 10 percent uplift in real costs over time might suffice, possibly less depending on the rate of return on capital inherent in the LRMC calculation. Presentationally this would have its difficulties unless depreciation policy was altered to reflect current costs, for accounts on the present convention would show misleadingly high profits with realistic tariffs.

Finally, by way of footnote, data in Table 5 are of interest. The table shows that despite the prominence accorded to it by the government as a counter-inflationary "loss-leader," electricity remains a relatively small household expenditure item.

Table 5. ***Customers' Expenditure and Consumption***

	1968–69	*1975–76*
Expenditure on electricity as a percentage of total household expenditure	2.52	2.63
Consumption per customer (kwh)	3,710	4,290

Coping with Inflation

It is to be hoped that our present period of high inflation will prove transitory, but it was preceded by a long period of mild inflation (indeed, a level of 4 percent per annum was then sometimes talked of as acceptable if full employment was to be maintained), and such a phase might well recur. Some developments which might never have been stimulated in the absence of high, as distinct from mild, inflation will, I believe, be of continuing benefit when the rate falls to acceptable levels. These are discussed below, albeit briefly.

Inflation Accounting

A switch from historic cost to inflation accounts is something of a traumatic experience for any business community, for it affects definitions of profit, distributable profit, tax, and general issues of accountability to proprietors. We, as other countries, have had prolonged public debate, but in my judgment the time for decision and action is close. In all probability the accounting profession will issue an Exposure Draft on its proposals within weeks, together with a timetable for introduction. This follows the acceptance by the government of general recommendations by a committee (the Report of the Inflation Accounting Committee) chaired by Mr. (now Sir) Francis Sandilands, CBE, published in September 1975. I have been closely associated with these processes, and the importance I attach to bringing accounts into line with current costs (stocks as well as depreciation) will be apparent from all I have said earlier. To me, realism — not only in published accounts but also in the financial appraisals that form the background of day-to-day management decisions — is at once the friend of industrial efficiency and the enemy of uncontrolled inflation.

There can be debates about method, and the repercussions of alternative methods, but it would be a digression to pursue them here. The important point is summed up in the answer to the question: What will be the effect on electricity prices? My answer is "none" *IF* tariffs are properly constructed to reflect long-run marginal costs. I have indicated earlier that there is a shortfall when this criterion is used, and if that were to be made good, the effect of bringing depreciation onto a proper footing would not be to increase prices but to show a true, instead of an exaggerated, profit.

Fuel Cost Variation Clauses

Fuel cost adjustments (automatic adjustment clauses) have been a matter of discussion for many years within our industry. Their use for industrial and certain commercial tariffs has long been established, but the subject for debate has been extension to other consumer classes. One result, across the years, has been a continuing tendency for domestic tariffs to lag behind industrial tariffs by the criterion of price in relation to cost. However, in May 1974 fuel cost adjustments were introduced for domestic and other tariffs to which they had not previously applied.

The advantages, which I submit to be of relevance in times of mild as well as sharp inflation, are fourfold: (1) removal of the uncertainty attaching to primary fuel price movements; (2) emphasis of the point that fuel, a cost outside the industry's control, is a considerable factor in electricity price increases; (3) avoidance of criticism from industrial and other consumers of disparity in treatment; and (4) avoidance of "cliff faces" in tariff rates due to delay in reflecting upward trends in fuel costs and the risk that increases so delayed will coincide with the need to recover increases in other costs.

What has public reaction been? There have been protests from consumer associations and other pressure groups and a recommendation from a parliamentary select committee that fuel cost adjustments be abolished. The disadvantages claimed relate primarily to domestic tariffs: The clauses are difficult for consumers to understand; consumers have difficulty in knowing precisely how much their electricity costs; and bills and consumer queries are more involved than they would be otherwise. The points about consumer comprehension were, we believe, valid only in the period immediately following the introduction of fuel cost adjustments in domestic and other tariffs. Recent experience of consultative councils (the independent bodies appointed by Parliament to represent consumer opinion with regard to electricity) is that fuel clauses are no longer a significant cause of consumer complaint. Experience has, of course, brought about improvements in our methods of explanation.

In my opinion, however, there is an important constraint upon the use of fuel cost adjustments. It might be argued that such adjustments should be calculated by reference to a zero base in order to bring home the full impact of fuel costs, but to go to this extreme would be to resort to average pricing, and this would be inconsistent with the pricing philosophy advocated here. In my view the basic cost of fuel should be included in the main tariff, leaving the fuel cost adjustment as a fine-tuning device.

Debt Recovery and Hardship Cases

Some years ago the industry, in anticipation of the time when price restraint ended and sharp increases were necessary to make good lost ground, initiated discussions with government welfare organizations and voluntary associations with a view to evolving liaison arrangements to ensure that persons entitled to financial assistance from the state were given an opportunity to make arrangements which would make it possible to continue electricity supply. Typically, this meant withholding disconnection action for a period of 14 days while the welfare authorities looked into the case and, subsequently, agreeing to continue supply while agreed deductions from statutory welfare payments were paid by installments to the Electricity Board (either through the consumer or directly by the authorities concerned). Liaison officers were nominated by the boards, and welfare authorities and voluntary associations were notified as to their names and whereabouts so that on-the-spot decisions could be given in cases of difficulty. Such arrangements were not a great departure, for the industry had traditionally sought to be sympathetic in hardship cases, but the formalization of arrangements proved their worth when we came to deal with problems of the kind discussed in the next section.

The Consumer

Billing and Collection

Tables 1 – 5 showed that increases in electricity prices in recent years have been much in line with price increases generally. Between 1968 and 1976 the relevant details were as follows: Index of Retail Prices (all items), 138 percent; electricity (domestic), 141 percent; and average earnings, 197 percent. In short, electricity (in common with all other items included in the Retail Price Index) decreased relative to earnings over the period. However, the 1976 tariff levels were reached by a marked increase toward the end of the period, and if one measures only over these latter years the following picture emerges (December 1973 to June 1976): Index of Retail Prices (all items), 59 percent; electricity (domestic), 113 percent; and average earnings, 61 percent. This clearly shows the consequences of damming up price increases by arbitrarily imposed price restraints. The rate of increase is as important to people as the absolute level, and it is perhaps due to this that we have seen an upsurge in the interest taken by pressure groups and members of Parliament in billing and collection and tariff structure, with an emphasis upon low income groups. These matters are discussed below.

Despite the escalation in electricity bills, the fact remains that consumers' paying habits have remained surprisingly constant, and in this respect the industry's cash flow has been correspondingly buoyant. The following is a brief description of the position. First, for domestic customers (billed quarterly for the main part) the interval between reading and billing is typically two days with a further day for dispatch; in the event of nonpayment a reminder is sent, typically after an interval of three weeks, and about two weeks after this, central billing offices send computerized lists of premises to districts for them to consider for disconnection, the emphasis being on the exercise of local knowledge and discretion. Second, 60 percent of consumers pay at boards' shops (we do a retail appliance business, and the shops have payment facilities), 20 percent pay by post, 10 percent via banks, and 10 percent prepayment meters. Finally, each quarter some 17 million credit consumers receive bills; 7 out of 10 pay without reminder; 19 out of 20 pay either before or during the currency of the reminder. Only about 3 in 2,000 are disconnected for nonpayment, and more than half of these are reconnected in less than two days.

As well as prepayment meters (which are virtually unique to the British Isles), we have a range of stamp schemes, weekly and monthly budget schemes, and pay what you like, where you like, at any time schemes, all of which are intended to help people on low incomes or otherwise in financial difficulty. In addition, there is publicity notifying persons who anticipate difficulty to contact their area board for advice, and as a backstop we have the arrangements with the welfare authorities referred to above. One might think that with this array of services the industry's standing with the voluntary social welfare organizations and others with similar interests would be good. Regrettably, this has not proved to be the case, for while the overwhelming mass of consumers have continued to pay their bills as promptly as ever, articulate pressure groups claiming to represent them have lobbied intensely for the abolition of the industry's statutory powers to disconnect supplies for nonpayment. The industry has resisted the pressures, which at times have appeared authoritatively backed. Our calculations indicate the consequences of losing this power (installation of extra prepayment meters where appropriate, greater numbers of court proceedings, consequences of a general "slippage" in payment times if well-established paying habits were disturbed by change in the status quo, and so forth) would be equivalent to the proceeds of an 8 percent tariff increase for domestic consumers. Government, which also experiences pressure from lobbyists and others, reached the conclusion that our statutory powers should not be withdrawn, but whether the pressure groups will persist remains to be seen. It is of aid to the industry that its stance for the protection of good payers against the effect of bad ones enjoys a groundswell of popular support. Certainly we have the support of the independent consultative councils appointed by Parliament to watch over affairs for electricity consumers and the support of trade unions with members in the industry.

There are distinct limits to the extent to which extended credit can alleviate distress. If new debt mounts faster than old debts are discharged, a day of reckoning must come; electricity must be paid for in the end. The industry has therefore continually urged that the only permanent way of dealing with poverty in relation to fuel is for government and its welfare agencies, as experts in this social field, to define poverty in terms capable of administrative interpretation and to alleviate it by outright payments. To a modest extent this is now being done. During the coming winter a government scheme will operate with the area electricity boards' cooperation. The boards will show on every domestic bill a predetermined amount of discount. The onus will be on consumers to claim a discount and to take suitable evidence to any Post Office that they fall in the defined group. They also take with them the electricity bill. The Post Office then issues a voucher for the amount of the discount, and the electricity boards treat this as cash. The industry does not bear the cost of administration or of publicizing the arrangements, but the taxpayer does, and I am sure that there are cheaper ways of achieving the same end.

Consumerist pressure groups have not been concerned only with seeking an end to disconnection powers. Some groups advocate wider extension of prepayment meters as an aid to the poor (although the annual costs of a coin-operated prepayment meter exceed those of an ordinary credit meter by £6 or £7 a year). There are also enthusiasts for token-operated meters, an idea which I believe to have been introduced on a small scale in Japan. We are looking at this as a long-term possibility, but there are potential demerits.

Energy Tariffs for the Poor

Our domestic tariffs can best be described as containing a fixed charge per consumer per quarter and a constant charge per kwh for electricity supplied. The usual way of expressing these charges is by means of a block tariff, for example:

First 70 kwh per quarter	4.25p per kwh
All additional kwh	1.25p per kwh

The 3p surcharge on the first 70 kwh is to cover the annual charge (interest, depreciation, operation, and maintenance) on a minimum connection from the consumer's dwelling to the public supply, together with the cost of providing an electricity meter and reading this meter, and an allowance for accounting and administrative costs. In short, the tariff is cost related.

Nevertheless, there are critics who claim that a tariff in this form is promotional; those who hold this view may do so either on energy conservation grounds or out of concern for the impact of high energy bills on the poor. In the latter case the argument runs that those who use the least electricity will be the poorest, and it is unfair that they should pay more per unit supplied. Earlier this year the government set up a group to review the scope for helping poor consumers by adjusting the structure of energy tariffs or by other means, such as introducing special concessionary tariffs or free allowances of gas and electricity. The report illustrated four possibilities and their effects.

FLAT RATE TARIFFS. Under flat rate tariffs there is no standing charge, but all revenue is raised from the unit consumption rate. These would help slightly over three-fifths and harm nearly two-fifths of the 13 million gas and 19 million electricity consumers. Help would range from 1p to 15p a week for electricity, from 1p to 25p for prepayment gas consumers, up to 12p for general credit gas consumers in the cheapest regions, and up to 32p in the dearest. Those helped for electricity would include at least 1.8 million "pensioner households," of which about 750,000 would be "poor pensioner households" in England and Wales, about 650,000 poor households in the United Kingdom with income approximately equivalent to or below supplementary benefit levels, and about 3.4 million council tenants (although they are not necessarily poor) in England and Wales. (These groups overlap, so the figures are not cumulative.) But those harmed, by between 1p and 50p a week or more, include for electricity at least half a million pensioner households, of which at least 120,000 would be "poor pensioner households," about 210,000 poor households with incomes up to about supplementary benefit levels, and about 1.4 million council tenants.

TARRIFFS WITH HALF THE STANDING CHARGES. If standing charges were halved, the balance of revenue would be recovered from the consumption rates. This would help and harm about the same number of electricity consumers, as would flat rate tariffs, but maximum help would be only 7½p a week, although harm could exceed 30p a week. For gas there would be no help to the three million (predominantly small) prepayment consumers; from 4p to 8p a week help to some of the three million general credit consumers, with harm to others of them; and help to some with harm to others of the seven million larger Gold Star consumers.

TWO-TIER INVERTED TARIFFS. Two-tier inverted tariffs would offer a cheaper rate for consumption up to a given level and a higher rate thereafter, with no standing charge. If, for the first 1,800 units of ordinary rate, unrestricted electricity (half the average consumption in England and Wales), the cheaper rate were set at two-thirds of the price necessary under a flat rate tariff and the higher rate were set 80 percent above the low rate (the level necessary to yield the same total revenue from the tariff, assuming no changes in consumption to take the maximum advantage of subsidized fuel or to avoid paying the cross-subsidy), this would help two-thirds and harm one-third of consumers in England and Wales. This tariff would help more consumers by greater amounts than the two previous examples, but the harm to the remaining consumers would also be greater. Help would range from 1p to 33p a week, harm from 1p to £1.60 a week or more. Among those helped would be at least 1.8 million pensioner households, including at least 750,000 poor pensioner households, 670,000 with income approximately equivalent to or below supplementary benefit level, and about 3.6 million council tenants. Those harmed would include at least 470,000 pensioner households (at least 120,000 of them poor), 190,000 with incomes approximating to or below supplementary benefit level, and 1.2 million council tenants. (We have also examined versions designed to double the amount of help, but the harm of £1.60 would then become £4.30.)

THREE-TIER INVERTED TARRIFS. The three-tier tariff discussed here is adapted from the one introduced in Japan in 1974 for certain domestic electricity consumption. There would be no standing charge and three consumption rates. The first 1,800 units of ordinary, unrestricted electricity might be priced 10 percent below the present unit rate; the next 1,800 units at the present unit rate; and units over 3,600 at the level necessary to yield the same total revenue from the tariff (which, in this example, and again assuming no change in the pattern of consumption, would be 50 percent above the present unit rate). This tariff would help slightly more and harm slightly fewer of the same consumers than the previous example of a two-tier inverted tariff; but the amount of help would be reduced to 1p – 23p a week, and the harm increased to 1p – £2 a week or more.

The conclusion reached by the group was that

> general tariff adjustments would afford some help to many poor consumers but they would significantly harm others and would raise, among other problems, the question whether other action would also be needed, at a cost to the Exchequer, to offset this harm. Help would be more specifically directed to particular groups by giving them concessions, whether in the form of special tariffs or allowances, though this would still be unselective to the extent that there is no obvious grouping which would both include all those needing help and exclude those who are not in need, and such schemes would involve practical difficulties of identification. Concessionary tariffs, however, could apply only to gas and electricity and such tariffs, if financed by other consumers, would require specific legislation. They could also have repercussions for counter-inflationary policy, the international competitiveness of industry, and for the implementation of industrial strategy. These difficulties could be avoided by giving the groups to be helped a monetary allowance towards the payment of whatever fuel they use; this would be tantamount to a general benefit uprating in so far as it applied to social security beneficiaries. The amount and cost of the help to be given would then be at the Government's discretion, but any Government subvention would raise serious public expenditure difficulties.

I believe this vindication of the industry's tariffs to have been entirely due to the fact that underlying them was the cost related philosophy I have attempted to describe here.

Conclusion

This then is my contribution: the British aspect of the interface between regulation and inflation as it affects electricity supply. I would like to offer three valedictory propositions in conclusion. First, the financial problems of electricity supply transcend, in large measure, not only international boundaries but also forms of ownership, public or private. Second, regardless of form of ownership, profit, return on capital — call it what you will — and realistic depreciation are essential to a pricing policy geared to the requirements of national resource allocation and energy conservation in particular. They should be part of a thread of continuity which links project appraisal, tariff policy, public accountability, and management data, accounting or otherwise, for financial realism is the enemy of inflation. Finally, marketing policy and public accountability should reflect the internal financial discipline. An industry so large, so important to national well-being, and yet, by reason of technology, inevitably a semimonopoly, must be pervaded by a sense of trusteeship.

Inflation and Public Utilities in Brazil: The Electric Energy Sector

Mario Bhering
and José Langier

Brazil has had inflation for a very long time, and by now it is fair to say that it has found ways to adjust its economy to the effects of inflation to avoid large misallocation of resources. Public utilities are most seriously affected by inflation because their prices are regulated. It is well known that under inflationary conditions public authorities are under pressure not to raise the prices they regulate, but any price limitation will in most cases reduce the revenues of the utilities in real terms. Even when revenues increase in real terms, they might not be sufficient to meet the resource requirements of the utility. The most important effect of inflation on public utilities is that it hinders their ability to obtain resources for expansion. Internal generation of resources is usually diminished in real terms, which reduces utilities' capacity to obtain external resources and to self-finance expansion.

Under these circumstances, public services might be curtailed and shortages develop. In Brazil, curtailment and shortages of electric energy services have been temporary, but in other public services, such as telephones, they have had longer durations.

Regulation in Brazil was adapted to permit monetary indexing of fixed assets to cope with the problems referred to above. This essay

NOTE: The views presented here are the authors' and do not represent those of any organization with which they are associated.

will show briefly how monetary indexing is applied to the electric energy sector and its effect on the total amount of resources available to the utility to pay back charges from past investment and to finance expansion. As the authors are not accountants, the subject will not be dealt with from that point of view. Information in this regard can easily be obtained from auditors (including foreigners) operating in Brazil. Furthermore, the distribution of the cost of service to consumers, electric energy rates, is not dealt with here because, under inflationary conditions, the authors consider the expansion of utilities more important than their operation. Finally, the second section is intended to be illustrative of the evolution of the variables concerning the electric energy sector and the rest of the Brazilian economy.

The Brazilian Economy and the Electric Energy Sector

The evolution of the Brazilian electric energy sector since World War II is interrelated with the development of the entire country. Table 1 presents some demographic statistics. There was rapid population growth from 1950 to 1975, when the population more than doubled. The urban population grew even faster, increasing from 36.2 percent of total population in 1950 to almost 60 percent in 1975. This urbanization process was caused by, among other things, the rapid development of the country.

As can be seen in Table 2, Gross Domestic Product (GDP) in real terms — at 1949 prices — increased more than sixfold from 1949 to 1973.

Table 1. ***Total and Urban Brazilian Population, Selected Years, 1950–1975***

	Total	*Urban (percentage)*
1950	51,944,397	36.2
1960	70,967,185	45.1
1970	93,139,037	55.9
1971	95,993,400	56.5
1972	98,690,200	57.4
1973	101,432,600	58.2
1974	104,243,300	59.0
1975	107,145,200	59.8

SOURCE: Brazilian Institute of Geography and Statistics, *Anuário Estatístico do Brasil 1975* (Rio de Janeiro: the Institute, 1975), Col. 36, pp. 60, 63, and 64.
NOTE: From 1971 on, the figures are estimated.

Table 2. ***Brazilian Gross Domestic Product, Industrial Product, Gross Capital Formation, and Electric Sector Investment, Selected Years, 1949–1973***

	Gross domestic product		*Industrial product as a percentage of gross domestic product*	*Gross capital formation as a percentage of gross domestic product*	*Electric sector investment as a percentage of gross capital formation*
	Cr$ millions	*Cr$ millions at 1949 prices*			
1949	233.3	233.3	22.3	13.8	—
1959	2,076.2	450.0	24.5	18.9	—
1970	206,564.7	1,002.2	26.2	21.0	8.9
1971	274,267.4	1,105.1	25.8	21.7	8.3
1972	359,132.7	1,236.4	26.1	22.0	8.8
1973	477,163.1	1,419.8	26.7	22.6	8.2

SOURCES: Brazilian Institute of Geography and Statistics, *Anuário Estatístico do Brasil–1976*, vol. 37 (Rio de Janeiro: the Institute, 1976), pp. 462 and 463; Fundaçao Getulio Vargas, *Conjuntura Economica* 27 (December 1973): Annex, p. 3, and 30 (March 1976): 111; and Centrais Electricas Brasileiras S.A.-Eletrobras, *Annual Report 1975* (Rio de Janeiro : 1976), p. 10.

Table 3. ***Brazilian Electric Energy: Generating Capacity, Production, and Consumption, Selected Years, 1950–1975***

	Generating capacity (Mw)			*Production (millions of kilowatt-hours)*			*Total consumption (millions of kilowatt-hours)*
	Thermal	*Hydro*	*Total*	*Thermal*	*Hydro*	*Total*	
1950	347	1,536	1,883	—	—	—	—
1960	1,158	3,642	4,800	4,481	18,384	22,865	18,346
1970	2,405	8,828	11,233	5,597	39,863	45,460	37,673
1971	2,426	10,244	12,670	7,714	43,274	50,988	42,487
1972	2,528	10,721	13,249	5,518	50,777	56,295	47,374
1973	2,859	12,495	15,354	5,822	57,497	63,319	52,842
1974	3,241	14,285	17,526	5,874	65,595	71,469	58,741
1975*	3,453	16,469	19,922	6,300	72,100	78,400	65,069

SOURCE: Comité Nacional Brasileiro da Conferencia Mundial de Energia, *Estatística Brasileira de Energia*, no. 21, 1975, p. 26.
*Estimated.

The nation's development had a significant impact on the industrial sector; industrial product as a percentage of GDP increased from 22 percent in 1949 to almost 27 percent in 1973. The development effort can be seen in the increase in the investment ratio (Gross Capital Formation/GDP) from 14 percent in 1949 to about 23 percent in 1973. A significant element of total investment has been in electric energy facilities, and during the 1970s, for which figures are available, this investment was more than 8 percent of Gross Capital Formation. Electricity facilities had to expand to meet the growth in demand occasioned by the larger and wealthier population, urbanization, and industrialization processes.

Table 3 presents statistics on installed capacity (thermal and hydro), production, and consumption of electric energy. From 1950 to 1975 the installed capacity increased more than ten times. Hydroelectric capacity represented more than 80 percent of the total installed capacity in 1975. Hydroelectric production from 1960 to 1975 increased by approximately 300 percent, while thermoelectric production rose by less than 50 percent, which indicates that thermal capacity serves as the electric system's reserve.

Beginning in 1950, the country has had to cope with a tremendous inflation. From Table 2 the implicit deflator of GDP can be derived, showing that from 1950 to 1974 prices increased by more than 40,000 percent! The general price index from 1962 to 1975 is presented in Table 4, showing an increase in that period of more than 4,000 percent. This means that the cumulative rate of inflation was approximately 34 percent a year!

Table 4 also presents the average electric energy rate index. The base year 1965 is used because in 1964 monetary indexing of fixed assets was instituted, allowing rates to be corrected for inflationary effects. Only after 1964 did utilities have their rate of return applied to the value of their investment, including the correction through monetary indexing. More details on monetary indexing and its consequences will be presented in a later section.

Institutional Development

Until 1934 electricity in Brazil was provided through contracts between local municipalities and the provider of such services. The main characteristic of the contracts was the pricing mechanism. The maximum rates suppliers could charge the consumer were set, and there was no direct relation to the cost of service. This could lead to either a risk to the supplier in obtaining his profit or to very high priced service, to the detriment of the consumer and with a large profit for the supplier. The maximum price was also partially linked to the gold standard, so that it varied with the exchange rate for Brazilian currency. To a certain extent this was a monetary index.

Table 4. ***General Price Index and Average Electric Energy Rate Index in Brazil, 1962–1975***

	General price index	*Average electric energy rate index*
1962	19.1	13.3
1963	33.5	20.0
1964	63.8	37.1
1965	100.0	100.0
1966	137.9	141.7
1967	177.0	208.3
1968	219.9	250.0
1969	265.6	325.0
1970	318.1	391.7
1971	383.1	475.0
1972	448.1	620.8
1973	515.9	683.3
1974	663.9	858.3
1975	847.9	1,166.7

SOURCES: Fundação Getúlio Vargas, *Conjuntura Econômica* 30, no. 3 (1976): 114; Departamento Nacional de Aguas e Energia Elétrica do Ministério de Minas e Energia, *Boletim Estatístico* 1, no. 4 (1968) and 5, no. 17 (1972); and Portarias do Ministério de Minas e Energia, *Diario Oficial da União.*

In 1934 the federal government enacted the National Water Code, changing the institutional setting for the electric energy industry, although many utilities continued to use the contract system mentioned above. New concessions for supply of electric energy services were granted under the new code. Among other rules, the National Water Code established that rates should be based on the cost of the service provided, including all the operating expenditures, depreciation, and a fair rate of return on investment. The latter was valued at its historical cost in Brazilian currency minus the depreciation. As long as inflation rates were moderate, the price system provided enough resources for expansion. At the same time, the consumers could buy the service at a rate which reflected its cost. Consumers were classified into the categories of residential, industrial, commercial, rural and others, and the electric energy price was based on the average cost of the service provided. In addition, the

National Water Code established a federal agency, the Departamento Nacional de Aguas e Energia Eletrica, to regulate electricity services.

By the late 1940s and early 1950s, growing inflation was creating problems for the electric energy industry in financing its necessary expansion. With the rate of return based on the historical cost of the investment, the internal generation of resources was not enough to maintain a healthy leverage to attract other funds. This situation led to state intervention.

The first direct involvement of the federal government was the incorporation of Companhia Hidro Eletrica do São Francisco, with the government holding the majority of shares and operating under the same rules applied to private utilities. The agency's objective was to develop an excellent site in Paulo Afonso, on the São Francisco River, to supply electricity to the Northeast, one of the country's poorest regions. With federal budget appropriations and international borrowing, the company built a hydroelectric plant at Paulo Afonso and transmission lines to the main consumer centers in Recife and Salvador.

In a similar fashion, various states also organized utilities to provide electric energy locally. Investment resources were provided for in state budgets.

As inflation continued during the 1950s and early 1960s, the federal government created a tax on electric energy to provide investment resources. Revenue was shared with the states and municipalities, but this was not sufficient, and part of the revenue of the federal excise tax and the import tax was also earmarked for electric energy expansion. In 1962 a compulsory loan charged to electric energy consumers was enacted to provide additional resources to Centrais Eletricas Brasileiras, S.A. (ELETROBRAS), a federally owned holding company.

The tax mentioned above is called the *imposto unico,* which means "sole tax," since it is the only one levied on electric bills, on the basis of 50 percent of the value of the "fiscal rate" (*tarifa fiscal*).[1] The compulsory loan is levied upon the actual cost of energy sold, and it is collected from industrial consumers at a rate of approximately 30 percent. In return, consumers receive 20-year 6 percent annual yield indexed ELETROBRAS bonds. All the proceeds from

[1]The fiscal rate corresponds to the actual average cost of service of energy sold for the entire country.

these funds are used in the expansion of electric service in the country.

With the exception of São Paulo and Rio de Janeiro, by the 1950s the largest consumption centers in the country were served with electricity by subsidiaries of American Foreign Power (AMFORP) and Brazilian Electric Power Corporation (BEPCO). Because of political unrest and poor financial conditions, in the early 1960s these foreign investors began to negotiate the sale of their assets in Brazil with the federal government.

In 1964 the government made two important decisions: It introduced a monetary indexing to establish the value of utilities' fixed assets for setting electricity rates during the year, and ELETROBRAS purchased the assets of AMFORP and BEPCO.

Later, it will be shown how the indexing works and what its effects are on utilities' investment resources. The concessions and distribution facilities in the areas served by AMFORP and BEPCO subsidiaries were later transferred to state utilities.

With monetary indexing, the federal and state governments' transfer of budget funds to the industry virtually ceased.

In summary, the present organization of the sector is as follows: Federal utilities, owned by ELETROBRAS, provide the bulk of supply and transmission, and state utilities distribute the electricity. Some state utilities also have generation and transmission facilities for their territories. The only remaining important areas served by a private firm are the metropolitan regions of São Paulo and Rio de Janeiro, served by LIGHT — Servicos de Eletricidade S.A. — a subsidiary of the Canadian firm, BRASCAN.

Concerning rate setting, the automatic readjustment of electricity rates with the exchange rate was replaced initially with a pricing mechanism which had almost no readjustment provisions and which based investment on its historical cost. This was followed by monetary indexing of fixed assets, with annual readjustment of rates. A business which had involved risk and monopoly gains, under the concept of maximum electricity rates the suppliers could charge the consumer, thus developed into an enterprise with almost no risk and controlled gains under the principle of rates being based on the cost of service, including a fair rate of return on investment with monetary indexing.

Monetary Indexing and Internal Generation of Resources

The internal generation of resources for investment in the Brazilian electricity sector is particularly important in view of the lack of an adequate local capital market.

When the cost of service includes a fair rate of return on investment, under inflationary conditions it is necessary to allow changes in the historical value of the fixed assets to reflect the effect of inflation to avoid a reduction in the real rate of return. In Brazil, these changes are allowed for through monetary indexing of the fixed assets.

Let us recall that, since 1964, "monetary correction" or indexing has been a policy in Brazil in several important economic areas. Readjustable indexed treasury bonds were issued in 1964 and in a way established a pattern for other indexed values. Almost all loans of over 12 months are indexed, and the utilities, which generally borrow at long term either from ELETROBRAS, the National Development Bank for local funds, or from abroad, know their loans will be indexed according to local or exchange adjustments resulting from the "crawling peg" system for the exchange rate. They also depend every year on the indexing of their assets. This is done at the beginning of the year, and it reflects the inflation of the previous year. The Planning Secretary of the federal government publishes the indexes by which the fixed assets should be multiplied to maintain their real value.

It is interesting to examine briefly the process of monetary indexing of fixed assets. Suppose that the rates for 1976 are based on the investment as of 1 January 1976. The new investment during 1975 then has a multiplier of one. Investment during 1974 is multiplied by 1.24 (meaning that inflation during 1975 was approximately 24 percent). That during 1973 is multiplied by 1.65 (meaning that inflation during 1974 was approximately 33 percent, giving the cumulative effect of 65 percent with the inflation during 1975), and so on for the previous years.

To determine the investment subject to return, on which the rates are based, the depreciation quotas of every year are also multiplied by the proper indexes accumulated and deducted from the total investment. Federal funds employed by the utilities are also indexed.

Table 5 shows the coefficients as they have been published by the Planning Secretary.

The balance sheet of a hypothetical utility shown in Table 6 presents the results of monetary restatements with their accumulated as well as historical values. It should be noted that construction work in progress is also subject to monetary indexing. The balance sheet also includes the monetary restatement of the previous year, thus representing the balance sheet as of 1 January of a given year, and it will be used to calculate the cost of service of this hypothetical utility. The monetary restatement of fixed assets has its counterpart on the liability side of the balance sheet, in the long-term debt and its current portion and as reserves for future share increase.

The cost of service with and without monetary indexing is shown in Table 7.

Considering that the internal generation of resources is the sum of the return on investment and the depreciation quota, it is important to note the difference between the internal generation of resources in the calculations with and without monetary indexing. One notices that with indexing the utility generates resources (Cr\$988 $\times 10^6$) that are more than twice the amount generated without indexing (Cr\$432 $\times 10^6$). The resources with indexing are sufficient to pay the current portion of the long-term debt (Cr\$446 $\times 10^6$), accrued interest (Cr\$100 $\times 10^6$), and dividends (Cr\$288 $\times 10^6$) shown in the balance sheet, leaving the utility with more than Cr\$213 $\times 10^6$ as retained earnings to be used for investment. Without indexing, the utility's internally generated resources are not enough to pay the

Table 5. ***Multipliers for Monetary Restatement of Fixed Assets in Brazil, 1938–1975***

Year	*Multipliers*	*Year*	*Multipliers*
1938	1,894.57	1957	170.71
1939	1,792.13	1958	145.07
1940	1,689.51	1959	105.78
1941	1,536.06	1960	80.28
1942	1,245.93	1961	58.03
1943	1,075.32	1962	37.53
1944	938.73	1963	17.04
1945	802.16	1964	9.80
1946	699.77	1965	7.70
1947	648.52	1966	5.64
1948	614.44	1967	4.60
1949	563.13	1968	3.68
1950	494.90	1969	3.09
1951	409.58	1970	2.60
1952	375.48	1971	2.16
1953	324.36	1972	1.86
1954	255.99	1973	1.65
1955	221.84	1974	1.24
1956	187.75	1975	1.00

SOURCE: Brazil, Secretaria de Planejamento da Presidência da República.

Table 6. ***Hypothetical Utility, Balance Sheet as of 1 January 19—***

	Cr$1,000
ASSETS	
Utility Plants	
— Plant in service, at cost	3,740,309
— Other properties, at cost	4
— Monetary restatement	4,107,035
	7,847,348
Less	
Accumulated depreciation	865,281
Monetary restatement	320,266
	1,185,547
Construction work in progress, at cost	3,166,897
Monetary restatement	802,632
Total utility plant	10,631,330
Current Assets	
Cash and banks	445.727
Accounts receivable	25,657
Other current assets	24,039
Total current assets	495,423
Other Assets	
Material and supplies	46,694
Others	67,553
Total other assets	114,247
	11,241,000
CAPITALIZATION AND LIABILITIES	
Capitalization	
Stockholder investment	
Common shares (at par value Cr$ 1.00)	1,258,000
Preferred shares (at par value Cr$ 1.00)	1,258,000
Reserves for future share increase	246,769
Statutory reserves	101,074
Retained earnings	396,476
Total stockholders investment	3,260,319
Long-term debt	6,047,829
Federal government funds, at cost	328,451
Monetary restatement	297,215
Total capitalization	9,933,814
Current liabilities	
Current portion of long-term debt	446,253
Accrued interest	100,058
Accounts payable	312,871
Dividends	228,220
Total current liabilities	1,087,402
Other liabilities and deferred credits	219,784
	11,241,000

service of the debt, the current portion of long-term debt, and accrued interest. The utility is unable to pay any dividend and must refinance part of its debt. It would not generate resources for investment.

Table 7. ***Hypothetical Utility, Cost of Service***

	With monetary indexing (Cr $1,000)	*Without monetary indexing (Cr $1,000)*
A — INVESTMENT SUBJECT TO RETURN		
01–Plant in service	7,847,344	3,740,305
02–Working capital[a]	220,354	127,740
03–Materials and supplies	46,694	46,694
04–Subtotal	8,114,392	3,914,739
LESS		
05–Accumulated depreciation	1,185,547	865,281
06–Federal government funds	625,666	328,451
07–Subtotal	1,811,213	1,193,732
08–Investment subject to return (4–7)	6,303,179	2,721,007
B — COST OF SERVICE		
09–Return on investment[b]	756,382	326,521
10–Depreciation quota	231,384	105,566
11–Internal generation of resources (9+10)	987,766	432,087
12–Reversion quota[c]	238,152	113,511
13–Operating expenses	334,358	334,358
14–Cost of service (11+12+13)	1,560,276	879,956

[a] According to current regulation, the working capital is equivalent to two-twelfths the cost of service, not including the reversion quota.

[b] According to current regulation, the return on investment varies from 10 to 12 percent a year. In this case the return was 12 percent.

[c] The reversion quota is a charge included in the cost of service, representing approximately 3 percent of plant in service to provide resources to the federal government to expropriate or buy electric utilities. The resources not used for this objective are utilized, under the management of ELETROBRAS, for investment in the electric energy sector.

Certainly, the balance sheet previously shown would be different without monetary indexing. For example, long-term debt would be much smaller because the borrowing of the utility is subject to indexing. This means that lenders would be losing the monetary restatement on their loans, and under those circumstances they would only lend to the utilities if the rate of interest were high enough to overcome the rate of inflation, so that the accrued interest would be much higher than the amount stated in the balance sheet. The stockholder's investment would be smaller because part of it originates from the monetary restatement.

Two comments should be made regarding monetary indexing. First, it does not stop inflation; just the opposite, it fuels it. But to what degree depends on the range of indexing in the country's economy. Brazil does not use a global indexing system; many prices are set on the basis of demand and consumption, including food prices, wages for qualified personnel, and so forth. Second, monetary indexing is a simplified method for handling the system of accounting based on the replacement cost of fixed assets. Some goods will cost more and some less, but on the average the new value of the fixed assets will be approximately the same as the indexed value of historical cost.

Because monetary indexing in Brazil is done on 1 January each year, there is an average 18-month gap between the expenditure on fixed assets and the first monetary restatement. This gap reduces the rate of return in real terms when there is inflation. Figure 1 shows the rate of return in real terms as a function of a constant rate of inflation

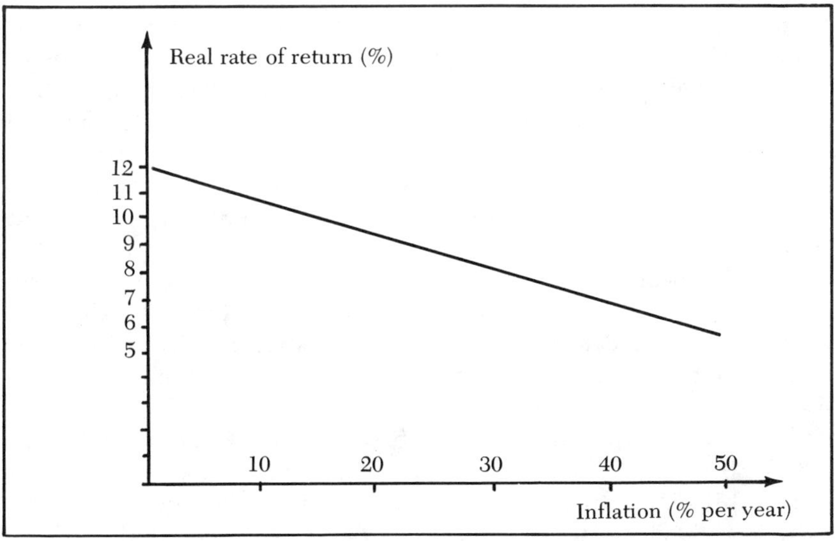

Figure 1. ***Brazilian Electric Energy Sector, Inflation and Rate of Return on Investment***

during a 33-year period in which the depreciation rate is 3 percent a year.

Actually, the rate of inflation is not constant. When it decreases over time, because the monetary restatement is delayed, it allows the utility to generate resources at a higher growth rate than the growth rate of investment cost. The opposite is also true.

To conclude, it is important to point out that, when there is inflation, monetary indexing is necessary. It allows public utilities with regulated rates based on the value of fixed assets to generate resources to meet obligations from past investment and to expand.

Regarding taxation, the situation can be summarized briefly. The monetary restatement of the utility plant value is not subject to income tax. Given the corresponding increase in the value of capital and long-term debt, the new revenues from power sales (if the rates are duly adjusted) will yield much more realistic profit values. Thus, the taxation of profits is also more realistic.

Conclusions

The regional characteristics of Brazil in 1975 are presented in Figure 2. Note the large hydroelectric potential available — 150,000 Mw — of which a little more than 10 percent is being exploited presently. It is also interesting that almost half of this potential is in the north, in the Amazon Basin, while consumption is mostly concentrated in the southeast. To exploit the Amazon potential means an industrial decentralization process toward the north or the transmission of large blocks of electric energy at distances greater than 2,000 kilometers.

It should also be pointed out that the fossil fuels available to Brazil are mostly imported, and the country has a commercial deficit in its foreign trade accounts.

For the period 1976–1979 the growth rate of electric energy consumption is expected to be 13 percent a year; for 1980–1985 the forecast is 11 percent a year. To meet this demand, the installed capacity to be commissioned in 1976–1979 is approximately 11,300 Mw.

Investment expenditure for 1976–1979 is expected to be around Cr$100 billion at June 1975 prices, representing approximately US$12 billion. This expenditure also includes funds for an additional 30,000 Mw, which should be commissioned after 1980. More than half of the investment is earmarked for generating

NORTHERN REGION
Production - 1,265 GWh
Consumption - 998 GWh
Population - 4,215 × 10^3 inh.
Area - 3,581,180 km^2
Per Capita Consumption - 237 kwh/person
Hydro Potential - 72,000 MW

NORTHEASTERN REGION
Production - 9,222 GWh
Consumption - 7,600 GWh
Population - 32,032 × 10^3 inh.
Area - 1,548,672 km^2
Per Capita Consumption- 237 kwh/person
Hydro Potential - 13,700 MW

WEST-CENTRAL REGION
Production - 1,687 GWh
Consumption - 1,527 GWh
Population - 6,328 × 10^3 inh.
Area - 1,879,455 km^2
Per Capita Consumption - 241 kwh/person
Hydro Potential - 3,000 MW

SOUTHERN REGION
Production - 7,557 GWh
Consumption - 7,867 GWh
Population - 19,258 × 10^3 inh.
Area - 577,723 km^2
Per Capita Consumption - 409 kwh/person
Hydro Potential - 25,000 MW

SOUTHEASTERN REGION
Production - 60,562 GWh
Consumption - 50,257 GWh
Population - 45,313 × 10^3 inh.
Area - 924,935 km^2
Per Capita Consumption - 1,109 kwh/person
Hydro Potential - 36,300 MW

TOTAL FOR BRAZIL
Installed Capacity - 19,578 MW
Production - 80,293 GWh
Consumption - 68,249 GWh
Population - 107,146 × 10^3 inh.
Area - 8,511,965 km^2
Per Capita Consumption - 637 kwh/person
Hydro Potential - 150,000 MW

SOURCE: ELETROBRAS, "Electric Power Sector" (Rio de Janeiro: 1976) Figure 1. Hydro Potential data from ELETROBRAS, unpublished.

Figure 2. ***Regional Characteristics in Brazil in 1975***

facilities. It is interesting to note that of the additional 41,300 Mw capacity, approximately 35,000 Mw will be hydro.

For this program 80 percent of the resources are already assured, provided the current regulations are maintained.

Because of the hydroelectric basis prevailing in Brazil, with a tendency to increasing investment cost, it will be less difficult to move into a nuclear power based system. On the other hand, countries with generating systems based on fossil fuel plants having relatively lower investment cost should have, at least while nuclear power is not a large share of their installed capacity, financial difficulties because their operating and investment expenditures will be relatively large. If one adds inflationary conditions, then this transition period will be really troublesome for their financial managers.

Four main conclusions from the Brazilian experience under inflationary conditions should be emphasized. First, under long-term inflationary conditions, with rates based on historical cost, a utility can maintain its services only with the help of government resources; in this case, conditions tend to favor state intervention. Second, under long-term inflationary conditions, monetary indexing of the fixed assets of a utility allows it to keep up with the supply of its services; in this case, monetary indexing extends the inflationary period, since it keeps fueling the inflationary process. Third, the monetary indexing of fixed assets is a simplified alternative to replacement cost accounting. Fourth, it is less difficult to go from a hydroelectric system with a large investment cost to a nuclear power system than from a conventional thermoelectric system to a nuclear power system. The transition period of the latter is overburdened by the large current expenditures inherited from the past and the large investment cost for future facilities.

One may add that with indexing the rates in Brazil have not been very high, and the electric utility sector has been able to cope with an exceptionally large expansion of the market.

Comment

James R. Nelson

The essays by Mario Bhering and José Langier and by B.H.F. Johnson are especially fascinating because they are the products of national backgrounds which appear to involve the alteration, or transgression, of economic laws which once seemed as immutable as physical laws.

The Bhering and Langier essay might be subtitled "The Economics of the Frictionless Surface," and Johnson's might be described as "The Economic Effects of Suspending the Law of Gravity."

Specifically, Brazil, the economic background of Bhering's and Langier's contribution, has produced the following economic rule: If prices must move upward, then try to assure that at least they all move together, and all move at more or less the same rate. Conversely, the paradox of the British economy, Johnson's milieu, is that — like the economy of the United States — it is much less developed with respect to general rules for dealing with the effects of inflation *on* and *in* particular economic sectors, precisely because it is so much more developed in a number of other respects. For example, Bhering and Langier point out that Brazil has never really possessed a capital market. In Great Britain, on the other hand, the world's most sophisticated international capital market has come rather suddenly up against a domestic rate of inflation in excess of interest rates which not only are very high, historically, but also higher than those now being charged anywhere else in the Western world. With a British rate of inflation of 15 percent to as much as 30 percent per annum, it would be a brave soul who would recommend that "real rates of interest" (money rates of interest minus rates of inflation) be positive. This would require money rates of 20 to 35 percent.

The Brazilian experience, and policy, have been the subject of much debate by monetary economists, but Brazil has probably not received the attention it deserves from the standpoint of *sectoral* economic analysis. Public utilities are notoriously capital-intensive industries. Many of them also have shown real rates of growth considerably in excess of the national average for the country in which they are domiciled. If prices of public utility services are held to lower percentage increases than prices of goods in general, additional inflationary pressures are added on both sides of the market: on the demand side, in response to relatively low prices for the output of capital-intensive industries, and on the supply side, in response to a lower rate of internal generation of investment funds. Since Brazilian electric power supply, in the present and in prospect, is about 80 percent hydroelectric, the dominance of front-end or capital costs is even more important than would be the case in countries which rely mainly on fossil-fuel generation of electricity.

Therefore, the terms of finance of Brazilian industry are of particular interest. It is the burden of Bhering's and Langier's message that the means is largely if not entirely self-finance. For an industry which is expanding, and expected to expand, at such a rapid rate, the *a priori* possibility of self-finance would appear to be quite remote, especially so if interest payments on debt are indexed to reflect changes in the general price level, along with other elements in the electrical revenue accounts. Thus it is not entirely easy to follow the Bhering-Langier discussion of self-finance as it operates in the electrical industry in Brazil. But three things can be said about Brazilian electrical finance as it relates to the characteristics of the supply industry as well as general inflation.

First, Brazil may still be in the fortunate position of being able to expand hydroelectric capacity at decreasing cost per unit of output. In a sparsely settled country with a massive hydro potential per inhabitant, some of the sites which are developed first may be developed because they are small and close to established markets, not necessarily because they are low cost when fully exploited.

Second, in a country with persistent demand-pull inflation, *more* self-financing of public utility development is always to be preferred to *less* self-financing.

Third, this is of particular significance if power suppliers are government owned, if all of their so-called external finance must be obtained either from commercial banks or directly from government budgets, and if there is no independent capital market and no prospect of one. Here the sectoral emphasis of microeconomics blends with the general emphasis of macroeconomics. What to do about public utility finance in the presence of inflation merges into the question of what to do about inflation in the presence of public utility finance.

The Brazilian experience also may serve to underscore one obvious attribute of the relationship between utility rates and general price inflation. Whether they are viewed from the standpoint of their relationship to economywide allocation of resources, or whether they are viewed as contributors to and claimants on the stream of national saving, public utilities may both suffer less themselves and operate as better economic citizens if the rate of inflation is high than if it is still officially designated as "moderate." If the rate of inflation is high enough, pressures are generated to equalize its effects throughout the economy. And if a high rate of inflation continues over a long period, as it has in Brazil, electrical rates may not only be fitted into the general inflationary pattern but also may even make up some lost ground. The public utility problem with inflation is likely to be worse when the rate of inflation is *accelerating,* or worse still if it is not only accelerating but also unadmitted as a permanent feature of the economy.

Which brings us to the recent and present British predicament. The Johnson essay is so thoroughgoing, and so sophisticated, that one is made to realize an intellectual value of inflation — it forces the rethinking and restatement of fundamentals as the familiar benchmarks are left behind in the upsurge. Thus, one is compelled to look once again at the economic function of monetary rates of interest, especially of money market rates. As Johnson points out in the latter context, "interest rates are geared to transient market conditions." All of this becomes connected with the meaning to be attached to long-run marginal costs, with special reference to the cost of long-run capital. This inquiry, in turn, cannot be dissociated from the concept of a (positive) real rate of return on capital, the existence of which cannot even be assessed, under inflationary conditions, without reexamining depreciation charges, which are based on the historical costs of capital assets.

One does not have to go very far in this review of fundamentals to arrive at a conceptual split in economists' analyses of capital markets.

On the one hand, the basic theory of money and banking was developed, in English-speaking countries, with relation to *current* assets and liabilities which never impinged on real capital formation beyond the relationship of short-term loans to changes in inventories. Long-term interest rates were supposed to be somewhat higher than short-term rates if the whole interest rate structure was expected to remain stable through time, but lower if all interest rates were regarded as unusually low. But what if all interest rates, no matter how regarded, are in fact *negative*, in the sense that average prices of all goods and services are going up faster than the price of money or the price of savings? Either the rate of inflation must slow down, or long-term rates must increase not only absolutely, but also relative to short-term rates. Hence the dilemma presented by Johnson. The borrowing rate for the Electricity Council now exceeds 16 percent. Yet, unless the rate of inflation in Great Britain is brought down rather considerably from its recent levels, even this "panic" rate of 16 percent is lower than what would be charged in anything like a free long-term capital market.

The idea of borrowing rates for utilities which start at levels of the order of 16 percent, and rise from there, is surely repugnant to anyone who is connected in any way with U.S. public utilities. Yet certain palliatives suggest themselves, *whatever the rate of inflation.*

The first has been adopted officially in Brazil and is clearly evident as an influence in Great Britain. This palliative has already been referred to as the "frictionless surface," or, less elegantly, "if you can't lick 'em, join 'em." The simple answer to external price movements which are, in effect, largely indexed in terms of each other is a price structure for utility services which is indexed with respect to all other prices. In periods of rapid inflation, this may be the only feasible course. The more rapid the rate of inflation, the more pronounced the consequences of a given interval of regulatory lag. But, as the Brazilian experience indicates, even this method of achieving price fluidity may not be entirely adequate (since any indexed adjustment must be based on what *has* happened) if the rate of inflation is already high and accelerating.

This first palliative would seem to be somewhat easier to introduce under conditions of public as opposed to private ownership. Unless inflation has become serious and deeply entrenched, its effects are probably in the direction of stimulating demands for relative price *cuts* by investor owned utility enterprises ("lifeline rates," and so forth). This idea of "social rates" is surely not absent from the management of publicly owned utilities, but there is less about the phenomenon of inflation, as such, which would serve to *increase* the effectiveness of consumer pressure during inflationary periods.

The second palliative has to do with indexing utility *costs*, or at least some of them. The impact of inflation on the utility industry is thus approached from the supply rather than the demand side. The most obvious type of cost indexing is that employed in the operation of fuel clauses. The least obvious, in the United States and practically everywhere else, is that which pertains to capital.

Here the advantage with respect to practical application may lie with private enterprise. For a public utility, no price increase is easy; even fuel clauses, which so often were introduced in the past with little or no public outcry, have become the focus of vigorous attacks by consumer movements. Moreover, the type of ownership of a public utility is not likely to muffle the protest if *all* costs are indexed. Indeed, if inflation becomes so pervasive a problem that this kind of general solution seems to be required, then the answer would seem to lie on the price side (with possible *downward* rate revisions permitted to regulatory bodies), and not on the cost side.

But there is one cost area in which private ownership has a tactical and perhaps even an economic advantage. That is the area of indexed securities. Government owned public utilities could, in principle, appeal freely to external capital markets without relying on internal government finance. In fact, the Tennessee Valley Authority has for years raised funds on the nation's capital markets. But such a right of appeal to these markets is not to be expected in principle and is probably not common, taking one country with another, in practice. Moreover, for a government owned enterprise to resort to open capital markets via the offering of indexed securities would appear likely to infringe on whatever the government's inflation control policy may happen to be at the moment (and whatever it may be, it is not likely to stress *recognition* of inflation).

Finally, this governmental hesitancy to recognize inflation cuts below purely tactical considerations of immediate political prestige and of lip-service to some current anti-inflationary "program." It can be traced down to the bedrock of any government's necessary insistence on its own sovereignty. A sovereign nation can both emit and control a national medium of exchange. Therefore, in practice, it can progressively debase this medium, but in principle it cannot admit its incompetence in an area within which its legal powers are more or less complete. Consequently, there is the greatest hesitancy in issuing securities which proclaim: "Although we are committed to maintaining the purchasing power of your money and of your savings, we are offering here, as a hedge against our failing to honor our own commitments. . . ." In short, the concept of sovereignty includes not only the subcategory of monetary policy but also that of monetary hypocrisy. Privately owned enterprises are exempt from the burdens imposed by either subcategory, and therefore they are free to issue indexed securities if they so desire. And be it noted: To the extent that *real* rates of interest may be low in periods of high money rates of interest, purchasers of indexed securities would be permitting utilities to raise new capital at a much lower immediate cost than would obtain if this capital were acquired via conventional debt or equity securities.

Comment

Joel B. Dirlam

The two economies whose electric utility policies are examined by Mario Behring and José Langier and B.H.F. Johnson are strikingly dissimilar in their stages of development, in their goals, and in the character of their inflations. These differences must be kept in mind in tracing the impact of inflation on policy. What is more, given the importance of the electric utility industry both as a source of energy and a component of capital expenditure, its behavior will not only be shaped by but also significantly affect the pace of inflation. Quite properly, neither Bhering and Langier nor Johnson deviates from his assignment to embrace monetarist, Keynesian, or structuralist doctrines. Nevertheless, a final evaluation of their essays and the policies they support requires choosing reasonable hypotheses about the unique qualities of the Brazilian and the British inflations.

Before arriving at this point, however, one is obliged from the wealth of issues surfacing in the two essays to sort out those which can be profitably reviewed within a brief compass. They seem to me to cluster about four polar questions and certain ancillary problems.

First, in an inflationary period, just what purpose is served by restating the accounts of a nationalized electric utility? Is it to provide managers with more reliable information, to make accounting and financial statements conform to economic trends, or to promote some kind of economic optimum use of resources? If restatement is desirable, how frequently should it take place?

Second, if restated costs are to be linked with changes in tariff structures, should the fact that the utility is nationalized affect adjustment principles and procedures?

Third, if at prevailing electricity prices there seems to be a need for new capacity, how should the expansion be financed? Again, should public ownership make a difference not only in the choice of financing methods, but also in the selection of a target rate of return?

Fourth, if major economic policy objectives are not the same in Brazil and Great Britain, how has this affected their utilities' responses to inflation? Conversely, to what extent have the rate and financing policies of utilities influenced the course of inflation in their respective countries?

The list is far from exhaustive, but it may serve as a basis for a comparison of the two contributions. I have endeavored to minimize the more general implications of a shift from historical cost accounting, a topic intensively explored elsewhere in this volume.

Purposes of Restatement

According to Johnson, restatement of assets is required in a period of sharply rising prices. Without restatement, net income will be exaggerated, and electric utility regulatory policy will be based on inadequate, if not misleading, data. Losses will be understated, profits overstated. One might add that even if a price freeze is imposed, the restatement could be useful. Investment in a nationalized industry might be determined by standards different from those used to set prices.

What are Johnson's standards for stating accounts? At a conference in 1975 he advanced a "fundamental" argument: If assets are valued correctly, there is no difference between "the cost today of continuing to use an existing asset, and the cost of using a new asset."[1] The value of assets as stated on a balance sheet should be their going-concern values, and depreciation constitutes the changes from year to year in these values. Actually, Johnson and the Sandiland Committee appear to advocate transforming fixed asset accounts into something akin to common stock, which, in conventional finance theory, is valued according to the market's estimate of the present value of net future cash flows.[2] It is still not clear

[1]B.H.F. Johnson and R.W. Orons, "The Relationship between Long-Run Marginal Cost and Accounting Practices, Especially during Periods of Inflation," UNIPEDE Tariffs Symposium, Madrid, Spain, 21–23 April 1975 (mimeographed), p. 11.

[2]"Balance sheet . . . accounts . . . value[s] should be shown [as] . . . the present value of the future cash flows that can be expected as a result of using the assets owned by the industry." B. H. F. Johnson, "Impact of Inflation," this volume, p. 107.

how this restatement will aid in guiding investment decisions, or in fact any other decisions. By making his accounting policy hinge on what he regards as the ideal method of estimating depreciation, Johnson not only suffers from a form of accounting myopia, but also ties his rate structure to interrelated forecasts that are bound to be highly debatable, if not impossible to quantify.

I use the term "accounting myopia" because he nowhere tells us *why* it is so important to recalculate depreciation, other than by a reference to what he regards as a proper statement of net income and net worth.[3] But when the going-concern value estimates upon which his restated depreciation is based are themselves dependent upon estimates not simply of the time-honored "useful life" of the asset in place, but of their future profitability, then his depreciation depends upon "earning power." And earning power in turn is a function of the price of the product, a relationship which, in a regulated industry, necessarily embodies some circularity of determination.

In Brazil, one gathers, the purpose of restatement is not so much to arrive at more meaningful net income and net worth accounts as to bring the debt and equity accounts into closer conformity with the changing value of the assets. Indexation provides an inducement for investors to absorb debt securities. In Bhering's and Langier's presentation (which expressly excludes pricing from consideration) restatement of the assets appears to have as its primary role generating resources for reinvestment. Their Table 7 shows how return on investment and depreciation can be more than doubled as a result of indexation. With the confidence that their loan will be repaid in amounts with approximately the same purchasing power, lenders should be satisfied with lower interest rates. Without restatement, obligations from past investments could not be met at the same time the enterprise expanded.[4]

I have perhaps exaggerated differences between the two approaches. Nevertheless, despite Johnson's concern about the adequacy of depreciation for financing investment,[5] his major emphasis is on achieving an identity between properly computed cost and price.

Indexation, restatement of accounts, or "monetary adjustments" may all be regarded as variations on one technique for justifying

[3]Ibid., pp. 103–104.

[4]Mario Bhering and José Langier, "Inflation and Public Utilities in Brazil," this volume, p. 136.

[5]Johnson, "Impact of Inflation," p. 101.

increases in electric rates. By providing a logical support for higher depreciation charges, or more substantial allowances for a return on invested capital, expressed in current monetary units, these accounting gimmicks can expand the flow of cash to the utility. The increased liquidity that results may be used for any purpose the enterprise finds desirable, including expansion.

Whether restatement will be likely to generate a rate level that does not make a special contribution to inflation cannot be determined simply by examination of the material in the two essays. In Brazil, we can see that the average electric energy rate index has risen more rapidly than the general price index, but part of the relative increase may be accounted for by the electric energy tax. In England, the price of electricity lagged the retail price index increase until 1975, when there was a spectacular jump, which Johnson views as insufficient because the electric industry would still fail to show a profit were accounts restated on a replacement cost basis. To be sure, the industry was compensated for its 1973 – 1974 loss, and no power station has been left in a partly finished state.[6]

Costs and Rate Structures

On the relationship between rates (tariffs) and restated costs, Bhering and Langier are silent, but Johnson is eloquent. To the latter, rates that do not coincide with long-run marginal costs must inevitably result in a misallocation of resources either as between customer classes or between all electric consumers and users of other resources. If there is a hierarchy of efficiency among plants in use, their capital charges on a new peak load plant, plus manning and maintenance, should equal the costs of retaining old plant, or of installing new base load plant minus its fuel savings. Central to the advocacy of long-run marginal cost as a basis for pricing is the belief that it will assure that customers pay their own way and that new investment will be made only when economically justified.

As a capstone of his discussion, Johnson provides an elegant demonstration of the theoretical equivalence between long-run marginal cost pricing and electric utility accounts that reflect inflationary changes. If one accepts his premises, there can be no quarrel with his conclusion that a switch from historical cost accounting to "inflation accounts" will have no effect on electricity prices if

[6]Ibid., pp. 101–102.

prices have been based on long-run marginal cost.[7] But this is because the most efficient plant necessary to satisfy new demand constitutes the basis for the long-run marginal cost computation. Yet we know that when investment costs are rising rapidly, long-run marginal cost pricing can lead to net income in excess of financial requirements. Johnson does not touch on this problem, perhaps because the British experience has been marked by insufficient, not excessive, profits. But he does indicate that with only a moderate increase in tariffs, British rates would approximate the "optimum."[8] One finds this difficult to reconcile with the meager profit, on historic cost accounting, shown in his Table 3.

There are, of course, other difficulties in relying on long-run marginal cost pricing. If utility rates are to serve as a basis for planning by industrial customers, they should maintain a minimum standard of stability. In a period of rapid inflation, however, when construction costs are shooting up rapidly, the tariffs (and the assets and depreciation estimates) must be changed frequently.

Without entering further into the merits of "replacement of the service cost" one may well ask why a nationalized industry in a country guided by socialist principles should embrace long-run marginal cost pricing. Indeed, it is curious that both French and British nationalized electric systems should have adopted a pricing principle designed to emulate the outcome of a competitive marketplace. True, the market under certain conditions may distribute resources and income according to principles said to be optimum. And Johnson rejects "socially desirable" alternatives to his firmly cost-based pricing in much the same manner and for the same reasons as do his counterparts in the free enterprise United States.[9]

But it is possible to defend standards other than long-run marginal cost as a basis for pricing. Neither the orthodox nor unorthodox Marxists have displayed much interest in the pricing theories of Aba P. Lerner and Oskar Lange. "By mandating nationalization of a sector, voters imply that it should provide goods or services different from — normally more, cheaper and less luxurious than — those dictated by 'real' demand, which results from an arbitrary and perhaps unjust structure of income and power. Voters thus imply that they are prepared to pay the price, in terms of sacrificed profits or

[7]Ibid., p. 116.
[8]Ibid., pp. 109–10.
[9]Ibid., p. 118.

even tax-financed losses in the nationalized industries."[10] Along similar lines, it is possible to argue that a broad anti-inflation policy might dictate preventing an immediate and equal response of electric rates to inflationary investment cost changes. In some circumstances, higher electric rates could intensify pressure for higher wages and prices in other sectors.[11] Perhaps the uneasy agreement on a "social contract" will be still more fragile if electric rates advance still further.

In Brazil, the choice for future power supply has been between hydro and nuclear, with major emphasis on the former. Fortunately for that country, it still has vast reserves of hydroelectric power sites unused but capable of economic exploitation should the center of population shift to the west, or the costs of transmission decline. The Itaibu station on the Paraná River, now under construction, will be the largest in the world. But for Great Britain the selection of the future source of energy is not simple. That country is faced with choosing to rely largely on nuclear power in the future — the plan of the Ministry of Energy — or, in the short run, remaining dependent upon relatively high priced oil fuel for thermal stations. In 1975 Johnson used fossil fuel plants in making his long-run marginal cost calculations. In October 1976 he was inclined to shift to nuclear plants because of the high cost of oil and the probability its cost would rise even further.[12] Yet the wisdom of engaging in further construction of nuclear power plants has been questioned by the Flowers Commission,[13] and its conclusions cannot be lightly shrugged off. They may entail a conservation program that would sharply diminish the rate of growth of consumption of electric energy.

Johnson concedes that it is possible to err in forecasting long-run marginal costs, but he is content to let the mistakes be corrected by asset revisions.[14]

---

[10] Michael Lipton, "What Is Nationalization For?" *Lloyds Bank Review*, no. 121 (July 1976): 35. Different views, substantially the same as Johnson's, may be found in Richard Pryke, *Public Enterprise in Practice* (London: MacGibbon & Kee, 1971); and Ralph Turvey, *Economic Analysis and Public Enterprise* (London: Allen & Unwin, 1972).

[11] Lipton, "Nationalization," p. 37. The financial integrity of Electricité de France has been sacrificed on the altar of stability of the consumers price index. *La Nouvelle Economiste*, 13 October 1975, p. 173.

[12] Johnson, "Impact of Inflation," pp. 108–109.

[13] Royal Commission on Environmental Pollution, *Sixth Report, Nuclear Power and the Environment*, Command 6618 (London: HMSO, 1976), Par. 474–84.

[14] Johnson, "Impact of Inflation," pp. 108–109.

If the demand for electricity levels off, or declines, long-run marginal costs, as defined by Johnson and measured by the cost of expanding investment to satisfy peak demand, will be zero regardless of the rate of inflation. Fixed assets will not be worth replacing, and the rates should reflect only the short-run costs of manning, maintenance, and fuel — at least as far as generating plant is concerned. Both Johnson and Bhering and Langier, however, assume that the demand for electricity will continue to expand.

Clearly, the Brazilian electric rates have been in excess of conventionally defined marginal cost because they have included not only the return on the capital invested, but also most of the investment itself. One can see an analogy here with the use of surcharges, or at least their proposed use, to enable gas utilities in the United States to obtain a share in production. Should the Brazilian rates be condemned as excessive? One hesitates to think so, because the cost of not expanding the system might be to check the rate of growth of the economy, inequitably distributed as its income is, and under the current power and class structure of Brazil there may be no alternative source of funds.

In these circumstances, Bhering's and Langier's conclusion that indexation tends to fuel inflation may be too pessimistic, at least as far as ELETROBRAS is concerned.[15] That Brazilian inflation reached high levels (over 30 percent) in 1974 and continued through 1976 surely cannot be attributed to indexing. By raising electricity prices, the monetary adjustment contributed to increases in the general price index. Nevertheless, it also provided an environment in which the Brazilian financial markets, including compulsory loans, could continue to function with interest rates at moderate levels. Perhaps endemic inflation that leads either to indexation, with constantly shifting rates, or price freezes and deficits makes long-run marginal cost pricing impossible to apply in any fashion that would permit it to realize its theoretical advantages.

Financing Expansion

This brings us to the third question, the most appropriate technique for financing expansion.

[15]See their essay in this volume, pp. 137 and 140. Indexing tends to encourage saving and prevent speculative holding of inventories and fixed assets. According to ECLA, when the rate of inflation has been reduced to 10 to 15 percent, the adjustability mechanism (that is, indexation) may become a serious hindrance to the combating of inflation. Economic Commission for Latin America, *Economic Survey of Latin America 1974* (New York: United Nations, 1976), pp. 68 and 80.

A large proportion of the generating and transmission plant controlled by ELETROBRAS has been internally financed, much of the incidence being borne directly or indirectly by its customers. Consumers large and small have advanced funds to ELETROBRAS or its affiliates. Electric bills include a tax on electric energy consumption as well as a 3 percent levy on net facilities. In estimating sources for expansion through 1979, ELETROBRAS appears to assume only about 28 percent will have to be obtained from sources outside the electric system.[16] While much of the funding may be strictly classified as federal or state budget investment, or as bank loans, examination of the sources and uses of funds for the electric utility system shows that of Cr$100.5 billion, only Cr$8.7 billion represents additional investment by the federal and state governments. The balance will be derived from compulsory loans, the energy tax, the assessment for purchase of private properties, and from servicing of investments in the electric system already made by federal and state governments and by banks. An examination of its balance sheet discloses that, to date, electric consumers have financed a large share of ELETROBRAS assets up through 1975.[17]

In Great Britain, depreciation has been inadequate, profits low or absent in recent years, and funds to finance expansion have been borrowed from the National Loan Fund. This intermediary in turn must depend upon the institutions that finance the British government's deficit. British deficits are now running about 10 percent of GNP, compared with a surplus in Brazil, although, taking into account various instruments for forced saving, this Brazilian surplus can perhaps be regarded as illusory.[18]

The electric industry pays an extremely high rate of interest to the National Loan Fund. The interest rate is high because the British government has been unable to keep inflation in check and actually employs high rates as an anti-inflationary technique.[19] If British

[16]See ELETROBRAS, *Annual Report, 1975,* Figure 3.

[17]It is not clear exactly how much. Bhering and Langier point out that part of the federal excise tax and the import tax were used in the 1960s for expansion of electric energy, as well as a compulsory loan in 1962. To what extent the government's current equity represents tax revenues from other sources I cannot say. Nevertheless, of the total Cr$ 1975 capitalization of approximately Cr$ 51 billion, only 9 billion reflected loans by foreign and local banks, the IBRD, EX-IM Bank, and suppliers. ELETROBRAS, *Annual Report*, p. 47.

[18]For British deficits, see *Lloyds Bank Review* (July 1976), charts. In 1970–1971 the deficit was only 2 percent of GNP. The Brazilian deficit was 1.7 percent of GNP in 1967 and had disappeared in 1973. In 1974 there was a surplus. ECLA, *Economic Survey of Latin America*, pp. 68 and 80.

[19]Or to overcome an exchange rate crisis.

inflation is to continue, one wonders whether it would not be advisable to shift to indexing in order to improve the tone of the financial markets. And one may well ask why it should be thought desirable to resort exclusively to borrowing for expansion. Why not stratify the capital structure? The nationalization statutes need revision. To the extent that the government supplies financing to the electric system, it should, as in Brazil, be offset by ownership rather than by debt.

In an economy where a large share of savings flows to nationalized firms,[20] is it necessary or desirable to use the market tests for directing investment?

It is Johnson's belief that allowance for adjusted depreciation and a "reasonable real return on capital" (about 5 percent on revalued net assets in the private sector) would enable the electric system to finance its expansion without resort to the National Loan Fund.[21] Surely, 5 percent is far from excessive. But just as in the case of long-run marginal cost pricing, one may inquire why investment in a nationalized industry should have to satisfy criteria devised for achieving an optimum distribution of privately owned resources. In a stagnating economy, where the state controls a large sector of industry and where costs are gravely distorted in many ways, how much credence can one give to an estimate, however carefully made, of the "return on capital"? If the social contract is not breached, if inflation is moderated, and if the vast losses in many of the nationalized industries disappear, perhaps a "real" return on capital could be estimated. But in the meantime, how much sense does it make to suppose that a rate of return can be found that reflects an "optimum" distribution of savings?

National Objectives and Electric System Policies

Although both electric systems are expanding, the Brazilian does so in a context of a rapidly growing economy. Even the current

---

[20]According to a recent estimate, 11 of the 20 largest firms in Brazil are state owned, and public investment accounts for between 11 and 12 percent of GNP. ECLA, *Economic Survey of Latin America*, p. 60. Another estimate gives 16 of the largest 20 as state owned. "Brazil," *Economist*, 31 July 1976, p. 21.

In Great Britain, the fixed investment in the national industries exceeds that of all the manufacturing sector by a substantial amount. John Redwood, "Government and the Nationalized Industries," *Lloyds Bank Review* (April 1976): 31. Total factor incomes arising in public corporations amounted to 10 percent of national income in 1972. William G. Shepherd, *Public Enterprise: Economic Analysis of Theory and Practice* (Lexington: Lexington Books, 1976), p. 108.

[21]Johnson, "Impact of Inflation," pp. 107–108.

recession has only slightly dampened the rate of growth.[22] Balance-of-payment difficulties have resurrected a policy of import substitution, and the government is trying to improve the lot of the most poorly paid workers — Brazil has perhaps the most inequitable of income distributions of countries with reliable statistics.[23] Nevertheless, in forging ahead with its program for expansion of the rail network, development of the Amazon region to the west, and additional investment in heavy industry, the Brazilian authorities need pay little heed to workers' pressures for higher wages.[24] True, in the past two years, the government has raised the minimum wage faster than the price index.[25] But this is a far cry from yielding to strikes in such a fashion as to channel funds not into investment, but into subsidizing constantly rising wages. The pattern of bargaining in England that prevailed until the recent shaky acceptance of the "social contract" approached "industrial anarchy."[26] P. Sargant Florence points out that if one's aim were to achieve rapid growth, nationalization in Britain has had conflicting and economically dangerous objectives: to control prices so as to prevent monopolistic exploitation, and (at least to the trade union members) to assure at least the same wage increases as workers in the private sector.[27] From their inception, nationalized industries were inhibited from raising prices, but were peculiarly susceptible to wage increases.

The English Electricity Council, then, is responsible for managing a moderately expanding sector in a stagnating economy that ranks income redistribution ahead of growth. At least it would be fair to say that inability to control wages, and hence ultimately prices, has created a different kind of inflation in Great Britain than in

[22]The GNP rose at an average of 10 percent in 1970–1974 and almost reached 5 percent in 1975. See Table 2 in the Bhering and Langier essay; and "Brazil," *Economist*, p. 11. In 1976, there is little likelihood of growth, but the state's commitment to large investment expenditures has not been weakened, and steel, railroads, oil, and, more important, electric power will continue to absorb large amounts of investment.

[23]The highest decile in 1970 was estimated to enjoy 47.79 percent of total personal income, and the highest 40 percent, 79.19 percent. Stefan H. Robock, *Brazil: A Study in Development Progress* (Lexington: Lexington Books, 1974), p. 142.

[24]According to one observer, the government fears that "premature or excessive income redistribution" would only mean sharing the poverty. Growth would be slowed because saving and investment would decline. Robock, *Brazil*, p. 144.

[25]"Brazil," *Economist*, p. 25.

[26]P. Sargant Florence, "Inflation in Britain," in Gardiner Means et al., *The Roots of Inflation* (New York: Burt Franklin, 1975), p. 101.

[27]Ibid., p. 97. See also R.J. Ball and T. Burns, "The Inflationary Mechanism in the U.K. Economy," *American Economic Review* 66 (September 1976):483.

Brazil.[28] In Great Britain, industrial production has dropped, unemployment rates have risen, and prices have continued to climb by annual percentages usually regarded as extremely inflationary. While Brazil takes measures designed to expand rapidly its production capacity in basic industries and diminish its dependence on high priced imports, even though the measures adopted perpetuate the inequitable distribution of income, the British Labour Party pursues a policy of further nationalization.

Given the divergent priorities of the two countries according to growth and equitable income distribution, the consequences of inflation in the two are bound to be different. For the electric utility industry in Brazil, at least that part of it represented by ELETROBRAS, the choices are easier than for the Electricity Council. And its future is rosier. Adjustment to a general price rise that is a direct consequence of maintaining real expansion, by no matter what means, has certain advantages over inflation resulting from continuous readjustment in income shares among small groups. Meeting sectoral claims "is likely to add up considerably higher than the total national monetary value of the product to be distributed.[29]

---

[28]See Lord Kahn, "Thoughts on the Behavior of Wages and Monetarism," *Lloyds Bank Review* (January 1976): 1–11; and Marcus H. Miller, "Can a Rise in Import Prices Be Inflationary and Deflationary? Economists and U.K. Inflation, 1973–1974," *American Economic Review* 66 (September 1976): 515–16.

[29]Florence, "Inflation," p. 102.

Experiments in Rate Structure

Lifeline — An Unfair Share?

Frank S. Walters

Electric service provides many of the basic necessities of life. This is a truism with which there is essentially no disagreement. Yet, because of this simple truth, the relationship between energy consumption and the fundamental needs of the family has occupied a unique position in recent years as the national dialogue on rate design has continued in the public forum.

However, *there is nothing unique* about the fact that some persons with low income may require some form of economic relief if their salary levels will not support the purchase of basic necessities in the open market. *What is unique* is the philosophical question as to whether or not resolution of the problem is a part of the tariff design function.

If we adhere to the traditional cost of service concept, special treatment in the price charged for the first several hundred kilowatt-hours of usage becomes a matter of equity between customer groups, since the "lifeline" approach is a deliberate departure from the cost pattern.

If we adopt a marginalist approach to costing and make an adjustment for excess revenue in the low consumption portion of the rate because of its price inelasticity, it can be argued that this is compatible with the cost pattern.

Thus, it may be said in the first instance that cost of service has been breached, and in the second instance that it has not; so we may well consider whether or not lifeline would provide an unfair share.

In its simplest form, lifeline implies a depressed price for a given number of kilowatt-hours each month, which are assumed to represent the energy required for a bare bones amount of lighting, refrigeration, and appliance usage, in other words, the basic necessities. Once this approach is taken, two choices confront the rate maker. Since customers using more than the lifeline quantity automatically buy the lifeline amount under the rate, such benefits as the adjustment may represent are extended to all customers taking service under the schedule, both large and small. On the other hand, if lifeline benefits were extended *only* to those customers using less than the lifeline limit, the preclusion of large use customers from comparable benefits would create a discriminatory pricing situation. Obviously, such a step would be undesirable.

A major variation on the lifeline theme which has been taking shape over the last few years has been called "fair share" by its proponents, although many disagree with that terminology. Under this approach special pricing is extended beyond the bare bones necessities level to include "average" kilowatt-hour usage for specific purposes such as cooking, water heating, and space heating. A standard of average energy use is then set for each application; the special rate is applied to average quantities, but a higher rate is applied to usage in excess of that amount.

Under lifeline the bare bones usage is usually a few hundred kilowatt-hours per month, or perhaps 4,000 kilowatt-hours per year. However, with fair share much larger usages are envisioned. Cooking and water heating may require 1,200 and 6,000 kilowatt-hours per year, respectively. Space heating annual usage may range from 10,000 to 20,000 kilowatt-hours or more, with wide variations depending on geographic location and size of dwelling.

The overall significance of this trend is that as more and more electrical usage is considered to be in the lifeline and fair share categories, the proportion of total sales remaining to carry the burden of compensation for the depressed price becomes dramatically reduced. This is best illustrated by a few examples.

Consider the case of a lifeline rate applicable to the first 300 kilowatt-hours of monthly residential consumption. Based on actual statistics for one utility, sales of electricity in the rate blocks up to 300 kilowatt-hours would be divided as follows. Sales to customers using 300 kilowatt-hours or less would be 30 percent of the total, whereas sales in the first 300 kilowatt-hour range but made to larger customers would constitute the remaining 70 percent. Thus, the lifeline benefit, intended for the small user, would serve to a greater degree as a discount on the first 300 kilowatt-hours sold to larger use customers. At 400 kilowatt-hours, sales to customers using less than the limit become 40 percent, and at a 500 kilowatt-hour limit they become 50 percent.

These statistics are based on bill frequency data in an area where the average residential use per customer is only 6,000 kilowatt-hours per year. If the same data are studied in a suburban area of higher consumption per customer, a greater mismatch occurs.

If residential usage is 10,000 kilowatt-hours per customer, the lifeline benefit extended to the small consumer (lifeline or less) shrinks further. At lifeline limits of 300, 400, and 500 kilowatt-hours, the benefit for these consumers would be 10, 20, and 30 percent, respectively.

It is quite apparent from these examples that much of the sociological benefit intended by establishing the lifeline rate goes to the *wrong* target. Although billing statistics of this kind will vary with the service area involved, these differences will not be sufficient to change the conclusion.

When the fair share doctrine is evoked and the "average" consumptions for large use applications, such as water or space heating, are included in the "special pricing," the leverage of these loads can be enormous — *if* their saturation is high.

Consider the first example, in which average residential consumption was 6,000 kilowatt-hours per customer a year with virtually no water or space heating. If water heating at 6,000 kilowatt-hours per year were added to one-half of these homes, the system average residential consumption would be increased by one-half of this amount — thus rising from 6,000 to 9,000 kilowatt-hours per year. If space heating were then added, at 15,000 kilowatt-hours per year, to one-third of the homes, the average would rise by 5,000 kilowatt-hours, to a level of 14,000 kilowatt-hours per year.

Carrying this "hypothetical" concept one step further, let us examine the revenue effect as fair share adjustments are made for water and space heating based on the average consumptions of 6,000 kilowatt-hours and 15,000 kilowatt-hours per customer, per year, respectively. Based on the assumptions of 50 percent saturation for water heating and 33 percent saturation for space heating, the system average use per customer would increase by 8,000 kilowatt-hours; 3,000 kilowatt-hours of the increase coming from water heating and 5,000 kilowatt-hours from space heating. If we assume that 4,000 kilowatt-hours of the initial average kilowatt-hour usage per customer had already been priced on a lifeline basis, only 2,000 kilowatt-hours would remain that could bear the burden of the additional adjustment to reflect fair share pricing. Therefore, if we further assume that the 8,000 kilowatt-hours for water and space heating were priced at one cent below the regular rate level, a deficiency of $80.00 (.01¢ × 8,000 kilowatt-hours) would result. Since there would remain only 2,000 kilowatt-hours to carry the compensating adjustment, the unit price of this energy would have to increase by four cents per kilowatt-hour above the regular rate level. Obviously, the leverage of such an approach could lead to unacceptable results in the marketplace.

In our example, 12,000 kilowatt-hours out of a total of 14,000 kilowatt-hours per year, per customer, or 85 percent of the energy consumption, would be sold at a depressed price resulting from the combination of lifeline and fair share adjustments.

I mentioned earlier that with lifeline in most cases a greater number of discounted kilowatt-hours would be sold to customers using more than the lifeline quantity than to customers using lifeline or less. However, if one considers only the latter category, namely, the small user, there is still a basic problem of whether or not the benefit goes to the specific consumers for which it is intended.

Average statistics tabulated for groups of customers may show that in areas where income levels are low the consumption of electricity is also low. However, it does not follow that the same relationship holds for individual customers making up the average. Customers with high incomes may have low electrical requirements if they are away much of the time, if they cook only a few meals at home, or if they have small families. Customers with low incomes may find it absolutely necessary to use large amounts of electricity — if they have large families, cook all their meals at home, and spend a great deal of time in their residence. A lifeline benefit for a fixed number of kilowatt-hours per month would reduce bills unnecessarily for the high income customer and would be a hardship for the low income customer with a large family.

When a lifeline rate is introduced, the discounted price may be established by a regulatory ruling of "no increase" for the early rate blocks during a rate increase proceeding, by establishing the price as a percentage of another rate block or a percentage of the average rate paid by the class, or on some other similar ratio. Once the discounted price level has been established, adjustment must be made elsewhere in the rate structure to compensate for the deficiency. If this is done by distributing the increase over the other blocks of the residential rate schedule, the burden on large use customers may be unacceptable. The alternative approach is to distribute the increase among other classes of business in addition to the high volume residential users to reduce the burden on individual bills.

Adjustments of the lifeline or fair share type distort the price cost relationship of the schedule because they are deliberate departures from cost. The amount of distortion obviously depends on the degree to which the price is depressed. Small excursions from the normal pattern can be accommodated reasonably well, but a more serious problem can be created by repeated lifeline modifications of the tariff structure. It is the long-range impact that is of greater concern since successive build-up of training rate blocks at artificially high price levels creates revenue instability when trailing blocks are required to carry substantially more than their share of responsibility for revenue production.

Implementation of a fair share rate structure would occasion severe administrative problems for the utility. Since the company normally has no record of the major appliances and other electrical equipment installed in the home of each customer, it would be necessary to make an inventory of these items for each of the hundreds of thousands of residential consumers served. Without such information customers could not be assigned to each of the end use categories of the fair share plan. Furthermore, problems of continuing the classification beyond the initial stage would require the establishment of a monitoring procedure which would have questionable reliability and would greatly increase expenses.

Since a customer could benefit from being billed in a category different from that to which he should be assigned, false claims would be encouraged and in all probability the situation would become uncontrollable.

Another very serious problem would arise in establishing average consumption levels on which the pricing would be based because of seasonal variation in usage. Air conditioning would be particularly difficult to handle equitably because historical weather patterns show that as much as 35 percent of the annual energy requirement for cooling might fall in the hottest month of the summer, and there would be no way to tell in advance whether that might be July, August, or September. To a lesser degree the same problem would arise with space heating, for as much as 20 percent of the annual heating requirement might fall in the coldest month.

Probably the most direct approach to the lifeline problem is what has been termed the "energy stamp" technique. Taking a cue from the food stamp program, energy stamps would be issued to low income consumers and would give them a discount on electric bills for their basic needs. Such a program could be administered by the experienced personnel of an appropriate government agency and should assure a fair and equitable distribution of the benefits.

By identifying specific beneficiaries, not only would the extension of benefits to high income users be avoided, but also a lower price could be offered to low income consumers within the same total revenue constraint.

The objectives of the lifeline–fair share approach are laudable from a sociological viewpoint. The purpose is to give economic assistance to those who need it. Yet, it is somewhat like engaging in target practice with a shotgun instead of a rifle — true, the shotgun may hit the bullseye, but the multitude of near misses tends to obscure the target.

It would be far better to identify the problem as a sociological one, provide a means of subsidy if that is judged to be the proper action, and thus remove the adjustment from the rate-making arena than it would be to create the illusion, with an artificial price tag, that the price of the utility's product is less than its real cost justifies.

The objectives of the lifeline–fair share approach are laudable from a sociological viewpoint. The purpose is to give economic assistance to those who need it. Yet, it is somewhat like engaging in target practice with a shotgun instead of a rifle — true, the shotgun may hit the bullseye, but the multitude of near misses tends to obscure the target.

Lessons from the Los Angeles Rate Experiment in Electricity

Jan Acton, W. G. Manning, and B. M. Mitchell

A number of utility systems have already begun experimentation with one or more time-of-day rates for their residential customers. In spring 1975 the Los Angeles Department of Water and Power (DWP) at its own initiative sought the approval of its Board of Water and Power Commissioners and the Los Angeles City Council to conduct a rate experiment with approximately 2,000 households. Researchers at the Rand Corporation would design and analyze the experiment. In summer 1976 the three major private utilities in California began to design peak load rate studies and demonstrations for their residential customers in response to the orders of the California Public Utility Commission in a generic rate case. In summer 1975 and again in summer 1976, the Federal Energy Administration (FEA) provided partial funding for a number of demonstration proj-

NOTE: This paper was prepared as part of a major study of the desirability and effects of new rate structures for electricity. The Rand research group has overall responsibility for the design and analysis of the study under contract to the Department of Water and Power of the City of Los Angeles. Partial support for the project is provided by the Federal Energy Administration. This paper does not necessarily represent the findings or opinions of the department or of the Federal Energy Administration. We are grateful for discussions with Michael Moore and Dennis Whitney of the department; James Boggis, Terrence Boley, and Roy Orson of the Electricity Council of London; and our Rand colleagues Frank Camm and Tom Glennan. The opinions and any errors should be ascribed to the authors.

ects designed to gain information about aspects of peak load tariff design, customer reaction, and equipment that might be suitable for administering the rates or helping customers adapt to its terms. As part of this program, the FEA has provided partial support to the Los Angeles rate experiment as well as the three other California rate studies mentioned above. Finally, the Energy Research and Development Administration (ERDA) has supported several demonstrations of bidirectional metering equipment which could, among other things, be used to implement a peak load pricing scheme for electricity.

With this considerable level of activity, as well as its great diversity in character, it is useful at the outset to ask what one can expect to learn from rate experiments and demonstrations. We will address this question in the context of the Los Angeles rate experiment, which is perhaps the most ambitious of the studies just reviewed both in scope and statistical design. After a brief introduction, we will present an overview of its objectives, scope, and methods of procedure. We will then consider, in separate sections, the analytical approach selected, the statistical design and choice of experimental rates, and some additional issues in experimentation. Finally, we will conclude with some observations about the expected transferability and generality of the results.

Introduction

Rate Structures and the Consumption of Electric Energy

The electric utility industry is a major sector of the energy economy of the United States. In 1973 it accounted for approximately 26 percent of total U.S. energy consumption and over 20 percent of U.S. fossil fuel consumption. The efficiency with which fossil fuels are transformed into electricity varies considerably, depending on the means of generation. The costs range from a fraction of one cent to several cents per kilowatt-hour (kwh) generated depending upon the type of fuel being employed and the nature of the generator (base load, intermediate, or peaking plant). Virtually all projections of energy supply and consumption show the *quantity* of electricity consumed in the United States growing in absolute amount and as a *proportion* of all energy through the end of the century. Consequently, public policies with respect to electricity will assume an increasingly central role in energy.

With the exception of direct rationing of electricity, changes in electric rate structures may be the most potent instrument available to policy makers for affecting both total quantity of electricity consumed and the time of day at which that electricy is used. Changes in the overall quantity consumed or the nature of the utility's load curve can, in turn, have a substantial impact on both the consumption of fossil fuels and the capital expansion requirements of the electricity industry.

Several recent cases before public utility commissions provide evidence of increased interest in altering electricity rate structures in the United States. These include generic rate cases in California, New York, Michigan, Connecticut, New Jersey, and Florida, as well as specific cases in Wisconsin, California, and New York. The theme of these cases and their findings have almost always included the following points: Marginal costs should be taken into account in the design of electricity rates; time-of-day tariffs should be applied to the largest industrial and commercial customers as rapidly as feasible; consideration should be given to extending time-of-day rates to intermediate-sized commercial and industrial customers in the near future, and suitable metering capability should be installed immediately; and additional study is needed to determine whether time-of-day or peak load tariffs will ever be beneficially offered to residential customers. The Los Angeles rate experiment grappled with many of these problems.

Objectives

Almost without exception, U.S. electric utility rates are based on a declining block rate structure in which customers pay a lower amount per kwh consumed as they move to higher levels of consumption. Much has changed since these conventional rate structures were developed, and four of these changes in particular prompt a reexamination of the theory and practice of rate setting. First, the high cost and shortages of fossil fuels require a reassessment of the rate structure. For many utilities, cost of fuel inputs has doubled or tripled in recent years, which has made many of their generation facilities economically obsolete. Second, the assumption of declining long-run incremental costs in electricity that has fostered the development of traditional tariffs may no longer be justified. In particular, it appears that new generation and transmission capacity may no longer enjoy economies of scale, at least beyond a certain point. Third, increased capital costs, delays in construction and licensing of new plants, and environmental costs may all affect the prices which should be charged for electricity. Finally, in a period of increased energy awareness and concern for prudent use of these resources, any rate structure which appears to reward greater consumption with quantity discounts should be closely reviewed.

Most analysts think peak load pricing is the most attractive alternative to existing rate structures. It is an old concept in economic theory,[1] but one which has been almost totally neglected in U.S. tariff design. The major questions in the design and analysis of peak load tariffs concern the calculation of marginal costs on which peak load rates would be based and the quantitative prediction of the changes in the amount and time pattern of electricity consumption which will result from alternative tariffs. Although considerable work remains to be done in order to have good estimates of marginal costs for different U.S. utilities, there is a substantial body of European writing and experience to draw upon.[2] We will concentrate our discussion on measuring the demand response to peak load tariffs.

From a policy perspective, the decision to adopt or reject a peak load tariff for a particular utility presents a problem in benefit-cost analysis. To assess the potential benefit of various rate structures, it is necessary to analyze data on the sensitivity of individual demand to changes in the rate structure and the amount of substitution that takes place between one period and another or from one form of fuel consumption to another. Any shift in electricity usage away from peak periods will permit savings both in fuel costs (because the most fuel costly units are employed to meet peak demand) and may permit capital savings (shifts away from peak lessen the need for new plant capacity and permit more efficient base load plants to be constructed to meet additional capacity requirements). Any savings in capital and operating expenses that result from changes in consumption patterns must then be compared with the costs of more complex metering of electricity use as well as the problem of implementation and administrative feasibility of these alternative rate structures. Depending on the magnitudes of these costs and benefits, significant overall social gains may be achieved by adopting one of the alternative rate structures. Conversely, if there is little behavioral response to an alternative rate structure, then a simple rate structure

---

[1]See, for example, Steiner (1957), Hirshleifer (1958), Williamson (1966), Bailey (1973), Panzar (1976), and the selection of articles in Nelson (1964).

[2]See Nelson (1964) and Turvey (1968).

is likely to be socially least costly. Only a demonstration of the effects of alternative rates will illuminate the matter and form a basis for policy.

Given the need to address such a fundamental question of benefit-cost comparison, some basic quantitative measures must be provided. Thus, the principal objectives of the Los Angeles project were as follows: (1) identify alternative electricity rate structures that may be superior to the rate structures currently in use by U.S. utilities; (2) demonstrate and measure the changes in energy consumption of a representative sample of customers in response to these alternative rates, holding constant the effects of other variables affecting energy demand; (3) analyze the distribution of the impacts among different types of customers, including changes in consumption of and expenditures for electricity by age, income, family size, housing type, and other important household characteristics; (4) determine the administrative, technical, and economic feasibility of these alternative structures; (5) estimate total energy use as well as the efficiency of energy use resulting from the alternative rate structures; and (6) estimate savings in operating costs (especially fossil fuels) and changes in capital costs that could be expected from systemwide adoption of alternative rate structures and project these savings to different utilities with specified generating systems and customer profiles.

A major objective of this project was to ensure that the experimental tariffs and the plan of analysis were sufficiently general that the results would be applicable not only to the current cost structure of the Los Angeles Department of Water and Power, but also to a wide variety of plausible conditions of electricity supply, including future cost increases and peak load conditions found in other utilities. The importance of such flexibility can be seen, among other instances, in the major and unexpected change in world oil prices in 1973 – 1974 as well as the current uncertainty regarding the cost and availability of nuclear power in the United States.

Why Have an Experiment?

Two methods of obtaining new data are potentially available. A utility may simply adopt a new rate schedule for an entire class of customers in its service area. In this case a single experimental tariff can be tested and its effects measured by analysis of the before-and-after variety, adjusting, where possible, for concurrent changes in circumstances. The alternative is to introduce a number of different rate schedules for a selected sample of customers while maintaining the current rate schedule for most other customers. We chose the experimental approach to obtain new residential data for a number of reasons.[3]

The first, and principal, reason for applying peak load rates to only a fraction of residential customers is that there is considerable uncertainty about customer response. Because there is so little U.S. evidence upon which to base a judgment, applying a full-scale time-of-day (or other peak load) tariff to all customers of a utility could be a costly error if the savings in capital and operating expenses did not offset the metering and other expenses.[4] Second, if a single peak load tariff were offered to residential customers as an optional alternative to their present rate structure, we would encounter a selection bias in the observed response. Generally speaking, only those customers who would expect to be better off under the peak load rate structure would select it. Consequently, we would have no evidence upon which to base an estimate of the quantitative response by other customers should the tariff be extended on a mandatory basis.[5] Third, the experimental approach allows us to observe the effects of several different tariffs instead of observing the effect of a single alternative. This not only permits cost-benefit analysis over a range of options, but also provides information that may permit fine tuning at a future time of any tariff adopted as a result of the initial test.[6]

Overview of the Los Angeles Experiment

In the next three sections, we discuss the methodological and statistical considerations that led to the specific set of tariffs in the Los Angeles experiment and the assignment of particular households to individual tariffs. The experiment consisted of approxi-

[3]In a related aspect of the study, we will conduct a before-and-after study of the pattern of electricity use among the largest industrial and commercial customers after a single time-of-day tariff is put into effect.

[4]The capital expense for installing the simplest time-of-day meter to DWP's 940,000 residential customers is estimated to be between $100 million and $200 million.

[5]On the other hand, if we were certain that the tariff would only be offered as an optional rate, it would not be a disadvantage to permit such self-selection.

[6]This point is developed further in the next section, when we discuss the use of a statistical design based on demand curve analysis in preference to the more traditional analysis of variance approach.

mately 1,800 households assigned to one of 40 different experimental rates for a 30-month period. An additional 400 households were selected for interview and observation as a control group. Because of somewhat different (although related) analytic issues, the experiment was divided into two parts: one for seasonal and one for time-of-day tariffs. The study consisted of six seasonal and flat (constant price) rates and 34 time-of-day rates.

Approximately 800 households within the City of Los Angeles were assigned to one of the seasonal and flat rates, which ranged from 2 to 8 cents per kwh. The peak season charge applied to either a four-month summer period or an eight-month winter period, and all rates were in effect at all hours, seven days per week. Approximately 1,000 households were assigned to one of the time-of-day rates. These applied to peak periods as short as three and as long as twelve hours. The peak period charge ranged from 5 to 13 cents per kwh, and the off-peak charges were either one or 2 cents per kwh. In our design of the experiment, we selected 17 different combinations of peak/off-peak charges for maximum expected statistical significance. Since we were also interested in the effect of a weekend exemption from peak charges, half of the subjects under each time-of-day rate were assigned to a tariff with a peak charge that applied five days per week, the other half to a peak charge applied seven days per week. This made the effective number of time-of-day tariffs 34.

Analytical Approach

Since a primary goal of the experiment was to provide general information about the nature of consumer responses to alternative tariff structures, greatest emphasis was placed on determining the underlying parameters that influence the quantity and time pattern of electricity consumption.[7] Statistical design procedures developed in a number of recent social experiments in income maintenance and health insurance were modified for the study. In order to gain the most useful information from the experiment, we must first identify the policy questions of greatest interest and then select an analytic approach that will yield the most precise information (with minimum statistical variance) about the policy questions. In our case, this essentially required a choice between an approach based on analysis of variance (ANOVA) or one based on demand curves.

[7]This section and the next on statistical design are deliberately nontechnical. A more rigorous treatment is provided in Manning, Mitchell, and Acton (1976).

Since we found the demand curve approach more suitable, we then had to identify the basic structure of the demand relationships to be estimated.

Policy Questions

Primary emphasis in the experiment was given to answering the following policy questions: (1) Under time-of-day tariffs, what is the *magnitude* of the change in quantity of electricity used in each time period (the load curve), and how does this response depend on (a) the length of the peak price period and (b) the levels of the peak and off peak prices? (2) Under seasonal tariffs, is there a significant *difference* in seasonal loads as compared with conventional tariffs? (3) Under all types of tariffs, what is the *level* of load as a function of the level of the rates in the tariff?

Answers to the first question are necessary in order to perform a benefit-cost comparison for alternative tariffs. We need to measure the changes in customer well-being (as measured by the economic concept of consumer's surplus) and changes in the utility's well-being (as measured by producer's surplus) and compare these changes with the added administrative and metering costs of a new tariff. Calculation of the change in consumer's and producer's surplus when prices of several related services are altered requires knowledge of the *change* in usage in both the peak and off peak periods.[8] It also requires a knowledge of increases or decreases in the consumption of alternative fuels such as natural gas. The first design objective was, therefore, to obtain reliable measures of changes in usage by period under a time-of-day tariff.

A closely related objective was to measure the sensitivity of consumer response to the length of time that the peak price is in effect in a time-of-day rate. Given uncertainties both about the degree of shifting customers can undertake in their pattern of consumption as well as uncertainties about the length of time that marginal costs are at their peak for a particular utility, it is necessary to examine the effects of varying the length of the peak period.

Seasonal tariffs, in which the peak period lasts for several months, can be implemented with existing residential meters and minor changes in billing and meter reading procedures. The major policy objective with respect to seasonal tariffs, therefore, was not to establish the precise magnitude of change, but to determine whether

[8]See Harberger (1971), Turvey (1968), and Besen and Mitchell (1975).

there would be *any* significant effect of raising the price per kwh for several months at a time and lowering it during the rest of the year, as compared with a uniform year-round price. If consumers respond to seasonal variations in prices by lowering use when prices are higher than current rates, this form of peak load pricing will necessarily result in a net welfare gain, since there are no important costs of converting to such a rate structure.[9]

The third policy objective centered on the need for reliable forecasts of the *levels* of loads during all periods under both conventional and peak load rate structures. Both investment planning for capacity expansion and the design of a particular peak load rate structure that will recover historical costs require accurate predictions of load by time period.

Analysis of Variance versus a Demand Curve Approach

The choice between an approach based on analysis of variance (ANOVA) and one based on demand curves is essentially a matter of deciding where one wishes to have the most precision and confidence in interpretation. If one is most interested in detecting the *existence* of an effect, then an ANOVA model is most suitable. If one is interested in determining the *quantitative relationship* between different levels of peak and off peak prices and the quantity of electricity consumed in each time period, then a demand curve approach is more suitable.

In attempting to determine the existence of a response, the ANOVA approach directs us to select a single alternative peak load tariff with a very high peak price and a very low off peak price. The observed response to this single alternative tariff is then compared to the pattern of consumption in a control group. For any given amount of resources devoted to the experiment, the average group can have a larger number of subjects than is possible in an experiment with several plans. Since the variance (or standard error) of measured response to any experimental rate goes down as sample size increases, the result of this ANOVA assignment is to measure with greater precision than would a multiplan experiment whether there is a behavioral response to a peak load tariff.

We can illustrate the strength (and some of the limitations) of this

[9]Of course, for distributional reasons it may be desirable to have seasonal tariffs that reflect variations in marginal costs even if no efficiency gains result.

approach in Figure 1. Suppose the current rate charges about 3 cents per kwh at all hours and that our alternative peak load rate had been set at 7 cents per kwh from noon to 6 P.M. and at 2 cents per kwh at all other hours. Suppose that control households were observed to consume, on average, about 200 kwh per month during the hours noon to 6 P.M. and experimental households an average of 160 kwh during those hours. If the difference is statistically significant (this will depend on sample size), then we could conclude that this particular time-of-day rate reduces peak consumption by about 20 percent for this sample. We are sharply limited, however, in our ability to answer other questions about the effect of peak load tariffs that might be of major policy interest. First, we cannot extrapolate these findings to other tariffs with very much confidence. For example, instead of 7 cents and 2 cents, the analyst or policy maker may wish to know the effects of a rate that charged 6 cents on peak and 2 cents during off peak hours. Unless he makes the strong assumptions that behavioral response is strictly proportional to peak period price, the effect cannot be determined. Second, this ANOVA single tariff comparison does not permit us to identify separately the effects of peak and off peak charges. Is the observed drop during peak hours due to the elevated level of peak price, or is it due to the reduced level of off peak price? Such information is crucial if we are to be able to judge the effect of still another tariff, for example, 7 cents on peak and 3 cents off peak. Third, use of a single comparison of one experimental group and one control group makes the experiment more vulnerable

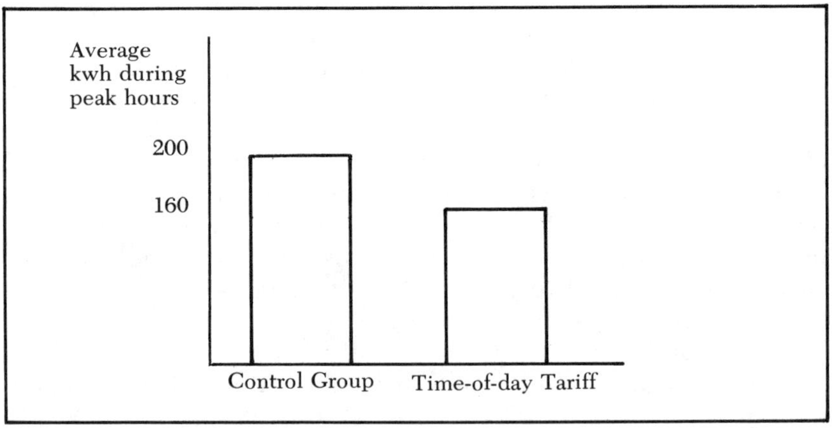

Figure 1. ***Illustrative Comparison of Peak Usage by Control and Experimental Groups in an ANOVA Experiment***

to flukes or spurious findings due either to unforeseen factors, statistical aberration, or mistakes in the conduct of the experiment. An example of such a suspicious finding occurred in one of the experimental plans in the United Kingdom's five-year rate experiment.[10] One of the three alternative rates used in that study (the load rate tariff) yielded a mean response that indicated a *positive* relationship between price and quantity of energy consumed. That tariff was the most complicated of the three forms tested. Since no one was willing to conclude that higher prices caused increased consumption, the finding was regarded as spurious and disregarded, which caused a significant loss in the size of the useful sample.

To a limited degree, these objections can be partially overcome by permitting more experimental tariffs to be used in the ANOVA design. Additional tariffs can be employed to identify the effects of off peak rates for different levels of on peak price. And an additional set of options can be introduced to determine the effect of length or location of the peak time period. But it is much more efficient, both in terms of statistical precision and in ease of comprehension and information processing, to employ a fundamentally different procedure based on demand curves. Since the principal analytic question is generally to determine the effect of different *variables*, or underlying factors, that contribute to different behavioral responses, it is better consciously to design the study to elicit those parameters at the outset. Once measured, those parameters can be used to calculate the effects of a variety of specific tariff alternatives. We drew additional support for our demand curve approach from the practical experience of the Electricity Council of London. After they had conducted their ANOVA experiment, the British peak load experimenters reached the conclusion that,

> with the aid of hindsight, the experiment might have been better directed to a more primitive problem. What are the price elasticities and cross elasticities of electricity demand by time-of-day, day-of-week and season-of-year? Such primitive, component information could be patched together to form views of the effectiveness of composite price structures without having settled those beforehand by somewhat arbitrary judgement.[11]

Model for Demand Analysis

Once it was decided to employ demand curves, the nature of demand equations that would be estimated had to be identified.

[10]See Electricity Council of London (no date).
[11]Boggis (1975).

Although statistical design can take place without an exact knowledge of the specification of the equations, the more information one has about specification, the better one is able to select a set of experimental tariffs to maximize expected statistical significance. In this section, we shall sketch briefly, and in nontechnical terms, the nature of the model underlying our analysis. The actual design was done in a manner that is not very sensitive to changes in exact specification over a range of alternatives. We employed a very general specification of the model for design purposes. Furthermore, we experimented with several specifications in order to determine whether the resulting allocations were sensitive to specification form. The allocations finally chosen were very robust over a set of likely final model specifications.

SYNTHETIC DEMAND CURVES. In the traditional ANOVA approach, the effects of an experimental tariff are compared with the effects of a control group. In many applications of demand curve analysis, a similar comparison is implicitly made, as researchers compare parameters estimated from a demand curve under one particular experimental tariff (for example, a peak charge from noon until 6 P.M. with different values of peak and off peak prices) with parameters of a demand curve estimated for the control group. We can increase the effective sample size (and therefore increase the precision of the estimates) by pooling the entire sample across all types of tariffs under observation (for example, those with peak charge from 9 A.M. to 3 P.M. can also be included in the analysis). This pooling is made possible by considering the entire *pattern* of demand under observation, not just one aspect, such as on peak consumption or total kwh consumed. If the day is divided into three-hour blocks of time (9 A.M. to noon, noon to 3 P.M., and so forth) in addition to the night hours (9 P.M. to 9 A.M.), we can consider all time periods simultaneously. Ignoring for the moment factors other than price that may affect consumption, the amount of electricity consumed in any one period is determined by the price in that period and the prices in all other periods. It is not necessary to know whether the particular price observed is a peak or an off peak price; the quantity of electricity consumed in that period is attributed to the full set of prices the individual faces in all periods. In economic terms, consumption in any one period can be predicted as a function of different values of own and cross-prices.

The practical import of this specification is to increase substantially the effective degrees of freedom. Once we have estimated the effect of each period's price on quantity demanded in each period (for example, effect on consumption between 9 A.M. and noon of prices in each of the four three-hour periods and the period 9 P.M. to 9 A.M.), we can estimate the effect of a large range of peak and off peak combinations, even combinations not explicitly observed in the experiment. We have designated this approach synthetic demand curves because we can synthesize the effects of any particular tariff by using as building blocks the parameter estimates for separate time periods.

PRICE-LENGTH INTERACTIONS. As noted above, we were interested not only in the effects of peak and off peak prices, but also in the length of time over which the peak charge applies. This is not only of intrinsic interest for policy analysis, but also is crucial to our synthetic demand curve approach. Consider the expected customer response to a peak charge during the hours noon to 3 P.M. We expect that the amount of electricity consumed during those hours may depend not only on the level of price in the preceding and following three-hour period, but also on whether all three (or two of the three) periods are at the peak rate.[12] This requires that we be prepared to analyze the separate effect of length of peak charge as well as level of peak and off peak prices.

GENERAL PRINCIPLES OF DESIGN. To further support our overall objective in addressing the primary policy questions articulated above, three additional principles of design are important: achieving a spread of experimental design points, allowing for nonlinear responses, and treating correctly other factors that may influence the pattern or level of energy consumption.

It is important for both statistical and analytic reasons to achieve a reasonably large spread in the values of experimental treatments. From a statistical viewpoint, we obtain more precise (lower variance) estimates of the effect of price by spreading the prices in the experimental tariffs. Suppose we are especially interested in knowing the effect of on peak charges in the range 4 to 6 cents per kwh. We could assign individual subjects to the values 4 and 6 cents for experimental study. Since actual consumption will result in a scatter

[12]It is impossible to know in advance what the net effect of these factors will be. On the one hand, peak prices in adjacent periods make it less likely that an individual will be able to shift energy use a few hours to take advantage of off peak prices. On the other hand, a long peak charge period makes it more worthwhile to purchase certain types of equipment (such as timers for large capacity water heaters) that could shift a major portion of energy use to an off peak period.

of points at each level of price, the observed pattern will be something like Figure 2A. Due to variability in individual responses or the luck of the particular statistical sample drawn, the demand curve actually estimated in a particular experiment may vary substantially from the true relationship between price and quantity (shown as the solid line). We have indicated two possible demand curves that might be estimated — the lines labeled 1 and 2. If, on the other hand, we selected more extreme values, say 3 and 10 cents, for the peak charge (Figure 2B), we would have considerable lower expected variance in the price parameter — in the range of interest (4–6 cents) as well as outside of that range. Of course, one does not generally wish to select values of peak/off peak prices that are too extreme, for to do so could increase substantially the cost per observation, increase participant refusal, or be too far removed from realistic policy alternatives to be of interest for judging other aspects of customer reaction. In the next section we will systematically consider how much variability is optional from a design perspective.

We also wish to allow for the possibility that customers do not respond in a linear manner to changes in price levels. Generally speaking, in order to detect curvature in the demand relationship we must observe at least three different levels of price. Figure 3 illustrates a possible demand response with curvature (line 1) that would

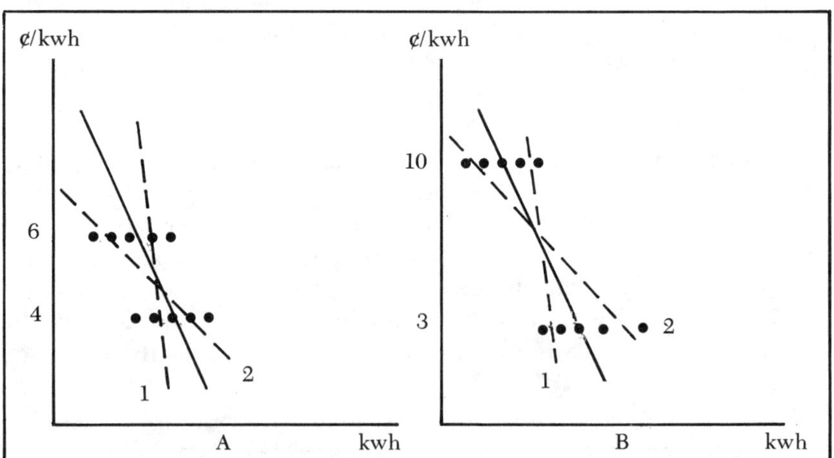

Figure 2. ***Illustration of Variability of Estimated Demand Curves Due to Differences in Spread of Experimental Rates***

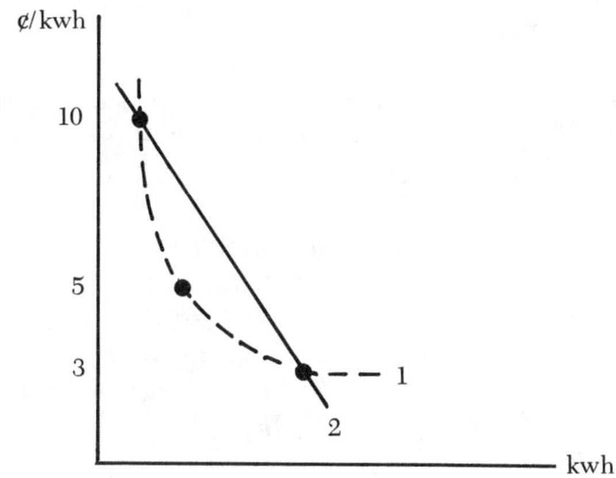

Figure 3. ***Illustrative Effects on Measured Demand Relationship when Three Experimental Rates Are Used instead of Two***

not be detected if we only observed individuals at prices of 3 and 10 cents (line 2).

The third design consideration is to assure that other factors which may be expected to affect demand are not systematically associated with some feature of the experiment. For example, if some factor such as income or ownership of electric water heaters were found in certain experimental plans but were absent in others, then the experiment would contain a built-in correlation that would be impossible to disentangle from the experimental rates.

Statistical Design and Choice of Experimental Rates

A rate study of the type considered here is a costly undertaking and requires careful planning to yield the greatest possible information. Because project resources were limited and observations are costly, we had to select carefully the number and types of households for participation. The problem was exacerbated by the fact that, generally speaking, the very things discussed in the last section as being most desirable from the viewpoint of analysis — greater numbers of observations and spread in design points — tend to be the most costly to achieve. The problem then was to design the study in a manner to maximize statistical significance and relevance of the results, taking into account the cost of each observation and the overall budget constraint.[13]

Broadly speaking, our procedure was to separate the statistical design problem into two parts: selection of the optimal set of experimental tariffs and the number of individuals assigned to each tariff, and assignment of specific individuals to particular experimental plans in accordance with the quotas determined in the first step. The first step made use of an Allocation Model, adopted from the pioneering work of John Conlisk and Harold Watts (1969) in the design of the first income maintenance experiment in New Jersey. The second step made use of the Finite Selection Model (FSM), developed by Carl Morris (1975) for use in the Health Insurance Study now under way at six sites throughout the country.

The Allocation Model

The Allocation Model was used to select the test set of design points (combinations of peak/off peak rates and length of peak charge) and to determine the optimal number of households (stratified by monthly electricity consumption) for each design point.[14] The basic procedure was to (1) specify the types of analytic models to be estimated; (2) assign weights to the different coefficients of this set of equations that reflect the relative value one attaches to alternative policies under study; and (3) select the set of observations that would give the maximum weighted statistical significance within the overall budget constraint. We discussed in the last section the type of analytic model upon which the estimating equations were based. The remaining inputs needed for the Allocation Model were a set of permissible design points, a set of weights for the policy parameters of interest, and an estimate of the cost of each observation on each potential design point.

[13]The importance of careful design is indicated by the magnitude of expense involved. The five-year British experiment cost in excess of $3 million. The overall cost of our experiment is expected to be between $3 million and $5 million over a four-year period. During that time, almost 7,000 household interviews will be conducted and about $360,000 will be used to purchase new meters.

[14]The Allocation Model can also be used to determine optimal design points also identified by nontariff characteristics (such as income or appliance ownership). We did not use the Allocation Model for this task because costs per observation do not depend significantly on such factors, and we were interested in the effects of these factors only as a secondary matter in order to study tariff effects. Consequently, we used the FSM to achieve balance in these nontariff dimensions and to assure that they were not correlated with any plan characteristic.

The selection of permissible design points is most interesting for present discussion.[15] The Allocation Model starts with a large initial set of potential design points and then determines a smaller optimal set to maximize expected statistical significance. We deliberately chose a wide range of potential peak/off peak price combinations that are more extreme than may be appropriate for the DWP situation at this moment. This was done for statistical precision as well as a desire to make the results applicable to future DWP circumstances or to those of other utilities.

We were guided by current operating conditions in the DWP as well as possible changes that may take place in capital and fuel costs. Under current circumstances, the *average* variable cost of producing electricity is sometimes as low as one cent per kwh. The short-run *marginal* cost, however, ranges between approximately 2 and 3.5 cents per kwh, depending on the hour of day and season of use. In addition to setting price equal to short-run marginal cost in each time period, peak load pricing rules also assign part or all of additional revenue requirements to cover capital expenditures to peak users.[16] In the DWP's current configuration, this may add between one and two cents per kwh to peak period prices. Thus, a peak load tariff under current circumstances in Los Angeles might have an off peak rate as low as one cent per kwh and a peak rate as high as 5.5 cents per kwh.

When we consider possible costs of supply five years from now (when tariffs might be in effect that are based on the results of this experiment), peak costs may be even higher. If the price of natural gas is decontrolled, then the short-run marginal cost at peak hours might well be in excess of 10 cents per kwh — not counting any charge for capital expenditures.[17]

The experiment consists of two types of peak period tariffs: seasonal and time-of-day rates. Although the design of the two aspects was coordinated, the two types can be considered separately for present discussion. Making use of the existing declining block tariff (which charges about 4 cents per kwh for a majority of households

[15]The other two types of inputs are discussed in detail in Manning, Mitchell, and Acton (1976), to which the interested reader is referred.

[16]For a discussion of different circumstances for determining how much capital to assign to peak and off peak users, see Panzar (1976).

[17]Gas turbines provide the peaking capacity for many U.S. utilities. They have an operating cost of about 5 cents per kwh at current, controlled prices of natural gas. Most analysts feel the price of natural gas would go up by at least a factor of two if it were decontrolled; see MacAvoy and Pindyck (1973).

observed), for control subjects we included four flat rates and thirteen seasonal rates. Table 1 gives the terms of tariffs that were potentially available for selection by the Allocation Model. All seasonal tariffs were broken into a summer period of June through September and a winter period of the other eight months. Note that tariffs that charge a higher amount in winter than in summer were allowed. Although the DWP's current cost structure would indicate a greater price in the summer, this "inversion" was included for generality as well as statistical significance. Higher level precision in estimating winter price effects is achieved by permitting greater variation in winter prices. In order to lower the overall cost of enrolling these customers, we permit some to face low summer prices. If we had excluded winter peak tariffs it would have required an increase in sample size of 40–50 percent to achieve the same expected degree of statistical significance.

Table 1. ***Potential Set of Seasonal Tariffs***

Declining block controls (¢/kwh)	*Experimental tariffs* Flats (¢/kwh)	*Seasonal tariffs* Summer (¢/kwh) / Winter (¢/kwh)
4[a]	2	4/2
	3	5/2
	4	7/2
	5	8/2
		4/3
		5/3
		6/3
		2/4
		2/5
		2/6
		2/7
		2/8
		3/4

[a]Average price per kwh for the majority of households.

The results of the Allocation Model assignments for seasonal and flat tariffs are shown in Table 2. In addition to 400 households on existing tariffs (labeled controls), two tariffs with flat rates of 2 cents or 5 cents per kwh at all times were selected. These households effectively served as controls for all experimental plans in the conventional ANOVA sense. The remaining rates served to estimate the demand curve by identifying the "end points" and the curvature of demand responses.

Table 2. ***Results of the Allocation Model, Seasonal and Flat Tariffs***

Tariffs summer/winter	*Number per plan*
Controls	400
2/2 (flat)	350
5/5 (flat)	110
5/2	140
8/2	50
2/5	150
2/8	20
Total	1,220

The potential set of time-of-day rates was greater because there were more parameters of interest to be estimated (level of peak/off peak prices, location of peak period, and length of peak period). The day was divided into four three-hour periods, plus one twelve-hour night period. We permitted off-peak rates of one, two, or three cents per kwh and peak prices of 4, 5, 7, 9, 11, and 13 cents per kwh. The length of peak rate could vary from three to twelve hours. A total of 47 tariffs were potentially available for selection; their values are shown in Table 3. Seventeen tariffs were selected by the Allocation Model, and the plans selected are shown in Table 4. In order to measure the effect of off peak pricing on the weekend, we selected at random one-half of the subjects on each plan to pay the peak price for

Table 3. ***Set of Potential Time-of-Day Tariffs***

Peak period	*Peak/off peak prices (¢/kwh)*
9 A.M.–NOON	11/3, 5/3, 13/2, 9/2, 5/2
NOON–3 P.M.	11/3, 5/3, 13/2, 9/2, 5/2
3 P.M.–6 P.M.	11/3, 9/3, 5/3, 13/2, 9/2, 5/2
6 P.M.–9 P.M.	11/3, 9/3, 5/3, 13/2, 9/2, 5/2
9 A.M.–3 P.M.	5/3, 13/2, 9/2, 7/2, 5/2
3 P.M.–9 P.M.	5/3, 13/2, 9/2, 7/2, 5/2
NOON–9 P.M.	5/3, 4/3, 7/2, 9/1, 5/1
9 A.M.–9 P.M.	5/3, 4/3, 7/2, 9/1, 5/1
9 P.M.–9 A.M.	11/3, 5/3, 13/2, 9/2, 5/2

the five weekdays and one-half to pay the peak price seven days per week. Therefore, the actual number of time-of-day plans under observation was 34.

Table 4. ***Results of the Allocation Model, Time-of-Day Tariffs***

Peak period	*Peak/off peak price*	*Number per plan*
9 A.M.–NOON	5/2	80
	9/2	60
	13/2	20
NOON–3 P.M.	9/2	40
	13/2	20
3 P.M.–6 P.M.	5/2	20
	9/2	80
	13/2	80
6 P.M.–9 P.M.	5/2	20
	9/2	60
	13/2	60
3 P.M.–9 P.M.	7/2	40
NOON–9 P.M.	5/1	120
	9/1	20
9 A.M.–9 P.M.	5/1	20
	9/1	80
9 P.M.–9 A.M.	5/2	160
Total		980

The results of the Allocation Model choices for time-of-day rates were broadly similar to the results for seasonal rates. Plans with extreme values of peak or off peak prices were selected to reduce variance (although the high cost of the former meant that relatively few households were assigned to them), and tariffs with intermediate values were selected to detect curvature. Again, one plan was selected with a peak rate between the hours of 9 P.M. and 9 A.M. Although this is the least costly time period for the DWP to supply electricity, the inclusion of this overnight rate permits demand curves to be estimated over a greater range of prices and produces an increase in statistical precision equivalent to an overall sample size about 40–50 percent larger if this tariff were excluded from the options.

Finite Selection Model

The Finite Selection Model (FSM) is used to achieve two desirable features of sample selection that cannot be achieved practically with the Allocation Model: statistical balance and the identification of particular households to be enrolled in the study. The FSM works in a manner similar to the Allocation Model. From a large number of households which are potential candidates for selection, the FSM chooses a fraction for assignment to tariffs previously determined by the Allocation Model. Balance is achieved by assuring that household characteristics that would be expected to influence the pattern of electricity use are proportionately represented in each plan. The FSM selects households with different values of income, appliance ownership, housing characteristics, and ethnicity so that none of these factors is systematically associated with any feature of experimental plans. The FSM also selects *particular* individuals for assignment to plans in accordance with quotas set by the Allocation Model. This is in contrast to the Allocation Model, which determined proportions of the sample to be enrolled on each type of plan, but did not designate *which* of the candidate households should be assigned to which plans.[18]

Our actual field strategy was to select approximately 200 neighborhoods, using the 1970 census. These were chosen from throughout the city of Los Angeles to represent the full spectrum of climate, appliance ownership, income, housing, and ethnicity. We then randomly selected 12,000 customers from these 200 neighborhoods using the DWP customer billing file and stratified customers by their level of electricity usage. Figure 4 shows the proportion of all DWP residential customers in each of these strata. In general, statistical precision will be increased by considerably oversampling in the high-consumption D Stratum. We deliberately sampled disproportionately from the four strata in accord with policy questions of particular interest.

One major question of general policy interest is the effect of price on the quantity of electricity used — especially as policy makers consider a revision of the rate level or the adoption of lifeline rates. These effects are best studied in the seasonal and flat tariffs. Consequently, those plans sample proportionately at the low end of the spectrum of usage (A) and oversample in the moderate and high strata of use (C and D). In contrast, response to time-of-day rates is especially important to observe at high levels of use — either be-

[18]The Allocation Model results are based on the characteristics of the entire sample universe, that is, a sample of infinite size, with average characteristics (such as income) exactly equal to the universal mean. In fact, due to costs of selecting eligible households, actual assignment to plans is made from a finite set of candidates whose *particular* characteristics may vary importantly from the universal mean.

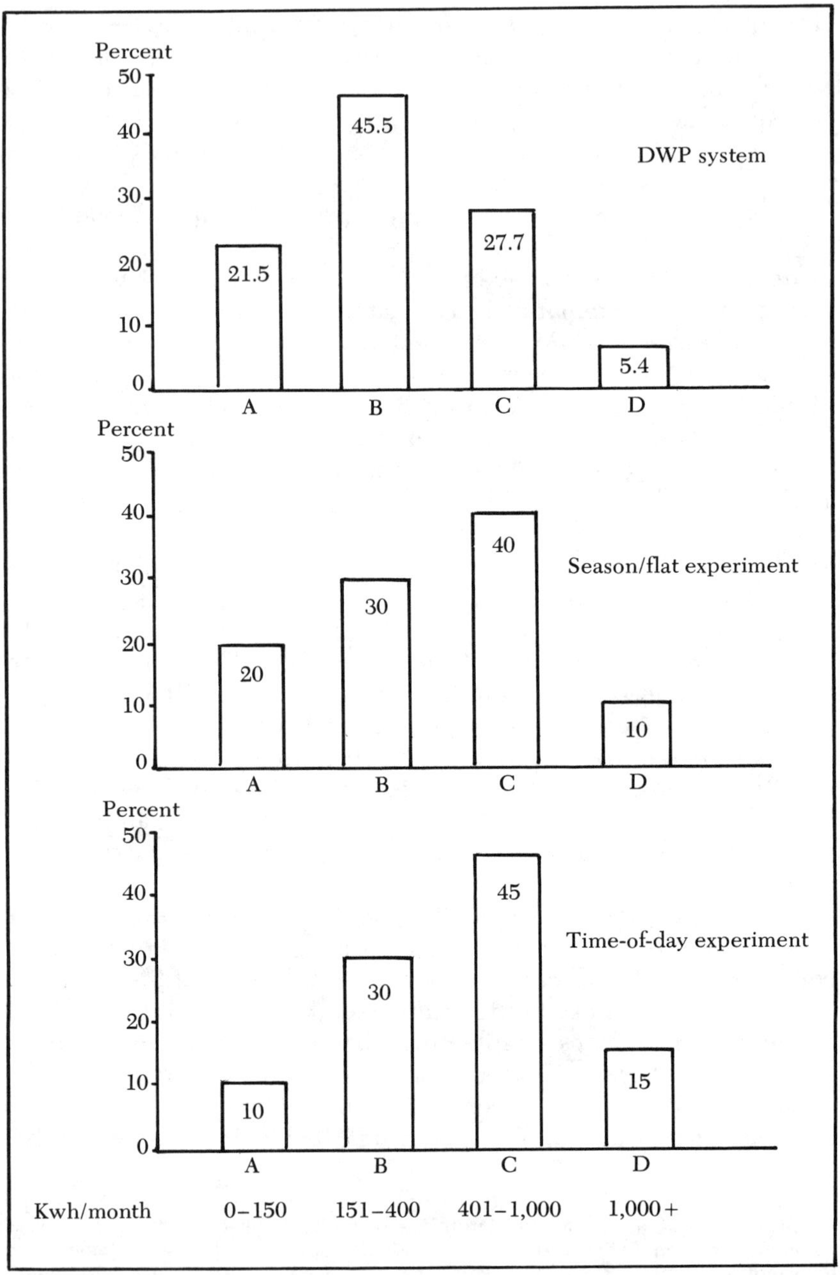

Figure 4. ***Proportion of Households in DWP System and Proportion on Experimental Plans***

cause these are the customers most likely to be offered time-of-day rates in the future or because we are particularly concerned about the effects on pattern of use of appliances owned by those customers. Consequently, the time-of-day tariffs undersample for customers at the low and medium levels (A and B) and greatly oversample customers above 400 kwh per month.

Results of Statistical Design

The preceding sections have discussed the assignments of households to experimental tariffs so as to yield maximum statistical significance for the given budget size. The design does not indicate how much precision to expect, only the best way to maximize the weighted value of statistical significance. In the process of determining the best assignments, the Allocation Model calculates expected variance of all parameters of interest. These variances are stated as a proportion of the overall precision of the equation (that is, as a fraction of its standard error).

The expected overall precision of the equation is unknown; indeed, if we had that information we would know the nature of peak load response and much of the study would be unnecessary. A first approximation to calculating expected precision can be achieved by looking at the five-year rate experiment conducted by the Electricity Council of London.[19] One inference from their data is that the variance under a time-of-day rate experiment might be as great as the mean level of consumption observed in that peak period. Using this information combined with DWP data, our calculations indicate that the typical standard error on parameters of interest will be around 9 percent of the mean level of consumption in the seasonal experiment and around 6 percent in the time-of-day experiment. This means, for example, that if 200 kwh were consumed per month during the peak charge hours of noon to 9 P.M., we would expect the standard error to be about 13 kwh per month.

Although the overall effects of the design procedures cannot be briefly summarized, it appears that we can expect to obtain statistical results that are highly accurate indications of what the effect would be if these same plans were extended to much larger numbers of households under similar circumstances.

Other Issues in Experimentation

The choice of analytic model, the permissible set of alternative tariffs for experimentation, and the results of the statistical design

[19]See Electricity Council of London (no date).

determine the basic character of the study. They do not, however, exhaust the set of issues that arise when designing an experiment or in interpreting the results. In this section, we discuss briefly the time horizon for the experiment, customer education, participation payments and Hawthorne effects, and administrative issues.

Time Horizon

In any study based on temporary participation by individuals, one asks: Is the study long enough? There are several facets to the question. Is it long enough for individuals to learn the terms of their experimental rate? Is it long enough to make major changes in lifestyle worthwhile? Is it long enough to permit cost recovery of any energy-saving investments that the household may wish to make? Are there important changes customers might make on the boundaries of the experiment (just before or after the experiment either begins or ends) that may reduce the effective number of months of "normal" behavior? Is it long enough to observe normal appliance retirements and conversions?

The Los Angeles experiment is designed to last 30 months, after which time households return to paying for electricity under the prevailing rate structures. We believe that this is a sufficient period to examine most of the response which is observable at all in this particular case. The character and degree of major capital investments that customers might make in response to peak load tariffs are quite limited in Los Angeles. Since natural gas is currently inexpensive and the climate is mild, few homes have major investments in electric heating. Storage heating devices are one of the principal means that European customers have for taking advantage of favorable off peak electricity rates,[20] and we might expect similar demand in the United States, especially in colder climates and areas without plentiful natural gas supplies. There is no comparable device readily available to store cool air at night for use on hot summer afternoons. Furthermore, if time-of-day rates were commonplace, appliance manufacturers would likely change the character of many appliances to make them more adaptable to the terms of electricity rates. Such changes in appliances cannot be easily reproduced in an experiment. Consequently, capital investment alternatives for most households will be limited to inexpensive timers to switch certain appliances off during peak charge hours. The one significant oppor-

[20]See Mitchell, Manning, and Acton (1977).

tunity we have to observe wholesale conversion of appliances is when a household moves. This is especially true of moves from apartments or houses with several appliances of one fuel to a unit with appliances of another fuel. For this reason, we have made every attempt to allow any household that moves to take its experimental rate to the new address as long as it is within the city limits.

The major evidence of response in Los Angeles will be the result of behavioral changes that permit households to use less energy on peak and perhaps shift some usage to off peak periods. For these reasons, we are determining in advance what hours people work, when they currently run the air conditioner, and when other appliances such as washers and dryers are used. We will attempt to determine whether shifts occur in any of these uses in response to terms of the tariff.

We believe that most of these behavioral responses will be observable in a relatively short period, so that during most of the 30 months we will see steady-state behavior. The experiment is designed to cover usage over two full summers and winters as well as part of a third summer for most households.

Customer Education

The experiment also offers the opportunity to engage in a considerable degree of education in assisting customers in taking advantage of the terms of their experimental rate. The appropriate degree of education to include in the experiment is not easily determined. On the one hand, we can certainly predict that if time-of-day rates were commonplace, there would be considerable general education and advice (as well as specialized equipment) available to assist households. To withhold all education in the experiment would lead to an underestimation of the effect if the tariff were available systemwide. On the other hand, any attempt to help individuals change the manner in which they use electricity runs the considerable risk of introducing an unexpected experimental effect in addition to the effect of the terms of the tariff itself, thus biasing the results of the study. Households may wish to please the person interviewing and "educating" them and may respond with a pattern of electricity use that is not representative (this so-called Hawthorne effect is discussed in the next section).

One could deal with customer education as an explicit experimental treatment and assign different amounts to different groups of households. For the present, we have adopted a simple strategy of providing the same, low level assistance to all participating households in the form of a brief handbook. It contains a number of suggestions for shifting energy use to off peak periods in order to lower the overall electricity bill. We are reserving the alternative of adding an explicit degree of education to part of the study at a future point in order to test the effect of such education.

Participation Payments and Hawthorne Effects

In order to experiment with a wide range of tariff alternatives, we selected many tariff combinations which may result in a higher electricity bill for the household. If we had excluded such tariffs, we would limit severely the relevance of options examined. In order to induce cooperation in the study (and not introduce a bias that would result from differential acceptance), we offer a lump-sum participation incentive payment (PI) to any household whose electricity bill goes up — *assuming no change* in pattern of consumption. Since the household retains any cost saving, this is a generous compensation criterion. Most households can be expected to make at least modest adjustments in their pattern of energy use, so this "no change" PI overcompensates them.

In theory, the household should treat the PI as it would a modest increase in its nonearned income. Since the payment will remain the same regardless of any changes in electricity use, the household should act as if it faced the full terms of the experimental rate. However, we cannot be certain that some (or all) households will not treat the PI as an offset to their bills and simply consume electricity exactly as before.

Although we cannot rule out the possibility of such behavior, we can test for its existence. Half of the households that receive PIs will receive their full payments quarterly throughout the study. The others will receive half the amount each quarter and the other half as a lump-sum payment at the end of the 30-month period.

A related issue is the so-called Hawthorne or experimental effect, in which behavioral responses are simply a result of conducting an experiment (or some unobserved aspect of the experiment) rather than of differences in the treatments applied to experimental and control subjects.[21] An example was offered in the dilemma raised by

[21] The original Hawthorne effect was observed in a study conducted over 50 years ago, when an attempt was made to see whether improved lighting increased worker

the option to educate households. Although we cannot rule out *a priori* such experimental effects, we can attempt to limit them in all obvious ways and test for their presence in the final results. In fact, several degrees of customer contact are under observation. These include the following: no direct contact at all; no interview, new meter placed outside; interview, no other change; interview, contract for new electricity rate, old meter; interview, new rate, new meter; interview, new rate, old meter, participation payment; and interview, new rate, new meter, participation payment. We thus can test separately for each of these factors as influencing customer response.

Administrative Issues

A number of administrative issues arise in the conduct of an experiment of this type, but three important ones are choice of meters, selection of interviewers, and rules for participation in the study.

We selected continuous tape recording cassette meters. Although these cost around $300 each (as opposed to $80 each for two-register meters plus a time switch to record peak and off peak kwh), the increase in information offsets the cost differences. Use of continuous recorders permits us to employ the synthetic demand curve approach, in which, in effect, each household serves as a control for every other household. If we had used only two-register meters, we would have been deprived of a significant number of degrees of freedom in estimating each demand curve.

In this study, DWP employees interviewed and enrolled participants. Generally speaking, only professional survey organizations, with trained interviewers, have been used in social experiments and other social research that expects to meet minimal standards of

---

productivity. Existing light bulbs were exchanged for brighter bulbs and productivity rose. Even brighter bulbs were tried; productivity rose again. Then the experimenter substituted bulbs with lower light output for existing bulbs. Productivity rose! It turned out that the experiment itself was increasing productivity.

It is not clear that rate experiments are vulnerable to precisely the same danger, because it is not clear what a better outcome is in each case. If energy use systematically rose (or fell) with every plan, we would not falsely ascribe any of the results to tariff levels; our conclusion would be that tariffs produce no effect.

Nevertheless, there is a danger that experimentation will affect the results. Perhaps a closer analogy is the so-called Heisenberg effect. Heisenberg, a physicist, found that the very act of attempting to measure certain very small phenomena changed the values of the phenomena because his measuring device was larger than that which he was measuring.

analytic rigor and representativeness.[22] The major successful exception of which we are aware is in the Electricity Council's five-year rate study which used employees of the Area Boards. Rand researchers and the Department of Water and Power cooperated in the training and supervision of about 45 DWP employees. The results were remarkably satisfactory. Interview completion rates were in excess of 90 percent (compared with normal survey experience of 80 – 85 percent), and some 93 percent of the households agreed to join the study (compared with about 85 percent in a number of other social experiments). Although this aspect of the study will be the subject of a special report, our general feeling is that with highly motivated people and careful training and supervision (four Rand survey researchers spent two weeks training the group of interviewers), a successful field operation can be conducted.

Finally, rules for participation in the study must be developed and made known to participating individuals. These should cover such issues as eligibility for enrollment, calculation and payment of the PI, conditions for disenrolling a household (fraud, failure to cooperate with interviewers, failure to permit the meter to be read, delinquency in payment), and continued eligibility when someone moves into or out of the house, the household changes residence, or in case of marriage, divorce, death, and so forth. These matters do not arise often, nor, taken as individual examples, are they very important, but failure to determine and adhere to such rules invites attrition of households, unexpected (and uncontrolled) experimental effects, and possible public backlash that can threaten the study.

Conclusion

The Los Angeles rate study has been designed to provide analysts with a data base on individual household responses to peak load tariffs. Given the dearth of information, it is important that the data base generated be sufficiently robust to answer a wide range of questions with some precision. In order to ensure that this level of quality is achieved we have used demand curves rather than ANOVA models; assumed that the functional form of the household response can be quite complex; selected price and policy options that bracket any reasonably likely prospects for electricity supply;

[22]In fact, the survey lore is replete with detailed stories about studies that have been attempted with nonprofessional interviewers and the disastrous results.

and provided tests for the existence and magnitude of experimental biases. We have relied on a recently developed, powerful statistical design method, the Allocation Model, to select those tariffs which minimize the variance of the answers to the policy questions of peak load pricing. A related algorithm, the Finite Selection Model, guarantees that the subsample on each tariff is similar to those on other tariffs and permits certain precision gains.

The design we have selected should yield estimates of consumer demand functions and responses to policy relevant tariffs of considerable statistical significance. Experience with the Allocation Model indicates that particular parameters on price and other variables of interest will be estimated with a variance generally less than 10 percent of the standard error of the equation. Furthermore, the variance with respect to particular policy questions will typically be less than 5 percent of the standard error.

We may ask what the generality of the results is likely to be. Will the findings be transferable to other situations? We believe there is considerable reason for optimism. Within the DWP system, the study should be useful in system planning and tariff design for a number of years. The high degree of statistical significance as well as the considerable range of tariff values studied should produce results that will guide major tariff revisions as well as the fine tuning of any peak load tariff that might be adopted.

The results of the study should be equally useful for analysis in other utility systems. This is especially true of utilities serving customers with a summer peaking load and a significant amount of air conditioning in place. Some elements of the study will even be useful to systems serving a fundamentally different type of residential demand, for example, a winter peaking system with significant electric space or water heating. This is true for two reasons. First, although electric space and water heating is not very common within the DWP at the present time, we are deliberately including a disproportionate number of such customers in the study. Second, the study will produce results on changes in habits in response to peak load tariffs for some uses of energy that are fundamentally the same regardless of locale. For example, if we measure customer responsiveness in the timing or amount of electricity used for lighting, clothes washing and drying, and small electrical appliances, that type of behavioral adjustment may be expected to be reasonably independent of climate and utility characteristics.

In conclusion, the general analytic design and expected statistical significance of the parameter estimates will produce results that hold promise of considerable analytic and policy interest.

References

Bailey, Elizabeth E. 1973. *Economic Theory of Regulatory Constraint.* Lexington, Mass.: D.C. Heath.

Besen, Stanley, and Bridger M. Mitchell. 1975. "On Measuring the Gain in Economic Welfare from Marginal Cost Pricing when a Related Market Is of Importance: The Case of Electricity and Natural Gas." P-5755. Santa Monica: The Rand Corporation.

Boggis, James G. 1975. "Some Practical Aspects of the British Experiment with Electricity Pricing." In C. J. Cicchetti and W. K. Foell, eds., *Energy Systems Forecasting, Planning and Prices.* Pp. 375–81. Madison: University of Wisconsin Press.

Conlisk, John, and Harold Watts. 1969. "A Model for Optimizing Experimental Design for Estimating Response Surfaces." In *Proceedings of the Social Sciences Section.* Pp. 150–56. New York: American Statistical Association.

Electricity Council of London. No date. *Domestic Tariffs Experiment.* Load and Market Research Report No. 121. London: the Council.

Harberger, Arnold. 1971. "Three Basic Postulates for Applied Welfare Economics: An Interpretive Essay." *Journal of Economic Literature* 9 (September): 785–97.

Hirshleifer, Jack. 1958. "Peak Loads and Efficient Pricing: Comment." *Quarterly Journal of Economics* 72 (August): 451–62.

MacAvoy, Paul W., and Robert S. Pindyck. 1973. "Alternative Regulatory Policies for Dealing with the Natural Gas Shortage." *Bell Journal of Economics and Management Science* 4 (Autumn): 454–98.

Manning, Willard G., Jr., Bridger M. Mitchell, and Jan Paul Acton. 1976. "Design of the Los Angeles Peak-Load Pricing Experiment for Electricity." R-1955-DWP. Santa Monica: The Rand Corporation.

Mitchell, Bridger M., Willard G. Manning, and Jan Paul Acton. 1977. "Electricity Pricing and Load Management: Foreign Experience and California Opportunities." R-2106-CERCDC. Santa Monica: The Rand Corporation.

Morris, Carl. 1975. "A Finite Selection Model for Experimental Design of the Health Insurance Study." In *Proceedings of the Social Sciences Section.* Pp. 78–85. New York: American Statistical Association.

Mowill, Ragnhild S. 1976. "Recent Research on Residential Consumption of Electricity." P-5703. Santa Monica: The Rand Corporation, August.

Nelson, James R., ed. 1964. *Marginal Cost Pricing in Practice.* Englewood Cliffs, N.J.: Prentice-Hall.

Panzar, John C. 1976. "A Neoclassical Approach to Peak-Load Pricing." *Bell Journal of Economics and Management Science* 7 (Autumn): 521–30.

Steiner, Peter O. 1957. "Peak Loads and Efficient Pricing." *Quarterly Journal of Economics* 71 (November): 585–610.

Turvey, Ralph. 1968. *Optimal Pricing and Investment in Electricity Supply*. Cambridge, Mass.: MIT Press.

Williamson, Oliver. 1966. "Peak Load Pricing and Optimal Capacity under Indivisibility Constraints." *American Economic Review* 56 (September): 810–27.

Time-of-Day Pricing: An Empirical Study

Larry L. Kehler

Peak load pricing of electricity has been of substantial interest to economists, utility executives, regulators, and consultants in the last few years. All of these interested parties support some "action," usually with a particular bias as to the feasibility of implementing such a rate form.

The Federal Energy Administration (FEA) has funded load management demonstration projects in several states over the last two years to test applications of experimental rate structures. These studies have served as a catalyst to experimental application of peak load pricing across the country. However, considerable controversy has developed as to design integrity, adequacy of sample sizes, validity of analytical methodology, and, most important, applicability of projecting results to existing operating utility systems.

This essay will not attempt to resolve or address these points of controversy, but simply will report the preliminary results and implications of one peak load pricing experiment of limited scope conducted in the state of Arkansas.

Background

The Arkansas Public Service Commission staff proposed to the FEA that a peak load pricing study be conducted in response to the expressed interest of consumer intervenors in Arkansas Power and Light rate proceedings in 1974. The commission and representatives of the utility jointly expressed the need for empirical data on the economic impact of any change in rate structure before it could be seriously considered for systemwide implementation in Arkansas.

The proposed study was to provide the following information: (1) empirical operating data which would show customer reaction to three cost based, time differentiated rate form alternatives in contrast to the current rate form; (2) data which would be representative of the total Arkansas Power and Light service area (residential, commercial, and industrial); and (3) an analysis of the impact of what might occur if the results of the experiment were implemented system-wide. This analysis would require an estimation of the impact of the new tariffs on each class of customers, as well as average customers within each class.

The key criterion for accomplishing these objectives was the development of practical, realistic rate alternatives which could be tested to determine the reaction of a unique and well-defined customer group within the state. The study was not designed to collect sufficient data to determine price elasticity curves or to gain behavior data which would have application outside Arkansas.

Design

The major design criterion for the study was to simulate the actions of the utility as if the test rates were being implemented systemwide. The first major design constraint was to rule out the use of voluntary participants. The experimental rates would be ordered into effect under state regulatory laws.

In response to the legal questions raised by implementation of mandatory experimental rates, a discriminatory precedent in geographically based telephone rates was cited. This precedent dictated that the experimental rates be tested in selected geographical areas in the state. After an analysis of the Arkansas Power and Light system, cities of 1,000 to 2,500 residential service units were found to provide sufficient diversity in kwh consumption history and demographic factors to represent the composite service area of the total utility system.

The methodology used for residential site selection was to evaluate the kwh consumption patterns and demographic factors of each site in terms of similarity to the composite data for the total system area. For commercial site selection, only kwh and kw billing history were used. The cities which most closely resemble the average Arkansas Power and Light residential customer group were Hamburg, Fordyce, and Wynne. However, final site selection required consideration of both the residential and commercial evaluations, for the residential experimental and commercial control groups must be in the same city, as must the commercial experimental and residential control groups. Hamburg and Wynne thus became the first and second choices, respectively, and were the primary sites for the combined residential and commercial analysis. Two additional sites were required for the commercial analysis only, and the towns of Beebe and Dumas were chosen for this purpose. The experimental conditions and site assignments are presented in Exhibit 1.

EXHIBIT 1

Hamburg	Wynne
Residential	*Residential*
Time-of-day	Time-of-day
Seasonal #1	Control
Seasonal #2	Regular control
	Blind control
Commercial	*Commercial*
Control	Seasonal #2
Beebe	Dumas
Commercial	*Commercial*
Time-of-day	Seasonal #1

In Hamburg, the primary residential experimental city, all residents were assigned either time-of-day, seasonal #1, or seasonal #2 test rates. In Wynne, the residential control city, three control groups were assigned: time of day, regular control, and blind control.

For the commercial sites, only one test rate was used at each site to minimize the constraints of trade difficulties that could arise in the commercial sector. Beebe became the time-of-day test site, Dumas the seasonal #1 site, and Wynne the seasonal #2 site. Hamburg served as the commercial control site.

The participants in each city were selected to represent the total system population through the use of sample optimization techniques. The historical consumption for system customers was grouped into 10 kwh use bands or strata, and the minimum sample size for each stratum was determined such that the sample could estimate the system consumption with ± 5 percent precision and 95 percent reliability. To ensure that the sample sizes would remain statistically valid during the course of the experiment, the optimal sample size of each stratum was increased five times where possible. This redundancy in sample design provided backup for lost participants due to moves, deaths, or other circumstances. The individual experimental customers were chosen from each stratum by random computer selection to maximize individual monthly consumption diversity.

Because of the concern for realism in implementation of the test rates, no participant interviews were conducted before or during the study. This meant that data on participants' applicance stock, necessary for sampling diversity, was lacking. Therefore, a special computer routine was incorporated into the sample analysis to select the maximum seasonal consumption diversity from each stratum of each city. It was felt that substituting seasonal consumption diversity for appliance diversity would provide the maximum range of diversity, while the technique also would eliminate the possibility of influencing participants through interview biasing.

A listing of each sample group and the respective number of participants is presented in Exhibit 2. Time-of-day rate participants all utilized magnetic tape meters for data and billing purposes, while seasonal and control group subsamples were selected to utilize these tape units for data collection only.

Rate Development

The study rate design was developed by Mr. David Johnson, at that time Chief Rate Analyst for the Arkansas Public Service Commission,[1] Mr. Ralph Teed, Manager of Rates, Arkansas Power and Light, and Dr. Robert Spann, an economist under subcontract to Touche Ross & Company for the study.

The primary tariff areas which the commission desired to test were: (1) increased summer-winter differentials, (2) increased tail block energy tariffs, and (3) time-of-day tariffs.

The rates were based on long-run incremental cost estimates made by Arkansas Power and Light of its operating system.

The "on peak" period was determined after extensive evaluation

[1]Mr. Johnson is now with Arkansas Louisiana Gas Company.

EXHIBIT 2

Sample Size and Location by Rate Type

	RESIDENTIAL	
Hamburg		
Time-of-Day	101 customers	101 tape meters
Seasonal #1	120 customers	41 tape meters
Seasonal #2	818 customers	41 tape meters
Wynne		
Time-of-day control	129 customers	129 tape meters
Regular control	115 customers	0 tape meters
Blind control	121 customers	0 tape meters
	COMMERCIAL	
Beebe		
Time-of-day	160 customers	160 tape meters
Dumas		
Seasonal #1	225 customers	23 tape meters
Wynne		
Seasonal #2	357 customers	25 tape meters
Hamburg		
Control	193 customers	22 tape meters

of the utility's historical load curve and was defined to include periods when there was a likelihood of operating at or near 90 percent of system peak. For pricing purposes, the study team chose 11 A.M. to 7 P.M. from 15 May through 15 October as the peak period. Winter demands, even at the time of greatest winter usage, are generally less than summer demands during the off-peak summer hours. Thus, the entire winter period was assumed to be off peak.

The long-run incremental cost estimates were translated into time period rates by application of appropriate time costs. Residential time-of-day rates were developed by estimating long-run incremental costs during the peak period as incremental energy costs plus the incremental cost of new capital facilities (such as production, transmission, and distribution plant) on an annualized basis, divided by the number of kilowatt-hours during the on peak period. For all other periods, long-run incremental costs were basically the incremental costs of energy, since these would be times during which idle system capacity is available. The long-run incremental cost estimates were then applied to system sales and adjusted to a set of rates so that the total revenues raised from the residential class under the experimental time-of-day rates would be approximately the same as the total revenues raised from the rates in force at the time the experimental rates were designed, assuming that participant usage remained constant.

A second residential rate was designed as a seasonal rate with no time-of-day differential. This rate allocated all incremental capital costs to the summer period and led to a summer-winter price differential of approximately three to one.

The third residential rate developed was a seasonal one in which production and transmission plant costs were allocated to the summer peak period, but distribution costs were spread over the entire year. This rate led to a winter-summer price differential of approximately two to one. In both seasonal cases, the revenues generated were approximately the same as those that would be generated under present rates from the residential class, assuming no participant changed his usage.

Three similar commercial rates were developed. The basic difference between these and the residential rates was an explicit demand charge. In the time-of-day commercial rate this charge was included based on long-run incremental distribution costs in order to take account of the fact that some amount of distribution plant is related to the customer's own peak demand. The energy rate during the on peak period was set equal to marginal energy costs during that period plus the cost of production and transmission facilities divided by the number of kilowatt-hours used in that period. The energy rates during all other periods were set equal to long-run incremental energy cost. The total revenues derived by these rates were estimated, and the rates then were adjusted downward in order to yield the same revenues that would be raised under existing commercial schedules, assuming participant usage remained unchanged.

There were two sets of seasonal commercial rates. The first was developed by assigning all incremental demand costs to the summer period with the exception of incremental distribution costs; these were applied to demand charges in both summer and winter periods. The energy charges were set at incremental energy cost averaged respectively over the summer and the winter periods. This led to a seasonal differential in demand charges of approximately three to one and a seasonal differential in energy charges of approximately 1.5 to one. In order to compare an alternative form of cost based seasonal pricing and rate flattening, a second commercial rate was developed which had a seasonal differential in energy charges equal to three to one and a seasonal differential in demand charges equal to 1.5 to one. The six rates tested in the study are presented in Exhibit 3.

Participant Communication

The Arkansas study was deeply concerned with participant reaction, not only in economic terms but also in terms of changed attitudes concerning energy use.

Because of the relatively small sample size, the attention given these "select" customers could influence their reaction to the test rates differently than if the rates were implemented systemwide. To minimize the possibility of such a "Hawthorne effect," all communications to participants were controlled. No direct individual contact was initiated, and only direct mailings or group meetings were used.

EXHIBIT 3

Experimental Rate Schedule

Residential customer class	*SUMMER**	*WINTER*
Time-of-day:	$3.00 customer charge 8.34¢ per kwh 11 A.M. to 7 P.M. 1.39¢ per kwh all other hours	$3.00 customer charge 1.24¢ per kwh 11 A.M. to 7 P.M. 1.17¢ per kwh all other hours
Seasonal # 1	$3.00 customer charge 4.14¢ per kwh	$3.00 customer charge 1.17¢ per kwh
Seasonal #2	$3.00 customer charge 3.53¢ per kwh	$3.00 customer charge 1.79¢ per kwh

Commercial customer class	*SUMMER**	*WINTER*
Time-of-day	$3.00 customer charge $1.95 max. kw demand 6.65¢ per kwh 11 A.M. to 7 P.M. 1.84¢ per kwh all other hours	$3.00 customer charge $1.95 max. kw demand 1.63¢ per kwh 11 A.M. to 7 P.M. 1.55¢ per kwh all other hours
Seasonal #1	$3.00 customer charge $6.18 max. kw demand 2.18¢ per kwh	$3.00 customer charge $2.03 max. kw demand 1.58¢ per kwh
Seasonal #2	$3.00 customer charge $4.65 max. kw demand 2.88¢ per kwh	$3.00 customer charge $2.96 max. kw demand 1.05¢ per kwh

*Summer is the billing months June through October.

The first communication to participants was a notice of the hearing that would be conducted before implementation of the rates. Notices were also placed in the newspapers of each sample city.

Approximately one week to ten days before the hearing a communication team visited each city and made a presentation to influential leaders outlining the study. The team described the design and history of the study and discussed typical bills that could be expected under the different rate conditions. The general reception was somewhat hostile, due to publicity about general rate hearings and the increased price of electricity. Participants wanted to know why they had been chosen from among the 29 possible sites to receive this special treatment.

The second communication to participants was an Oregon energy calendar, a document that suggests many very general energy saving techniques for all types of energy. An accompanying letter asked individuals to read the calendar and suggested that they record their electrical consumption in the space provided each month on the calendar.

The last document sent to each participant was a booklet prepared by the study team. This publication was a major undertaking and described to each participant his particular rate structure and suggested different energy conservation techniques which he could utilize if he so desired. For time-of-day customers this was a relatively easy document to prepare, but for the seasonal customer it was very difficult to recommend methods of conserving energy in one season and increasing use in the off season.

Follow-up meetings were conducted in the test cities, some at the participants' request.

Preliminary Results

The data have been evaluated for December 1975 to May 1976, which falls in the off-peak period. After conducting a complete covariance analysis, no significant differences could be found between any of the sample groups. No great shifts could be expected so early in the learning curve. Data for the summer peak period, June through October, are currently under analysis, and the results of the peak pricing period should be available soon.

Other results which are of interest and which affect the feasibility of time-of-day pricing include metering difficulties and customer reaction.

The magnetic tape meters utilized in the Arkansas study are of a popular design used for load research. To shorten delivery time, meters were purchased from three different manufacturers. During the summer, failure rates approached 30 percent in some meter groups. These failures were due to foreign substance build-up on electrical contacts and were not limited to any specific manufacturer.

It is very unlikely that magnetic tape meters would ever be utilized during large-scale implementation of time-of-day pricing; therefore, the specific difficulty experienced in Arkansas is not a significant factor. What is important is that time-of-day pricing requires nonstandard metering technology, and the likelihood of problems arising from a changeover must be considered in the feasibility analysis of time-of-day rate forms.

Customer reaction to the study has been vocal in many instances and suspiciously quiet in others. After the first orientation meeting in each city, most participants seemed to adopt a wait-and-see attitude. At two sites legal petitions were collected to halt the study, but there was insufficient support. The most negative reaction comes from the high kwh consumer, who, because of the flattened tail blocks, is paying substantially greater year-round energy costs.

It is apparent from questions asked by study participants that there is continued misunderstanding about the details of how the rates apply. In a recent meeting in the commercial site, Wynne, attended by approximately 50 percent of the local participants, only two individuals indicated an understanding of how the peak demand charge was determined. A large number of people were also certain the test rates applied to residential rates in their city and could not be convinced that the increase in bills was due to fuel adjustments under the current rates.

This behavior is not unusual, as any utility billing desk clerk would testify. However, it is a serious matter when the planned effort to educate and communicate with the experimental group appears to have failed so badly. A basic understanding of energy utilization on the part of the user is essential before the total load management impact of new rate forms can be measured.

Conclusion

The economic impact on the Arkansas Power and Light operating system in implementing any of the test rates remains to be determined. The design and methodology of the study outlined here offer an adequate estimate of the load and revenue impact of the test rates, but the study data do not permit an evaluation of the education costs required to influence consumption patterns.

Stated another way, the emphasis of the Arkansas and other studies has been on the production aspect of time differentiated pricing. Will the increased load factor justify the increased metering and billing cost? Will the flattened peak demand delay capital investment? These questions are basic and necessary to the issue of new rate forms, but the experience in Arkansas indicates that the marketing and consumer education aspects of the issue are equally important. If the average consumer, residential or commercial, does not comprehend the alternatives in time differentiated rate schemes, the potential benefits of such plans are lost in the frustration of higher utility bills. On the other hand, the educational costs required to enable consumers to comprehend and benefit from better load management may be very substantial.

The major observation to date in the Arkansas study is the realization of how difficult it is to educate consumers about efficient use of electrical energy. Any future evaluation of the feasibility of time differentiated rates should consider the implementation cost of consumer education as a key element of that analysis.

Ratemaking Objectives and Rate Design Options

Robert G. Uhler

There were four major reactions to the increase in electric rates that followed the escalation of oil prices in late 1973.[1] These were: (1) state regulatory commissions' generic rate design hearings that highlighted peak load pricing and marginal costing; (2) Federal Energy Administration (FEA) load management demonstration projects and FEA intervention in state regulatory proceedings; (3) state and federal legislative efforts that focused on time-of-use rates and lifeline proposals; and (4) the nationwide Electric Power Research Institute (EPRI) rate design study to examine peak load pricing and other aspects of load management.

Generally, all four activities have raised much the same rate

[1]For utility customers, the Arab oil embargo in particular and the energy crisis in general was felt through higher electric prices. Based on National averages, residential annual usage of electricity increased from 7,066 kilowatt-hours (kwh) in 1970 to 7,691 kwh in 1972, a 9 percent increase. The average annual bill increased only $27.73, a 19 percent increase over the two years. Between 1973 and 1975, usage grew by only one percent, while the electric bill jumped 36 percent. On some systems and for particular customers, price increases were even more dramatic.

For utilities, increased fuel costs were reflected in higher revenues and higher operating costs. Between 1973 and 1974, the operating revenues of investor owned electric utilities increased 27 percent. Operating expenses, however, jumped 45 percent. Interest charges went up 27 percent, while income after dividends fell 7 percent. Customers were paying $15 billion more in 1975 than they did two years earlier for about the same amount of electricity — 1.7 trillion kwh. Consumers and investors perceived the problem of higher costs from two polar perspectives — higher electric bills and lower dividends. Regulators and utility executives were caught in a crossfire. Politicians ducked and maneuvered.

design and load management issues. Figure 1 illustrates some of the questions being investigated in the EPRI rate design study.

The diagram, of course, is an oversimplification, but it does contrast the rate design and load management options available to utility executives and regulators. The first major choice is the conceptual basis for *costing*. This has been popularized as the average versus marginal cost controversy, with the "traditionalists" favoring average or fully distributed costs (FDC), while the "economists" prefer marginal or long-run incremental costs (LRIC).

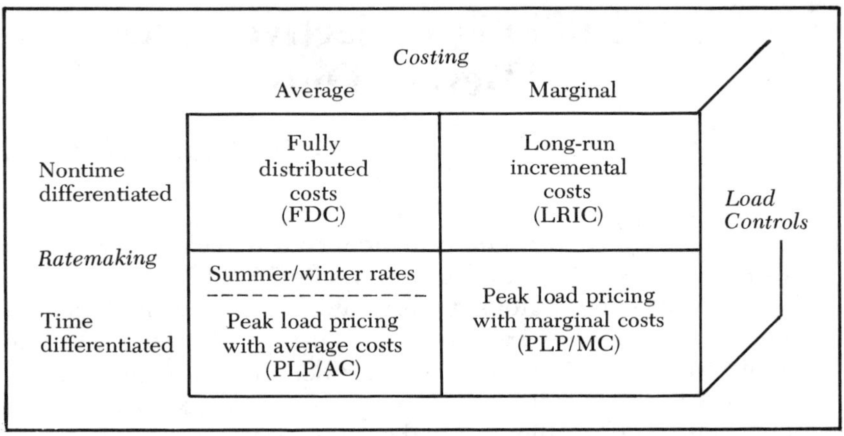

Figure 1. ***Rate Research Matrix***

On the *ratemaking* axis, as shown in Figure 1, the second major choice — a time-of-use differentiation — is under scrutiny. Here, for example, a summer/winter differential could be accommodated with present rate forms and existing meters. While such rates have been implemented by a number of utility systems with pronounced seasonal peaks, a more difficult question involves the diurnal differentiation of rates (that is, peak load pricing). This would require a more sophisticated and more expensive metering configuration. Combining the costing alternatives with the time-of-use ratemaking choice generates the four broad options shown in the drawing. Other rate design refinements, such as a demand charge, would be possible but are not depicted.

LRIC, an early costing proposal of the marginalist school, was examined at great length in Wisconsin. More recently, an approach that adds a time-of-use dimension has surfaced as long-run marginal cost or LRMC. This version of peak load pricing (PLP/MC) captures the marginal cost concept as well as the notion of time varying costs. It is also possible to design time differentiated rates based on average costs (PLP/AC).

Continuing to simplify, the quality of electric service provided utility customers also represents a choice. This third axis or dimension is shown in the rate research matrix in Figure 1 as "load controls." Customers, for example, might permit installation of a radio or ripple switch on their heating or cooling appliances, particularly if the equipment has some energy storage capability. The direct control of the switches would be vested with the utility so that specific loads could be centrally managed during peak periods. In practical terms, this changes the quality of service rendered to the customer and should be coupled with a price incentive that represents the cost savings realized by the utility. Other load management options, such as interruptible rates, red lights during peak periods, or similar schemes are possible.

Given this three-dimensional representation of choices in Figure 1, it is possible to discuss the consequences of each in practical terms. Moving from left to right, for example, raises the revenue constraint issue as well as a problem economists call "second best." Similarly, moving downward might create needle peaks on some systems, with the associated phenomena of revenue erosion and lower load factors. In addition, singling out a particular set of customers for either marginal costing or peak load pricing poses the legal question of "undue" discrimination. Finally, the imposition of load control devices might be contrary to the mandate to serve that underlies utility operations in many states.

Other important issues are not so easily portrayed. Many regulators, for example, hold that the provision of electric service should be reliable but at the "least" cost attainable. This, in itself, requires a difficult trade-off between quality of service, generally described as a level of reliability, and cost. Moreover, for regulated utilities, a public service commission must perform an additional balancing act. This involves the determination of a rate of return on investment sufficient to ensure the continued financial integrity of the company, but one that does not overburden the utility's customers with excessively high electric bills. These two issues are not illustrated but are of major concern to regulators.

Ratemaking Objectives

Regulators generally have relied on historical costs to set rates and to determine revenue requirements for pragmatic reasons, particularly the reasonableness of the results. Similarly, utility executives seeking stability of both rates and revenues have avoided tinkering with ratemaking. Such considerations have influenced the evolution of existing costing methodologies and rate forms and will not be quietly overturned. They are being questioned, and in some states new costing ideas and rate design concepts have been mandated. For example, some commissioners seeking an efficient allocation of resources prefer marginal costing as the basis for ratemaking to obtain better price signals. Thus, the multidimensional choices of electric utility ratemaking pose challenges and provide opportunities for both utility executives and regulators.

The selection of a particular ratemaking procedure, of course, is coupled intimately with the objectives of the regulator or the utility executive. Realizing the allowed level of revenues over several years, for example, is a major concern of company officials, while income redistribution or conservation might be of great importance to some regulators. A second simplified diagram illustrates the relationships among a few ratemaking objectives and three rate design options. An economist might assess the various trade-offs as indicated in Figure 2.

Traditional nontime differentiated rates may underprice peak period service, which in turn might contribute to inefficiencies in system operations and expansion. Furthermore, such growth might result in higher costs and the need for repeated rate increases. Time differentiated rates based on *marginal* costs, however, might signal the higher costs associated with an expansion of peak demand. They may also produce "excess" revenues, which would necessitate use of an adjustment process, such as the "inverse elasticity rule." This might provoke cries of unfairness. On the other hand, peak load pricing based on *average* costs might be a practical compromise in some cases. And, although the rate design study is examining such questions, it is *not* evaluating the objectives of ratemaking. The emphasis of the study is on means, not ends — rate design options, not ratemaking objectives.

There is a consensus that "something" could be accomplished with changes in rate design and the adoption of load management. This follows because higher electric rates are unpopular, and the growth in peak demand seems to aggravate the problem. There is general support for the idea that, in some cases, time differentiated rates could slow the growth of peak demand or could shift loads to off peak periods, and this would be beneficial to both a utility and its

Ratemaking Objectives	*Rate Design Options* Traditional (FDC)	Time differentiated (PLP/AC)	(PLP/MC)
Revenue requirement	✓	✓	?
Fair apportionment of cost burden	?	✓ ?	✓
Economic efficiency/ conservation	?	✓ ?	✓
Income redistribution	✓	✓	✓

Figure 2. ***Ratemaking Objectives and Rate Design Options***

customers. There is disagreement, however, about exactly which rate design changes should be adopted, precisely what form load management innovations should take, and, specifically, on which systems such modifications would be cost effective.

Attempts to do "something" have varied considerably. One legislative suggestion, for example, would have state commissions insist that utilities set rates based on marginal costs, including differences in cost incurrence attributable to daily and seasonal time of use. Similarly, one FEA spokesman urged the immediate implementation of time-of-day pricing based on marginal costs for customers where the cost of metering would be trivial. This advocate claimed that even for residential customers the benefits of time-of-day pricing would outweigh the added implementation costs. However, at least one regulatory commission believes that the impact of rate design changes should be determined experimentally before such rates are implemented across the board.

Much of the rate design debate centers on the marginal cost controversy rather than on peak load pricing. For example, in a minority opinion, two California commissioners called a recent decision a radical departure from reasonable rate setting practices. They complained that the majority opinion floated into the heavens of theoretical economics and charged that the record did not support such a drastic departure from traditional practices. The majority argued that conservation, that is, an efficient allocation of electricity, should be the keystone for rate structures. The minority criticized the majority for unfurling the fashionable banner of conservation. Furthermore, the dissenters denounced marginal costing as cloudy and branded the inverse elasticity rule as arbitrary — a flawed concept for rate setting where "whim is king."

Earlier, the Wisconsin Commission had found that marginal costing was an appropriate guide for designing rates but had decided that the inverse elasticity rule for adjusting revenues was not satisfactory. In addition, the Wisconsin regulators had accepted time differentiated rates as desirable. However, one dissenting commissioner said that some of the expert witnesses were like mountain goats who leaped and gamboled in the "upper atmosphere of theoretical economics." In Michigan and West Virginia, marginal costing was rejected, while in New York the concept was endorsed.[2]

Unlike some of the reactions to higher electric utility prices, the rate design study is structured as a formal research program but is responsive to practical needs. The study is aimed at examining *how* to proceed with time related rates. By contrast, others, such as the FEA, are convinced that the implementation of peak load pricing and load management should begin now. The FEA does acknowledge that the transition from present rate structures to new rate designs requires attention and that the specific cost basis for ratemaking is debatable. The nationwide rate design study is providing this close look at implementation and a careful examination of the costing controversy.

The magnitude of the recent increases in electric utility rates

---

[2]The Public Service Commission of New York concluded that "marginal costs do providė a reasonable basis for electric rate structures." Earlier, the NYPSC had ordered the companies to prepare time-of-day rates based on either incremental or embedded costs (7 January 1976). Thus, New York has moved forcefully in its *Opinion No. 76-15* (10 August 1976) to require peak load pricing based on marginal cost studies.

underlies the four responses noted earlier and underscores the need for the million dollar rate design study. While it is probably correct that some "rate reform" is necessary, the specifics are arguable. Time-of-day pricing for some customers might make sense under certain circumstances, but not all. The trick, of course, is to design rates that help consumers, that is, the realized benefits of rate reform should exceed the costs that are incurred. And this must be determined by each utility and each commission, given their particular set of circumstances and ratemaking objectives.

To facilitate this process, the rate design study is examining load management by pricing as well as by various direct control methods. Although the peak load pricing rate design option occupies center stage, the participants of the study are approaching quite broadly the problem of serving cyclical loads. A progress report follows.

Background of Rate Design Study

In late 1974 the National Association of Regulatory Utility Commissioners (NARUC) asked the Electric Power Research Institute (EPRI) and the Edison Electric Institute (EEI) to study the technology and cost of time-of-day pricing. The resulting joint effort, the Electric Utility Rate Design Study, has been under way for about a year in the field. It is examining various methods of controlling the peak period uses of electricity and the feasibility of shifting loads from peak to off peak periods.

A *Plan of Study,* prepared by representatives of EEI and EPRI, focuses on the control and management of peaks, as well as on the possibility of lessening electric system peak demand growth. Moreover, the plan underlines the economic role of pricing in managing load growth and calls specifically for a careful evaluation of peak load pricing. The research is being done by several consultants and ten task forces.

The study is also examining peak load pricing based on alternative costing methodologies, namely, average and marginal costs. Specifically, the plan provides for an appraisal of marginal costing for ratemaking within the limit of aggregate revenue requirements as determined by conventional methods. Finally, the *Plan of Study* affirms the concept of basing rates on the cost to the utility of providing service within the regulatory "just and reasonable" standard.

The study of peak load pricing for NARUC was divided into ten research topics:

1. Peak load pricing
2. Elasticity of demand
3. Rate design–load management experiments
4. Costing for peak load pricing
5. Rate design
6. Cost benefit analyses of load management
7. Metering
8. Equipment for using off peak energy
9. Load controls and penalty pricing
10. Customer acceptance of load management

The Research Team

In brief, over 150 men and women are organized into three committees and ten task forces (one for each research topic). In addition to EEI, EPRI, and NARUC, others, such as the American Public Power Association, the National Rural Electric Cooperative Association, and several governmental agencies, are participating to achieve a diversity of institutional perspectives and to take advantage of related research activities conducted by these groups.

The task forces have submitted reports on their portions of the research (the consultants' work complements these efforts). Their preliminary findings are discussed in the next section.

The eleven participating consultants, their respective research areas, and the level of funding are indicated below.

Consultant	*Topics*	*Level of Effort*
Temple, Barker, & Sloane	Overview	$103,000
National Economic Research Associates, Inc.	1-5	276,000
Ebasco Services, Inc.	1, 4, and 5	150,000
Elrick & Lavidge, Inc.	10	70,000
Arthur D. Little, Inc.	7, 8, and 9	65,000
J. W. Wilson & Associates, Inc.	2	25,000
Power Technologies, Inc.	6	35,000
Systems Control, Inc.	6	35,000
Gordian Associates Inc.	6	35,000
Energy Utilization Systems, Inc.	6	11,000
J. Daniel Khazzom	—	12,000
		$817,000

Although a considerable amount of the consulting work has been completed, the preparation and review of final reports will extend to the end of 1976. Some of their findings are noted in the next section.

Progress of Research

Peak Load Pricing

Both Task Force 1 and NERA have completed a review of electric utility ratemaking in the United States. In particular, the task force has assembled rate histories from a score of utilities covering the years 1925–1975. NERA has concentrated on an historical overview of ratemaking practices in the United States, with particular emphasis on the interplay between regulatory objectives and rate design. NERA also is reviewing rate setting theory and practice in Great Britain and France.

Both NERA and EBASCO as well as the task force have prepared reports on the theoretical core of the rate design study, that is, developing methodologies for time-of-use pricing in the United States. In brief, NERA has set forth a framework for marginal cost based time differentiated rates, while EBASCO has suggested alternative approaches to peak load pricing based on several costing methodologies. These include average costing and marginal costing. The task force has outlined its thoughts on peak load pricing based on average costs.

Elasticity of Demand and Load Management Experiments

Task Force 2 has surveyed the studies of the elasticity of demand for electricity and has concluded that they shed little light on the likely response of customers to time-of-day rates. The task force notes the need for substantial experimentation to gather data and to develop methodologies for estimating elasticity at peak. NERA and J. W. Wilson have submitted reports on elasticity of demand. Task Force 3 has identified and is monitoring 40 different tests presently under way. From this work, the specification of further experimentation will be made. Such efforts will be necessary to reduce the uncertainty concerning customer response to peak load pricing and other forms of load management.

Costing for Peak Load Pricing and Rate Design

Seven utilities agreed to provide data for detailed work under these topics. EBASCO and NERA are working with these companies to develop and apply alternative costing methodologies for peak load pricing. The utilities and the consultants with whom they are working are the following:

Utility	*Consultants*
Carolina Power and Light Co.	EBASCO
Dayton Power and Light Co.	NERA
Minnesota Power and Light Co.	EBASCO
Omaha Public Power District	EBASCO
Portland General Electric Co.	EBASCO & NERA
Tennessee Valley Authority	NERA
Virginia Electric and Power Co.	EBASCO & NERA

Task Forces 4 and 5 have been working with the consultants and are providing a critical appraisal of their costing methodologies and ratemaking approaches. In addition, the ratemaking task force has prepared a report that describes its analysis of peak load pricing.

Cost-Benefit Analyses of Load Management

Four consultants, Task Force 6, and four participating utilities are working together to develop methodologies for assessing the costs and benefits of load shifting. Each consulting firm is perfecting its own approach within the context of one of the four companies, as shown below:

Utility	*Consultant*
Virginia Electric and Power Co.	Gordian Associates, Inc.
Northern States Power Co.	Power Technologies, Inc.
Southern California Edison Co.	Systems Control, Inc.
Buckeye Power, Inc., & South Central Power Company	Energy Utilization Systems, Inc.

Meters, Equipment, and Controls

Task Force 7 has completed an extensive survey of metering equipment. In addition, Arthur D. Little has analyzed alternative metering configurations. Little has also assessed equipment that could take advantage of peak load pricing and has appraised load control devices. Task Forces 8 and 9 have surveyed the literature and have assembled technical reports on the engineering aspects of shifting or controlling loads.

Customer Acceptance of Load Management

In connection with assessing customer attitudes toward electric utility rates and load management controls, Elrick and Lavidge has completed a nationwide market research survey of residential, commercial, and industrial users of electricity. E&L's report indicates an awareness of peak problems and an understanding of time-of-use pricing. In addition, Task Force 10 has evaluated the literature in this field.

Reports to NARUC

The *Plan of Study* specifies three reporting requirements: brief quarterly progress reports, an interim progress report, and a final report. Progress reports were sent to NARUC in March, June, and September 1976. The interim report, submitted to NARUC in October 1976, was to outline the major issues and indicate the progress of research. An updating at the NARUC annual meeting was planned for 16 November 1976.

A *Final Report* will integrate the findings on the various topics. It will include an assessment of the overall research results and will recommend directions the industry and its regulators might follow in rate design and load management. Moreover, it seems likely that a comprehensive experimental program will be necessary starting in 1977. The *Final Report* was planned for submission to NARUC in March 1977.

Conclusion

At this time several observations can be made: (1) the *Plan of Study* addresses the rate design and load management issues in a practical way; (2) the organization structure permits a diversity of views; (3) the funding is adequate for a one-year appraisal; (4) a comprehensive assessment of the issues and alternatives will be completed by March and will be included in the *Final Report* to NARUC with recommendations and conclusions; (5) recommendations for continued research efforts in 1977 on behalf of NARUC have been made; and (6) the information needed to make reliable estimates of the benefits from various rate design and load management options will require a considerable utility-specific data collection effort (for example, experiments to assess the price elasticity of demand of residential customers to time differentiated rates).

The marginalist challenge to existing ratemaking practices must be taken seriously on its conceptual merits as well as on its attractiveness from a practical standpoint. It is too early to tell whether the revenue adjustment process associated with marginal costing is reasonable and whether other technical problems of implementation (such as fuel adjustment clauses) can be overcome. Both marginal and average costing, however, should be tested against the same criteria.

The traditionalists will be hard pressed to defend the status quo — particularly nontime differentiated rates for certain classes of customers. Some analysts believe that the most valuable service — power delivered at the time of the system peak — is underpriced, with the result that generation mix and system expansion decisions may be uneconomic. Whether the benefits of improving price signals are greater than the possible implementation costs is the crux of the rate design question, and whether the benefits of controls outweigh their costs is the heart of the load management investigation.

The rate design study will provide empirical information and analytical methods for analyzing these questions and will make specific policy recommendations in early 1977. Research, of course, is a complement to judgment, not a substitute. In this regard, the rate design study will make a substantial contribution to the analytical capabilities of decision makers — both utility executives and regulatory commissioners.

Comment

David L. McNicol

I have no major criticisms of Frank Walter's paper. I will add some footnotes and elaborations to his argument,[1] but my purpose is to set lifeline rates in a broader context.

The textbooks say that public utility regulation should be a substitute for competition when competition itself is infeasible.[2] Lifeline rates have no place within this conception of regulation.[3] Instead, they must be understood as a social welfare measure.

I wish to focus on the use of government control over prices to provide benefits to specific groups, which is one aspect of lifeline rates. The discussion will be built around two contrasting sets of measures. The first of these originated in the 1930s: (1) Social Security; (2) unemployment insurance; and (3) aid to the blind, aid to the permanently and totally disabled, and other forms of categorical assistance. The second set of measures was adopted or seriously considered during the 1960s and 1970s: (1) Medicare; (2) food

[1]The issue is lifeline and fair share rates, and rejection of these measures does not require acceptance of all aspects of existing rate structures. I shall also *not* be concerned with the question of "government intervention, yes or no." Throughout these comments I assume that the government is responsible for: (1) conducting monetary and fiscal policy to promote full employment and stable prices; (2) providing public goods; (3) preserving competitive markets, especially via the antitrust laws; (4) regulating prices where competition is impossible; and (5) making such redistributions of income as society chooses via the political process. I shall be primarily concerned with the means of making redistributions.

[2]See, for example, James Bonbright, *Principles of Public Utility Rates* (New York: Columbia University Press, 1969), p. 10.

[3]Declining block rates would not be economically warranted if long-run average cost were constant or increasing. In that case, economic efficiency argues for charging

stamps; (3) reduced transit fares for those over 65; (4) free transit; and (5) gasoline rationing.

To the economist's eye, the distinction between these two lists is one of means. In political terms, the distinction is one of degree. While both assume a federal responsibility for social welfare measures, the expressed goals of the earlier programs differ from later ones. Social insurance was the idea behind the programs of the 1930s. Their purpose was to protect individuals from major economic disasters: prolonged unemployment, severe disability, poverty in old age. The programs of the 1960s and 1970s arise, instead, from the notion that everyone should have equal access to basic necessities. These two ideas — social insurance and equal access to necessities — are not only associated with different means but also have sharply different implications for the extent of federal responsibility for welfare measures. Consequently, questions about "how" tend to be bound up with disputes over "how much." It is that tangle which needs to be sorted out.

Government intervention in the economy did not begin with the New Deal, but the New Deal was associated with a major shift in views on the responsibilities of government. Before the Great Depression, the federal government acted to promote economic development and adopted measures, such as rate regulation, the antitrust laws, and child labor laws, for curbing what were described as abuses of competition. During the 1930s, a consensus developed that the federal government should, in addition, to some degree protect individuals from the effects of market forces.

Economists tend to assume that this goal primarily requires the federal government to conduct monetary and fiscal policy so as to maintain overall stability in employment and price levels (with unemployment insurance serving as a useful backstop).[4] This emphasis is understandable, if only because the pivotal fact of the Great Depression was massive, prolonged unemployment. But the under-

---

each group the marginal cost of the service provided. There is no argument, on grounds of economic efficiency, for inverted block rates. In particular, the appropriate degree of conservation would be indicated by marginal cost prices. It may also be worth noting that the econometric evidence suggests that the long-run average costs of electricity generation are decreasing or, perhaps for large systems, constant. See Malcolm Galatin, *Economies of Scale and Technological Change in Thermal Power Generation* (Amsterdam: North Holland Publishing Company, 1968), which provides references to the earlier literature.

[4]Monetary and fiscal policy does not require government control of particular markets. This is what is meant by statements to the effect that "Keynes saved capitalism."

lying principle — government responsibility to cushion the effects of economic forces — is much broader.

To some, the issue is the way in which economic activity is organized. Complaints, especially about price increases, often seem to embody the belief that markets exercise a power analogous to governmental power. Granted that premise, it seems a simple extension of democratic principles that individuals should have a right to be heard and that costs should be allocated "fairly." Markets do not grant due process, and it is perhaps for that reason that they have become increasingly unpopular. But if there is anything more unpopular than the market these days, it is government regulation, and the reason is much the same. Government regulation can, and does, have capricious effects on the lives and livelihoods of individuals. Therein lies a paradox.

Generations of economists have grown old and died explaining to distracted freshmen the virtues of the market, as opposed to government control, in the production and distribution of goods and services. But if the question is one of the "rules of the game," there is perhaps little to say in a nonpartisan vein.

The rules of the game may not, however, really be at issue. Low income families tend to spend a larger fraction of their incomes than do higher income families on housing, food, clothing, medical care, utilities, and transportation. Consequently, a rise in the prices of any of these goods tends to increase the degree of inequality in real income. I suspect that changes in the distribution of income, caused by price increases, are the problem.

It has been popular in recent years to suppose that we are entering an era of shortages, especially of energy, and declining real income. While I do not accept these premises, those who do are likely to believe that it is particularly important for society to ensure that "basic necessities" are "fairly" distributed.

Because this position has found concrete expression in some programs, it warrants consideration. A "fair" distribution of "necessities" would presumably be provided through such programs as gasoline rationing, food stamps, life linerates, rent control, and Medicare. But how would "fairness" be judged? While in many cases people agree that equality is required for equity, equality and equity (or justice or fairness) are not the same. It is possible, and I think common, that market controls undertaken in the name of equality produce situations that are regarded as inequitable.

Gasoline rationing provides a good example. If families were used as a basis for issuing ration coupons, those that included two or more commuters would suffer disproportionate hardships. This suggests issuing coupons to drivers, but, especially in central cities, there are many families with two or more licensed drivers who do relatively little driving. The arithmetic is such that issuing ration coupons on the basis of drivers would allocate "too much" gasoline to some and "too little" to others. Basing gas coupons on cars owned would favor families with two, three, or four cars and provide an incentive for individuals to acquire junkers to increase their gas ration. Gasoline rationing could not be conducted without some simple basis for distributing coupons, yet none of the practical alternatives would produce a clearly "fair" allocation of available supplies.

The roots of problems such as this lie in the notion of "basic necessities." It is intelligible to speak of the basic necessities of life: food, clothing, shelter, medical care. As a situation becomes life threatening, people are more likely to agree on what division of supplies is fair. But, in concept, the programs of the 1960s and 1970s extend beyond the poor; and the necessities in view are not those required to sustain life, but goods and services required for a middle class life in the United States in the latter part of the twentieth century. What are these necessities? It is all too often forgotten that "average" is a statistical abstraction that describes relatively few individuals accurately. Some people choose to marry, some do not; some couples choose to have children, some do not; some people prefer to live in the city, others prefer the country; some eat to live, others live to eat. Above very low income levels, the notion of necessities must yield to the fact of wide differences in preferences. There is, then, no basis for argument on what is "fair," and it is ultimately for this reason that government programs such as gasoline rationing will be regarded as inequitable.

The burden of these comments is that the notion of basic necessities involves endless difficulties that obscure the real issue, namely, the establishment and maintenance in the face of changing circumstances of what is determined by the political process to be the appropriate distribution of income.[5]

[5]Direct transfers can cushion the effects of economic forces. Social Security benefits, for example, were fairly rapidly adjusted to take account of inflation, and the benefit levels under a negative income tax could similarly be adjusted to account for price changes. A system of direct transfers could not, in practice, achieve a finely tuned distribution of income in the face of a changing situation, but neither could gasoline rationing, lifeline rates, and so forth.

The terms "income redistribution" and "income transfer" are not yet part of the American political vocabulary, but the ideas involved are familiar. There is a strand in American thought which holds it to be unconscionable that some should do much better than others because of the accident of birth or the misfortunes of life. A majority probably would not accept this language but would agree that no one should be permitted to fall below some minimal economic level. Both positions justify, within differing limits, government actions to redistribute income.

The two broad types of means for influencing the degree of economic inequality are illustrated by the lists given previously.[6] Medicare, food stamps, lifeline rates, and so forth, provide transfers in kind, that is, benefits are tied to the consumption of particular goods and services. The alternative is direct transfers. Social insurance programs fall into this category, and a negative income tax would provide a way of making direct transfers in an organized way. A transfer of any given size could be made by either type of means. Suppose, for example, that it is determined that $5,000 is required to purchase the basic necessities for a family of five. The minimum income under a negative income tax could be set at $5,000. There is, then, a real choice among means, *given the level of benefits to be provided.*

The distinction between transfers in kind and direct transfers is significant. First, the administrative costs of making direct transfers tend to be less than the cost of making transfers in kind, since the latter usually require detailed policing. Costs are further increased because, as Walters stresses, for each one dollar of benefits in kind provided to some group (such as low income residential users) it will usually be necessary to provide unintended benefits of, say, 25 cents to some other group (high income residential users).

A third and more subtle cost has to do with the value that recipients place on transfers in kind. Suppose, for example, that an individual is permitted to buy $100 in food stamps for $40 and that he then, as often happens, illegally sells the $100 in food stamps for $80. The individual is left with a net benefit *in cash* of $40. The fact that he freely chose to sell the food stamps is proof that he would rather have a net benefit of $40 *in cash* than $60 *in food stamps*. However, it costs taxpayers $60 to provide a benefit of $40. Taxpayers and the

[6]The measures of concern here are directed to reducing the degree of inequality in results. Another and somewhat less controversial category is measures designed to reduce inequality in opportunity.

recipient would both be better off if they split the difference and replaced food stamps with a direct transfer of $50. Even recipients who do not sell the $100 in food stamps would be as well off with a direct transfer of $60, and taxpayers would be better off to the extent that administrative costs are saved. The general point is this: It never costs donors more, and typically costs them less, to provide benefits of a given amount by direct transfers.

There is another problem with providing benefits via the manipulation of particular prices. Prices play the role of a signal. For example, a rise in the price of electricity provides a stimulus for better insulation of buildings. Similarly, higher gasoline prices would, over time, favor mass transit and lead to changes in residential and industrial locations that reduce commuting. Overriding such price changes locks parts of the economy into an uneconomic mold, which means that the total value of goods and services available is reduced.

Views on "how much" equality are matters of personal and social values. Facts can be useful in clarifying values, but values cannot be established as "true" or "correct," or rejected as "false" or "incorrect," on a factual basis. I note this familiar point because there is a basis, provided by the preceding comments, for agreement on *means*. Given that benefits of some amount are to be provided, direct transfers are superior to transfers in kind for two reasons: (1) It costs donors less to provide one dollar directly than to provide benefits in kind of one dollar; and (2) indirect transfers typically result in distortions that reduce the total value of goods and services available.

Lifeline rates provide an apt illustration of the themes that have run through this discussion. The idea of lifeline rates was triggered by the increase in electricity rates that followed from OPEC's quadrupling of the price of oil. From this perspective, lifeline rates appear to be a way of cushioning the effects of a sudden change in the economic situation. However, they are intended to be permanent, and in this respect they are, like food stamps and reduced transit fares, a way of transferring income. One of the major points of the preceding discussion is that the apparent distinction between cushioning the effects of market forces and redistributing income is bogus. The issue is the distribution of income.

I take no position here on what degree of economic equality is "fair" or "just." But, given that society chooses through the political process to modify the distribution of income that results from market forces, direct transfers are the appropriate means. On the theory that it is as well to be hung for a sheep as a lamb, the suggestion is: Replace the current plethora of government measures designed to alter the distribution of income with a single, comprehensive program along the lines of a negative income tax.

There is also a simpler less controversial point embodied in these comments. I have tried to persuade you that two issues are closely related: the trend toward more government regulation and problems of the distribution of income. These are, I think, two sides of the same coin. We do not have a consensus on either, and I do not think that they can be resolved separately.

Contributors

Jan Paul Acton Economist, The RAND Corporation. Dr. Acton received the B.A. degree from San Diego State College and the A.M. and Ph.D. degrees from Harvard University. He serves as Principal Investigator for the Electric Rate Study being conducted by the Los Angeles Department of Water and Power. His numerous publications in the energy utility field include "Electric Rate Structures in Project Independence," "Electricity Conservation Measures in the Commercial Sector: The Los Angeles Experience," "Conserving Electricity by Ordinance: A Statistical Analysis," "Selected Econometric Studies of the Demand for Electricity: Review and Discussion," and "Regulatory Rationing of Electricity under a Supply Curtailment." His works have appeared in a number of journals including the *Journal of Political Economy, Land Economics, Law and Contemporary Problems,* and numerous RAND monographs.

Stanley Bazant, Jr. Senior Engineer, New Mexico Public Service Commission. He received the B.S. degree from the University of Iowa and attended the John Marshall Law School. Mr. Bazant has served as South American Regional Manager and Bolivian Utility Operation Specialist with the Harza Engineering Company. His areas of responsibility with the New Mexico Public Service Commission include, among others, utility plant valuation, depreciation, rate base and rate of return, jurisdictional separation studies and reviews, service cost allocation, and rate design. He also testifies as an expert witness before the Commission. Before joining the staff of the Commission, Mr. Bazant was employed by the Commonwealth Edison Company.

Mario P. Bhering former President of Electrobrás (1967-75), the national electric utiltity holding company of Brazil, and now consultant to the Brazilian electric utilities. He graduated in Rio de Janeiro with a degree in civil engineering. Sr. Bhering participated in the founding of CEMIG, the electric utilities company of the state of Minas Gerais, and served successively as Commercial Director, Vice President, and President. He is a former president of CIER, a commission fostering the integration of electric utilities in South America, and currently heads the Brazilian delegation to that group. Since 1974 he has served at the invitation of the Brazilian government as a member of the Administrative Council of Itaipu Binacional. He also serves as Vice President of the Brazilian Delegation to the World Energy Conference. Sr. Bhering has represented Brazil at a number of world and Latin American energy conferences.

Joel B. Dirlam Professor of Economics, University of Rhode Island. He holds the Ph.D. degree from Yale University. He was visiting Professor of Economics, University of Paris I, 1970 - 1971, and Directeur, Centre d'Economie Industrielle, Universite d'Aix- Marseille II, Aix-en-Provence in 1973. Dr. Dirlam serves on the editorial advisory board of the *Antitrust Bulletin* and is a member of the Advisory Committee on Petroleum and Natural Gas, Federal Energy Administration. His publications include "Market Structure, Regulation, and Dynamic Change" (with Walter Adams), *An Introduction to the Yugoslav Economy* (with J. Plummer, 1973), and "The Process of Inflation in France" (1975).

William H. Fletcher Executive Vice President, Indiana Telephone Corporation and Public Telephone Corporation. Both of these companies have published some form of price-level adjusted financial statements for many years. Mr. Fletcher received the A.B. degree from DePauw University, the M.B.A. in accounting from Northwestern University, and the J.D. degree from Harvard University Law School. He serves as Executive Vice President of Peoples Loan & Trust Company of Wichester, Indiana, and is Financial Vice President and Treasurer of Liberty Fund, Inc. He has been engaged in the practice of public accounting, and for many years served as a partner in Arthur Anderson & Co., where he was engaged in auditing, accounting, and tax matters.

Myron J. Gordon Professor of Finance and Political Economy, Faculty of Management Studies, University of Toronto. He received the B.A. degree from the University of Wisconsin and the M.A. and Ph.D. degrees from Harvard University. He has served as consultant to the U.S. Federal Communications Commission, the U.S. Department of Justice, and the Canadian Prices and Incomes Commission. Within the American Accounting Association, he was a member of its Committee on Accounting Theory and Chairman of its Committee on Managerial Accounting. Dr. Gordon has served as both Vice President and President of the American Finance Association. He is a member of the editorial board of *Accounting Review.* His numerous publications include, among others, *The Cost of Capital to a Public Utility* (1974).

B.H.F. Johnson Financial Adviser, The Electricity Council, Great Britain. The Electricity Council is the general coordinating body of the federally organized electricity supply industry in England and Wales. Mr. Johnson first served with the London and Home Counties Joint Electricity Authority and then with the South Eastern Electricity Board. He has been with the Electricity Council since

1958. He is a Member of the Chartered Institute of Public Finance and Accountancy, a Fellow of the Association of Certified Accountants, and a Member of the Accounting Standards Committee and the Inflation Accounting Steering Group. The latter two groups have responsibility for developing accounting and reporting standards. Mr. Johnson also serves as chairman of several electricity supply staff committees.

Douglas N. Jones Specialist in Public Utility and Natural Resource Economics, Economics Division, Congressional Research Service Library of Congress. He received the B.A. degree from the University of New Hampshire and the M.A. and Ph.D. degrees from Ohio State University. He taught at the U.S. Air Force Academy, Colorado, and has been lecturer, adjunct, and visiting professor at other universities, including Ohio State University. Dr. Jones also has served as Regional Economist to the Secretary of Commerce and as a congressional legislative assistant. His publications have appeared in various professional journals and congressional committee prints. He is the author (with Angela Lancaster) of *Electric and Gas Utility Rate and Fuel Adjustment Clause Increases, 1975.*

Larry L. Kehler Manager, Management Services, Touche Ross & Co., St. Louis. He received the B.A. and M.B.A. degrees from Indiana University. Mr. Kehler is project manager for the Arkansas Public Service Commission, Federal Energy Administration funded study of electrical energy demand management, an eighteen-month study of electrical energy pricing of three rate forms in nine experimental customer groups. Other areas of his consultancy include computer modeling, cost allocation, compensation administration, and organizational planning and development. He is a member of the Institute of Management Consultants, American Society for Personnel Administration, and the National Association of Accountants.

José David Langier Special Advisor to the President of ELETROBRAS and Assistant to the Economic and Financial Director of ELETROBRAS. He received the B.Sc. degree from the Federal University of Rio de Janeiro and the M.A. and Ph.D. degrees from Michigan State University. Mr. Langier has served as Senior Economist of the Organization of American States. He is the author of *Economical and Nutritional Diets Using Scarce Resources.*

William W. Lindsay Assistant Chief, Office of Economics, Federal Power Commission. He received the B.S. and M.A. degrees from the University of Pittsburgh and the Ph.D. degree from Ohio State University. He has authored various articles dealing with public utility economics and regulation and has taught courses in these subjects in the U.S. Department of Agriculture Graduate School and the Industrial College of the Armed Forces. From 1958 to 1962 Mr. Lindsay was Director of Rates and Research, Public Utilities Commission of Ohio. From 1964 to 1975 he served as Chief, Division of Rates and Corporate Regulation, Bureau of Power, Federal Power Commission.

Willard G. Manning, Jr. Economist, the Rand Corporation. He received the B.S. degree from the California Institute of Technology and the Ph.D. degree from Stanford University. Mr. Manning has served on the Harvard University faculty as an assistant professor at the School of Public Health and the Kennedy School of Government. Since joining the Rand staff he has pursued research in the economics of health, energy, and television. Recently, he has collaborated in a study of European experience with peak-load pricing and load management and in the design and analysis of the Los Angeles experiment, which is testing forms of peak-load pricing for residential customers.

David L. McNicol Senior Staff Member, President's Council of Economic Advisors. Dr. McNicol received the A.B. degree from Harvard University, and the S.M. and Ph.D. degrees from the Massachusetts Institute of Technology. Before joining the Council of Economic Advisors, he held various positions with Charles River Associates. In addition, he taught at MIT and served as a member of the faculty at the University of Pennsylvania. He has written a number of articles and papers dealing with various theoretical and applied aspects of public utility pricing. Dr. McNicol will become a member of the faculty of the California Institute of Technology in late 1976. He is a member of the American Economic Association, the American Statistical Association, and the Econometric Society.

Bridger M. Mitchell Senior Staff Economist, The Rand Corporation. He received the B.A. degree from Stanford University and the Ph.D. degree from the Massachusetts Institute of Technology. As a Brookings Economic Policy Fellow, Mr. Mitchell worked in the Office of the Secretary of Health, Education and Welfare and later directed the analysis of national health insurance issues for HEW. During 1978 he will be a German Marshall Fund Fellow and a visiting international scholar studying pricing and supply practices of European utilities. His research findings in the fields of energy, health care, statistical methods, and telecommunications have been published in a wide variety of professional journals, including the *International Economic Review,* and *Econometrica.*

James R. Nelson Professor of Economics, Amherst College. He received the B.A. degree from Oberlin College and the Ph.D. degree from Harvard University. He served as Director of the Office of Economics, Department of Transportation, and as Chief of the United Kingdom Branch of the Economic Cooperation Administration. He is past chairman of the Transportation and Public Utilities Group of the American Economic Association. Dr. Nelson has written many articles in the field of public utility economics and regulation, and he is the editor of the authoritative collection of papers entitled *Marginal Cost Pricing in Practice.* He also is the co-author (with D. F. Cavers) of *Electric Power Regulation in Latin America.*

John L. O'Donnell Professor of Financial Administration, Graduate School of Business Administration, Michigan State University. He received the B.A. (Hons.) and M.A. degrees in economics from Cambridge University. He came to the United States in 1951 and earned the M.B.A. and Ph.D. degrees from Indiana University. Professor O'Donnell has served as Acting Director, Bureau of Business and Economic Research, Michigan State University, and as Chief-of-Party, Michigan State group in Turkey, and as an adviser to the Mission Director, USAID/Turkey in Ankara. He has authored numerous articles, monographs, and books and is active as a financial consultant. He has devoted particular attention to the current problems facing public utilities.

Joseph M. Quigley Financial Vice President and Secretary, Northern Illinois Gas Company. He received the B.S. and M.A. degrees from the State University of Iowa. Before joining the Northern Illinois Gas Company, Mr. Quigley served as a public utility audit manager with Arthur Andersen and Co. His publications include "Levelized Revenue Requirement for Return and Depreciation." Mr. Quigley is a frequent participant on programs in the fields of public utility regulation, finance, and energy utilization.

Sylvia M. Siegel President and member of the Board of Directors, Toward Utility Rate Normalization (TURN). Ms. Siegel is a graduate of Wayne State University. She has appeared before regulatory agencies as a representative of small consumer interests. In 1973 she organized TURN, a public interest group that focuses on matters pertaining to energy and public utilities. As an advocate of consumer interests, Ms. Siegel has been a frequent participant in regulatory proceedings, and she also has testified before congressional committees. More recently, TURN has launched a consumer conservation education program, with a pilot study in San Francisco, which is designed to promote more efficient residential use of electricity, gas, and water.

Robert G. Uhler Executive Director, Electric Utility Rate Design Study, Electric Power Research Institute. The Electric Utility Rate Design Study is a joint effort of EPRI and the Edison Electric Institute to examine time-of-day pricing for the National Association of Regulatory Utility Commissioners. Mr. Uhler received the B.S. degree in commerce, the B.A. in languages, and the M.A. in economics from Ohio State University. He formerly served with the Federal Power Commission where he was Chief of the Division of Economic Studies of the Office of Economics. Mr. Uhler has taught at West Point and at Vanderbilt University. He has testified extensively before the FPC, the Atomic Energy Commission, and the Nuclear Regulatory Commission. He also has testified on rate design matters before the House Committee on Interstate and Foreign Commerce and the Senate Commerce Committee.

Richard Walker Senior Partner, Arthur Andersen and Company. He joined Arthur Andersen immediately after attending the University of Illinois. He has had extensive experience in all aspects of public utility regulation and management. Mr. Walker has testified before state and federal commissions, courts, congressional committees, and state legislative bodies. He has been involved with the use of accounting data for ratemaking and managerial purposes, having designed and installed automated accounting systems for public utility firms. His publications include articles in the *Duke Law Review, Investment Dealer's Digest,* and chapters in a text book on public utilities. He is a member of the American Institute of Certified Public Accountants, the Illinois Society of CPAs, and the Federal Power Commission's National Gas Survey, where he serves as Chairman of the Technical Advisory Committee on Rate Design. He also serves on the Energy Finance Advisory Council of the Federal Energy Administration.

Frank S. Walters Vice President, Rates and Regulatory Practices, Potomac Electric Power Company. He received the B.S. degree from the Massachusetts Institute of Technology. Mr. Walters has served as an expert witness before various regulatory commissions. He is a past chairman of the Rate Research Committee, Edison Electric Institute, and a past chairman of the Rate Section of the Southeastern Electric Exchange.